AFFECT IN THE CURRICULUM

Toward Democracy, Dignity, and Diversity

AFFECT IN THE CURRICULUM

Toward Democracy, Dignity, and Diversity

JAMES A. BEANE

TEACHERS
COLLEGE
PRESS

Teachers College, Columbia University
New York and London

Published by Teachers College Press, 1234 Amsterdam Avenue
New York, NY 10027

Library of Congress Cataloging-in-Publication Data

Beane, James A., 1944–
    Affect in the curriculum : toward democracy, dignity, and
diversity / James A. Beane.
        p.   cm.
    Includes bibliographical references.
    ISBN 0-8077-3000-9 (alk. paper).—ISBN 0-8077-2999-X (pbk. :
alk. paper)
    1. Affective education.   2. Curriculum planning.   I. Title.
LB1072.B43   1990
375′.001—dc20   89-27204
                                                                        CIP

ISBN 0-8077-2999-X (pbk.)
    0-8077-3000-9

Printed on acid-free paper

Manufactured in the United States of America

97 96 95 94 93 92 91 90   8 7 6 5 4 3 2 1

To
Catherine O. Beane
and
Barbara L. Brodhagen

Contents

Preface

The term *affect* has been with us for several centuries, during which its definition has evolved from emotional reactions in the absence of reason to a dimension of human thought and action that is integrated with cognition or thinking. Applied to schools, affect most frequently refers to those aspects of education that have to do with personal and social development. The purpose of this book is to explore how those aspects have appeared in the curriculum and to suggest ways in which their present forms should be restructured to promote not only personal and social development, but efficacy as well.

To do this, several problems must be confronted. First, the meaning of affect is still somewhat ambiguous. Second, the educational terrain is cluttered with proposals and programs regarding affect in the curriculum, and these are often in serious conflict with one another. Third, this area of work has suffered from a good deal of ahistoricism, with the result that those who currently either propose or subscribe to particular versions of affect in the curriculum are largely unaware of their roots or of contradictions within them. Finally, if we define personal and social development broadly, it includes not only self-esteem, to which *affect* is usually attached, but values, morals, ethics, and other aspects of communal living. Because this takes in almost everything that schools are concerned with, it raises the very difficult question of what the schools *ought* to stand for and work toward. To say the least, this is very controversial territory. However, given the confusion and contradiction presently plaguing affect in the curriculum, it is an area in need of serious attention.

Much of the writing about affect in the curriculum is aimed at promoting various programs or activities that will supposedly enhance personal and social development. In this book, I will take a quite different approach by looking at the field as a whole and proposing grounds upon which any proposals or programs within it ought to be based. Chapter 1 suggests a definition of affect and describes its relation to learning, the various places where it might be found in the school, and a framework that might be used in making and evaluating proposals regarding affect in the curriculum. In Chapter 2 I attempt to escape the problem of ahistoricism by describing the origins of various versions of affect in the curriculum and tracing the routes they have traveled during the twentieth century.

Chapter 3 presents a crucial part of the case for restructuring affect in the curriculum. It is here that the themes of democracy, human dignity (and related moral and value principles), citizens' rights, and developmental psychology, as well as the nature of emerging social trends, will be explained and presented as the appropriate basis of affect in the curriculum. Then, in Chapter 4, we will see how the historical versions of affect presently appear in the curriculum and how they stand in light of the themes developed in Chapter 3. Chapter 5 takes up the question of how the major themes of democracy, dignity, and diversity might be brought to life in the school. This includes consideration of how young people ought to be viewed in that context, the possibilities for developing relations between the school and society, and examples of curriculum, teaching, and institutional arrangements that are closely aligned with those major themes.

In Chapter 6, I propose and describe conditions for the kind of reasoned discourse that is needed to bring us out of the present confusion over affect in the curriculum and point us in the direction of appropriate and coherent action in this area. The localized level that I suggest for this discourse is intended not only to consider how the major themes might be brought to life in the school, but to do so by means that themselves reflect those themes. Finally, in the last chapter we will recall the framework for making and evaluating proposals for affect in the curriculum and see how my claims fit within it. At this point, I will also suggest the promise that those claims hold for enhancing the personal and social efficacy of young people.

As one way of understanding the case I will argue, it might be helpful to explain how my thinking has developed regarding affect in the curriculum. In my early work as a teacher and student of curriculum I was dismayed by the way young people were manipulated by the "system" of schools, particularly their personal histories as students in undemocratic institutions. My sense was that if we turned our efforts toward democratic forms of curriculum planning that were sensitive to personal characteristics, we might make progress toward humane, person-centered schools. This was, of course, a dominant theme among many of us who began our education careers in the 1960s.

By the mid-1970s the prospects for democratic school restructuring and student-centered forms were, so to speak, yesterday's news. The education field was generally enamored with management systems borrowed from business and the military, and affective concerns were more and more relegated to separate courses on "affective education." It was clear that schools were becoming even more impersonal and custodial. Thus my attention became concentrated on the effects of school experiences on the self-concept and self-esteem of young people. Richard Lipka and I began to construct what we have come to call the "school as bad guy" metaphor, in which most present institutional features and curriculum forms are seen as debilitating to the self-perceptions of young people (and adults) who live and work daily inside the schools. We constructed a theory of affect as antecedent and outcome of experiences in school and argued for institutional restructuring on that basis (Beane & Lipka, 1986). This theoretical work was coupled with practical efforts to develop self-esteem projects in several schools and to protest practices such as corporal punishment and ability grouping. The idealized school we portrayed pursued diversity, cooperation, personalness, interaction, problem solving, participative governance, and other features.

At the same time we consciously attempted to continue the work of our friend Louis Raths on topics such as creating emotionally secure climates and encouraging cognitively based valuing. Although in constructing our ideas, we interviewed young people of all ages, our work became increasingly focused on middle schools, partly because of our concern for the drama of early adolescence, but mostly because it was at this level of schooling that people were most visibly attempting to be sensitive to the characteristics of learners (Beane & Lipka, 1987).

As this work developed, I also attempted to recapture the dimensions of curriculum planning that held promise for reempowering teachers and learners. Conrad Toepfer, Samuel Alessi, and I restated the case for thoughtful, cooperative curriculum planning at the local level, a case that seemed urgent (and still does) as curriculum discourse and decision making became more centralized, and teaching and learning more mechanized. To make our statement consistent with our theory, we intentionally described alternatives available in curriculum planning and withheld our own biases about which alternatives ought to be chosen (Beane, Toepfer, & Alessi, 1986). It is our continuing belief that the purpose of theories is to inform democratic discourse rather than monopolize its outcome. Among us we also had enough experience with schools to know that specified theories, or top-down versions, are contested on local grounds and resisted behind closed classroom doors. Thus we were guided by respect for professional judgment and by practical facts.

This book is by no means a rejection of those earlier efforts. Instead it extends the previous ideas to consider problems about which I have become increasingly uneasy. The theory and research work on personal affect in the institutional context called for a thorough restructuring of the school, including a reorganization of curriculum plans around personal and social issues. However, it was often miscast as another variation of the part of the self-esteem movement concerned with self-gratification, academic achievement, or development of personal coping mechanisms. This gross misinterpretation may be due partly to the fact that while we made statements about social, economic, and political injustice, we did not sufficiently address overt resistance to it. I now tend to think that the misinterpretation also had to do with the reluctance of many people to understand affect as broadly defined and to see our work as a focus on one aspect of it. We should have said more forcefully than we did that being sensitive to young people in school is only part of a larger struggle that includes trying to reform the conditions under which they live on the outside. The critical analysis of social issues that we recommend as part of the curriculum should have been framed as critical awareness and ethics leading to social action.

The work on curriculum planning has also left some feeling of uneasiness. We ended that effort by discussing some of the more obvious issues that ought to be on the minds of educators, particularly the troubling symptoms of problems among young people, the litany of issues that continue to face our society, and the increasing tendency to look for simplistic solutions like raising school standards and tightening controls on students. I began to wonder whether we should have been more explicit about the kind of curriculum and institutional reorganization such issues demand. This uneasiness increased as the rhetoric of school reform heated up. Specifically, there has been much talk about "restructuring" schools but it has almost altogether avoided the question of whether the subject-centered, academic approach is itself a major part of the overall structural problem of schools. In other words, no matter how much we tinker with the institutional features of schools, nothing of significance is likely to happen if curriculum forms ignore issues that pervade the lives of students and the larger society.

Thus the line of work I followed was not so much incorrect as it was incomplete. This was specifically true insofar as what I now call "affect in the curriculum." One cannot help but notice how this theme is emerging in the spirit of school reform. The emphasis on moral education has now turned mostly toward behavioristic shaping of conduct, compliance with social conventions, and preference for the "high culture" literacy of classical humanism. The press for higher-order thinking skills has been situated in the narrow context of academic excellence. The work on self-esteem has been placed largely in separate courses tied to glossy "curriculum" packages that claim to develop mechanisms for coping with the residue of personal and social problems.

Taken together these ideas present the impossible promise of quick-fix solutions. The need for long-term efforts in which affective issues are a central feature of the school, addressed with thoughtful and serious restructuring, is simply ignored. Moreover, the real problems of young people and the larger society are obscured by an endless array of promises for school adjustments that will supposedly make things right. Meanwhile, more and more young people fall through the cracks in the system, self-destructive behaviors increase, and gaps in social, economic, and political positions widen. In short, the present school excellence reform movement, including its versions of moral education, is more and more revealed as a smoke screen of superficial activity that is neither good nor right for young people.

It is the uneasiness growing out of these conditions that finally drives this work. Somehow we ought to be doing better than we are with how we place affect in the curriculum. Somehow the discourse about this theme should be more informed and reasoned than it is and should involve wider participation. Somehow our thinking about affect ought to be less narrow and more forward looking than it is. Somehow we ought to do better with young people in sharing the legacy of our democratic and humane principles and liberating them to see beyond the limitations on personal and social efficacy that continue to plague us.

Acknowledgments

This book, like almost all others, could not have been written without invaluable support from many people. The main work was done while on sabbatical leave from St. Bonaventure University and on an appointment as an Honorary Fellow in the Department of Curriculum and Instruction at the University of Wisconsin at Madison. I am, of course, grateful to both institutions for extending these courtesies, without which the work would probably not have been completed.

Several friends at Madison were particularly helpful. Michael Apple served as a gracious host and careful critic, teaching me a great deal along the way and also offering encouragement during those "doldrum" periods when the flow of ideas was little more than a trickle. Alan Lockwood offered numerous critical suggestions, pointing to serious gaps and suggesting where I might look to fill them. Professor Apple's infamous Friday Seminar group graciously offered me a chance to present my ideas and made a number of crucial suggestions about fundamental aspects of the work. In particular, Jim Ladwig seemed almost daily to find a new source for me to read, spent many hours in informal conversation talking through ideas, and made many suggestions that led to significant changes in how I framed the book's content.

Back at St. Bonaventure University, my good friends and colleagues in "The Group," namely, Peggy Burke, Huang Xiaodan, and Chris Gaeta, not only read and reacted to various chapters, but helped form the concepts I have tried to describe. As usual, they constantly reminded me that democracy, dignity, and diversity are really useful only when they come to life in the everyday experiences of the young. And so, of course, did Professor Robert Harnack of SUNY/Buffalo, who encouraged me to see this work through on precisely those grounds.

Help also came at unexpected times. My friend Dick Ulasewicz spent what should have been a social evening explaining how, as a teacher, he viewed the relation between private and public values in the classroom. Paul and Peter Apple talked with me about how they viewed the authority rights of school officials. An unknown truck driver, in a diner somewhere between Wisconsin and New York, told me that people in schools "moralize too much, and kids don't learn how to think for themselves." And my old friend Mary Pitz somehow knew exactly when to send two letters to her "other son," saying simply, "keep at it."

Thanks go to Carole Saltz, Sarah Biondello, Ron Galbraith, Susan Liddicoat, and Nina George at Teachers College Press for their continuing interest in my work and their sharp, but humane, editorial reactions. Much appreciation is due also to Myra Cleary, whose meticulous and professional copyediting of the manuscript has resulted in this volume's final format.

In more ways than they can know, this work, as always, was driven by Jim, Jason, and John Beane. Their experiences in school and the way they talk about them offers an endless supply of issues, concerns, and examples. The fact that they must live out their lives and try to find happiness in an increasingly difficult world is never far from my thoughts.

In the end I come to the two people who had the greatest influence on this work and to whom I wish to dedicate it. Catherine O. Beane, now in her eighties, first taught me the meaning of dignity, respect for cultural differences, and the importance of democracy, not only by her words, but by the continuous commitment she made to live them out in everyday life. Her early teaching of "nonprivileged" children and her recent work in an urban soup kitchen give elegant symmetry to a life led for others; it is a life that defines the concept of "caring."

Barbara Brodhagen, my good friend and wife, would probably say that she only read the manuscript and commented along the way. Can it possibly be that she does not know how many ideas she contributed and how many things were rewritten because of her suggestions? Only her sense of genuine caring could prevent her from realizing that it was by her encouragement that the first and last words were written and that the old excitement, half-forgotten for too long, was brought back to life.

It is probably the case that these many people still see much that should be different in this work. So it is that regardless of their help I take sole responsibility for the way it all came out in the end. Perhaps their concerns will be somewhat lessened in knowing how much their help and support continue to be appreciated.

Living and Learning in the Affective Domain

Not too long before undertaking this book I attended the annual conference of a large professional association. On the program were several sessions described as addressing "affective education." In these sessions I found the speakers were actually promoting commercially prepared programs that involved workshops for teachers on how to use various activities collected in nicely bound, attractive booklets. In practice, the teachers were to engage students in these activities one period a day or every other day over the course of a semester or two. According to the speakers, these programs would enhance the self-esteem of young people and go a long way toward stopping them from using drugs, getting pregnant, getting arrested, and failing in school. The activities themselves had a familiar ring: in fact, many were exactly the same as some developed 20 years ago in the halcyon days of humanistic education, human relations, and values clarification (oddly enough they had been copyrighted again by these new program developers). Given the claims of the speakers, the content of the programs, and the prescribed methods, I felt as if professional time had stood still. Indeed, I wondered, had we come no further than this? Had our understanding of affective education made no progress over the years? Had we learned nothing from research or practice with these kinds of programs? And, in the end, why was the audience so thoroughly taken with what the speakers had to offer?

No doubt my reaction to this experience would appeal to other groups that have recently made forays into the field of affect in the curriculum, particularly advocates of reviving so-called "character" education. However, in the rhetoric of didactic teaching of moral virtues and behavior shaping used by this group, we hear also voices from the past advocating an old approach that gathered little support in research or, ultimately, in practice. So here too we may ask the same questions. Have we made no more progress, come no further?

Why are so many educators so thoroughly taken with the promises of the conservative restoration?

The answers to these questions are both simple and complex. On the one hand, they come down to the fact that the issue of how to appropriately place affect in the curriculum, even after all these years, is still filled with ambiguity and disagreement. Little progress has been made toward developing a broad and coherent theory or framework that defines the place of affect in the curriculum and sets the grounds for evaluating claims that are made about how it should be addessed. On the other hand, resolving this ambiguity and working toward a coherent theory are extremely complicated. To begin with, there is still disagreement about how to define affect, resulting in a wide variety of opinion about how it should be placed in the curriculum. To attempt such a resolution is a harrowing experience as it requires the realignment of diverse and sometimes apparently oppositional views and, finally, a statement about how work in this area should proceed in both theory and practice.

Nevertheless, the present disarray in the field demands such an attempt, because almost everything we do in schools has to do with affect. Clearly we are in an era when troubling symptoms evidenced in the behavior of young people, adults, and institutions suggest the need for a new look at affect in the curriculum. Many voices from many directions are responding to this need with various proposals, some competing and some complementary. As the ambiguity of the postindustrial age presents greater problems in the personal and social arena, this renewed attention will undoubtedly become more widespread. As issues related to cultural diversity, human rights, the distribution of wealth and justice, corruption in business and government, the ethics of technology and technicization, and so on more fully enter the public conscience, or at least its consciousness, the concern over affective issues will be even more heavily emphasized. If schools are not reasonably prepared to explicate a coherent framework for placing affect in the curriculum, they will stand open to continuing criticism from the outside and to the empty promises of "fluff" programs from within. Worse yet, they will make little contribution toward helping young people and their communities to participate in efforts to address the affect-loaded issues that face them now and in the future.

Suggested proposals for work in this area are becoming almost as commonplace as the reports of trends themselves. Such rhetoric is important for those who work in schools, because many of the proposed solutions are situated in the schools, even though the issues themselves may be located in the larger society. The notion that the schools should (or can) solve social problems is certainly not new; it has been a primary force in the field of education in general and curriculum development in particular (Cremin, 1961; Kliebard, 1986). Thus the renewed attention to affect in the curriculum turns out to be an inevitable response to the trends and how they are perceived.

The underlying theory appears to be this: When large-scale social problems appear, we may react with legal and legislative action, but in the long haul the best solution is to educate the present generation of young people to "cope" with their own problems and/or to help create a more ethical and moral society. So it is that talk about self-esteem, values, morals, ethics, character, and so on once again surfaces in discussions about what the schools ought to be doing. And right behind this talk follows a parade of suggestions about how to do it. Of particular interest is the way in which current trends are interpreted, especially as solutions are situated in the schools. Suggestions for responsive affective activity in the curriculum are a product of these interpretations. Their specific content in different versions depends on the answers to several questions. How are social data interpreted? Who is interpreting them, and what are their motives? And what ends are the proposed solutions aimed toward?

TOWARD A DEFINITION OF AFFECT

Over several centuries, the term *affect* has generally been used to refer to mental aspects of human nature that are differentiated from reason (*Oxford English Dictionary*, 1961). Those aspects include feelings or emotions like anger, fear, love, and others that were thought to arise from stimuli without reasoned analysis. This conception of mental structures is rooted in classical theories that describe distinctive and exclusive mental states. However, modern work in psychology and philosophy has offered a different approach, in which such states and related processes are integrated. Research in psychology has demonstrated that in the presence of stimuli, and except for the most base visceral reactions, thought and feeling occur simultaneously in human experience (Mandler, 1984). For example, the experience of love is not, as is often claimed, simply an emotional response to physical attraction. Although it is partly that, it is also based on past experiences, reactions to which have led to particular preferences. We are attracted to other individuals because we have learned that certain characteristics evident about them represent desirable or preferable traits. The love of one person for another may appear more or less rational, but even the label of irrational is not the same as that of arational. In forming attachments, then, emotional responses are joined and partially formed by (thoughtful) recognition of symbolic traits. Such situations represent purposeful action behind which is some sort of thinking or "social intelligence" involving both affect and cognition as we react or respond to them (Berscheid, 1985; Rorty, 1980). As Ellen Berscheid (1982) succinctly put it, "Who performed the frontal lobotomy on interpersonal relations?" (p. 38).

While research on relations among mental states and processes is most frequently considered to be only a psychological matter, the case for integration may also be constructed from a philosophical view. Feelings and emotions are not empty occurrences; rather they are feelings about or emotions tied to something. That "something" is the content of problematic situations that call for some sort of reaction or resolution. Again, no matter how irrational (not arational) a reaction or proposed resolution may seem, it is based on some degree of belief that it is appropriate in the given situation. As Dewey (1939) put the case in speaking of the role of reflection in the formation of impulses and habits:

> The result is formation of desires and interests which are what they are through the union of the affective-motor conditions of action with the intellectual or ideational. . . . For, wherever there is an *end-in-view* of any sort whatever, there is affective-*ideational*-motor activity; or, in terms of the dual meaning of valuation there is union of prizing and appraising. (p. 31)

Here, then, we may argue that cognition and affect operate simultaneously, rather than that a reaction or proposed resolution is devoid of thought. Thus as affect and cognition are seen to coincide, we must be concerned about the kind of thinking that enters into situations, not simply describe their emotional tone.

This intersecting of mental states and processes brings us closer to a more complete and realistic theory of human experience than does one that separates them into an either/or description of cognition and affect. When we are angry at a person or idea, our state reflects both emotional turbulence and the presence of learned experience with the object of our anger. When we are happy with some situation, our state reflects emotional and physical comfort as well as intellectual satisfaction and equilibrium. To resolve or extend such states, we must apply intellect of one sort or another to attain or maintain satisfactory situations; that is, we must think and act in a purposeful way.[1]

As we begin to recognize the place of cognition in a complete understanding of affect, however, we must be careful not to overstate its role. Certainly the quality and clarity of thinking have much to do with the quality of those dimensions of humanness that are related to affect; yet we must not be tempted to marginalize the affective dimensions—including feelings and emotions—because they are necessarily a part of what it means to be fully human. Unfortunately our obsession with "science" in the twentieth century has often pointed in exactly this direction, especially as we have placed a premium on "cold logic" and rational-technical calculation in social policy planning. A good example is the dominance of standardized testing and other quantitative measures in defining appropriate school practices and worthwhile learning. This kind of thinking simply presents another version of distinctive mental states and processes rooted in an incomplete and inaccurate view of what it means to be fully human. To rephrase Berscheid's question, we will attempt to undo the "lobotomy" that has been performed on affect in schools.

The content of experiences that we think about centers on two types of satisfaction in personal and social activity. One involves what is "desired" or makes us or others "feel" good. The second involves what is "desirable" or is "best" for us and/or others. In either case we think and act in terms of preferences and choices that emerge from our beliefs, aspirations, attitudes, and appreciations, all of which, in turn, rest on what we "think" is good or right. Thus, whether we are concerned with personal issues (such as self-perceptions) or social issues (for example, human relations), the question of what is good or right brings values, morals, and ethics into the definition of affect.

One very useful way of thinking about affect in these terms was developed by Philip Phenix (1977) in an attempt to align it with the area of ethics (concerns about what we "ought" to do). In his view, affect has five levels:

1. *Organic needs* rooted in the search for personal homeostasis
2. *Subjective feelings* or the search for pleasure that characterizes hedonistic ethics
3. *Interests* or aspirations expressed in conative values related to the ethics of self-realization
4. *Judgments* by which the individual reflects upon and organizes the first three levels and intersects them with social interests in the community through critical ethics

5. *Idealizations* that are located in the continuing search for creative growth as both an individual and a society expressed through the ethics of progressive norms

Importantly, these five levels are viewed as objects of educational efforts in both individual and integrated forms, because ultimately they become synthesized in human behavior. This suggests that educational forms that focus on only one or a few levels are incomplete and inadequate, a point that I will emphasize later as a crucial grounding for a coherent theory of affect in the curriculum.

In a similar fashion, Albert Wight (1971, 1972) extended the meaning of affect beyond the usual interpretation. Wight described affect as involving an elaborate set of goals based on self (self-control, self-concept, and self-esteem), others (interpersonal and intercultural relations and responsibilities), and the environment (natural and technological). From this view he proposed a "taxonomy" in which personal experiences result in and are influenced by dispositions to action, personal guiding systems, and action orientations, which, in turn, lead to action itself. He claimed that this process involves increasingly complex cognition as it is applied in life contexts such as self, interpersonal relations, society, learning, work, aesthetics, and the natural world.

In sum, then, we may now define affect as an aspect of human thought and behavior that has a number of constitutive elements. It refers to a broad range of dimensions such as emotion, preference, choice, and feeling. These are based on beliefs, aspirations, attitudes, and appreciations regarding what is desired and desirable in personal development and social relationships. Both of these are connected to thinking or cognition, because they are informed by what has been learned from past experiences and they influence purposeful action in terms of values, morals, and ethics. The nature of such influence may range from the barely conscious to the carefully reasoned. Finally, affect is connected to behavior as both an antecedent and a consequence. Thus it is both a constitutive aspect of learning and an appropriate object of educational efforts.

While I have been speaking of affect as a noun, it is also used as a verb; for example, "to *affect* someone." In this sense it refers to the influence of one or more of those dimensions of thought and action included in the definition above. Much of our work here, especially in later chapters, dealing with planning and carrying out experiences for young people in schools will focus on such influence as it does and might occur. To represent this possibility I will refer to how we "place affect in the curriculum" as an expression of the deliberate attempt to influence the personal and social development of young people.

As we begin to explore the place of affect in the curriculum, the definition of affect will be extremely important. The dimensions by which it is constituted imply that it involves a complex interrelationship of preference, thinking, and behavior as these reside in and emerge from thought and action regarding self and others. To ignore the range and complexity of these meanings and instead rely on only one (such as the personal dimension) would be to arrive at an incomplete version of affect in the curriculum.

AFFECT AND SCHOOL LEARNING

Affect permeates the entire school and the experiences of young people within it as a powerful antecedent, as an aspect of transactions, and as an outcome, planned or otherwise. We have already seen that affect is not simply an isolated and differentiated aspect of human nature. Rather it is a crucial component that integrates with other dimensions in both inner states and outward expressions. In this sense, a theory of learning or schooling that ignores or denies affect is incomplete and inhuman.

When young people arrive at school, for the first time and every day thereafter, they bring with them their whole selves, including the affective aspects. Even before actually starting school, children typically construct some belief system about it, using what they have heard from adults, siblings, the media, and other sources. These belief systems may amount to fear, anxiety, excited optimism, or a combination of those. Once children are in school, each day adds new experiences that may confirm, change, refine, or otherwise alter their existing belief systems, preferences, or attitudes toward themselves or others in general or specifically in relation to school. Because these aspects reside within the individual and are integrated with other mental and physical characteristics, they cannot be left at the school doors or set aside in order to focus on those other characteristics. The child who is afraid or lacking in confidence is not likely to barge into new experiences as if those feelings or beliefs did not exist. Nor can the enthusiastic and optimistic child easily betray or suppress those feelings. In the case of the former, anxiety and fear may be manifested in psychosomatic symptoms that inhibit participation altogether.

Affect enters into the transactional phase of school experiences not only as an antecedent, but as an ongoing function in learning situations and as an object of their tone. In the attempt to fully learn, we seek not only intellectual meanings, but their affective organization and integration as well. This organization involves the search for personal meanings that we may use as part of our system of beliefs, attitudes, preferences, and the like, as well as guides for future experiences. The greater the opportunity for finding such meanings, the more likely that learning will be complete and satisfactory; the lesser the opportunity, the more likely learning experiences will be unsatisfactory, frustrating, and disengaging. Moreover, an individual's personal and social affect is also influenced by the tone of school transactions. Work on "positive" and "negative" affect carried on for many years suggests that while some dissonance is a necessary condition for learning, its extremely negative forms, like fear or extreme anxiety, inhibit both engagement and problem solving (McLeod, in press). In addition to its role in the antecedent and transactional phases of learning, affect is an important and appropriate object of school efforts as a purposeful outcome. This point may be argued from three directions. One is that schools have responsibility for educating the "whole" person. Because affect is an inseparable part of that wholeness, it must be part of the educative ends that schools seek to promote. The second argument is that affect is an unavoidable part of the learning process and, therefore, an inevitable part of its outcomes. We have seen how affect enters into the antecedents and transactions of schooling and that school experiences influence affective states. This means that school experiences result in some form of affective learning whether they are meant to or not. The very existence of schools and compulsory attendance laws are both value expressions of which young people are reminded every day. To suggest that schools not take affect into account and deliberately plan for it is foolish because it would assume young people are not human beings subject to affective states. Yet the desire for an "affect-free" school is argued by some who want to focus on the acquisition of information alone. Work in the area of the "hidden curriculum" has revealed the fundamental fallacy in their argument; that is, when the hidden curriculum is ignored, its effects "blindside" other efforts and often distract them altogether (Giroux & Purpel, 1983; Overly, 1970).

The third argument is that education in schools is supposed to result in some kind of improved thinking *and* behavior, or at least a better version than if someone did not attend school at all. Young people should not simply learn about ideas, but should also learn to apply them in the direction of "good" lives. This requires that they develop some organization of preferences, appreciations, and attitudes on which to act. It is exactly this affective dimension that brings learning out of mere passivity and accumulation of information toward full, active participation and meaningful outcomes (Dewey, 1916). To deny affective purposes is thus to abdicate an important responsibility of schools and to restrict the possibility that our educational efforts will come to worthwhile ends.

I have thus far argued the case for deliberate affective purposes from a psychological and philosophical position. However, it can (and must) also be argued from a sociological perspective in terms of the school and the classroom as culture. Among the aspects of antecedent belief systems are those about other people and one's relation to them. Children coming to school, even for the first time, have prior beliefs about others based on age, ethnicity, physical characteristics, gender, neighborhood location, and other variables. Such beliefs are informed by prior experience and the particular information network of which young people are a part. These beliefs shade the expectations that young people carry into settings within the school; they also emerge from learning experiences in the same ways (confirmed, refined, or changed) as other aspects of affect. The degree to which these belief systems contribute to a just, moral, and efficacious sense of community is a legitimate and crucial concern of schools in a democratic society.

More will be said about this when we examine the affective domain as it has been addressed in proposals regarding affect in the curriculum. For the moment, though, we will leave this point by noting again that affect and cognition are inextricably interrelated across the whole range of human activity, including school learning experiences. Neither functions in isolation from the other. It is only when we fully recognize and apply this fact that we have the best chance for promoting real, worthwhile, and legitimate education in schools based on a complete theory of how learning and its outcomes occur. The continued separation and fragmentation of cognition and affect is surely one of the saddest aspects of contemporary schools.

THE PLACE OF AFFECT IN THE CURRICULUM

Before looking further into how affect enters into the program of the school, I want to comment on the term *affective education*. At one level this term may appear useful insofar as it suggests a particular kind of education that directly addresses the dimensions of affect as I have defined them, particularly in courses or other arrangements set aside specifically for that purpose. However, upon analysis it is clear that the term actually reduces the meaning of affect and thus inhibits discourse about its place in the school. Affect is one dimension of humanness and functions simultaneously with other dimensions in learning experiences. Therefore, education *must* be affective and cannot be otherwise, just as it must be cognitive and cannot be noncognitive. The term *affective education* suggests that somehow affect can be isolated for episodes in which its form will be educated, a notion I have suggested is unproductive with regard to cognition and now claim is equally restrictive with regard to affect. In light of this understanding I would further argue that we should avoid use of the term *affective education* and instead speak of the place of affect in the curriculum.

In its broadest sense, affective learning is concerned with personal-social development. It includes knowledge, skills, behaviors, and attitudes related to personal interests, social relations, and the integration of those two. Though curriculum has been defined in many ways (Beane, Toepfer, & Alessi, 1986), I will use it here to mean all of the experiences of learners in the context of the school. When combined, those definitions indicate that affect is situated in the curriculum in all experiences that involved self-perceptions, values, morals, ethics, beliefs, social predispositions, appreciations, aspirations, and attitudes. Further, it is situated that way whether the affective learning is planned or accidental, overt or hidden, and no matter what content or process it is related to.

Where, then, might we look for affect in the school? Roberts (1972) suggests that we might think about personal awareness, creative behavior, interpersonal awareness (within and across groups), subject orientation (relevance and preference), specific content (personal meanings), affect in teaching styles and methods, and adult models. In sum, affect enters the curriculum in any experience that influences (or attempts to influence) how young people see themselves, the world around them, and their place in that world. Wherever personal-social development is involved, either implicitly or explicitly, there is affect in the curriculum

Some examples of where affect is found in the school might help clarify what is meant by this definition. One such place is in proposals or programs that make direct claims about affect in terms of self-perceptions, moral development or education, character education, values education, citizenship, or ethics. Another is proposals or programs in which such matters are implicit, but integral. Here I mean career education, substance abuse education, human growth and development or sex education, suicide prevention programs, peace education, and the like. A third is in programs involving areas like art, music, drama, and others in which explicit claims are made regarding "appreciation" of objects and forms.

A fourth place where affect might be found is in various subject areas of which affect is either an explicit or implicit part. In the former case we may include social studies, English/language arts, home economics, and others where attitudes and values have played a traditional role or where teachers have sought to promote personal-social meanings. In the latter case we might include aspects of science that consider affective meanings in areas like environmental issues, technology, and human growth. A fifth is in programs that are often thought to be affect-free. Perhaps the best example of this is mathematics, the area most often considered to be purely cognitive. Mathematics does in fact have affective implications. For instance, teaching about ratios and proportions may seem to be only a mathematical exercise. However, it takes on value and moral dimensions when applied to comparison shopping where nonreturnable bottles are cheaper on the shelf but more expensive in terms of the environmental effects of disposal. Similarly, teaching about averages as abstract categories obscures individual differences when applied to the social meaning of the "average" person. In these examples, what is taught has affective meaning, whether explicitly raised or not, in the predispositions that are promoted.

Another illustration might be found in computer classes, where the attempt to promote "computer literacy" says a great deal about the relative importance attached to technology as an economic force and where neglecting to explicitly consider the ethical issues of technology suggests that its human effects are largely irrelevant. In this example we may also see that affect can be found by examining not only what is included in the school program, but what is left out or marginalized. The possibilities for affective meaning are at least partly defined by what the school chooses to reveal about particular topics. Whether certain concepts or problems are included or excluded, emphasized or deemphasized, places boundaries on what young people are encouraged to explore.

A sixth place where affect can be found is in the institutional features of the school that largely define the hidden, but powerful, curriculum: the school climate, the placement of young people in labeled groups, the rules and regulations, the reward and punishment system, the distribution of power in decision making, the grading system, teacher expectations, adult behavior, and so on. A seventh is in the experiences and attitudes young people bring to school, their expectations and anxieties about it, and their developing dispositions about school and education, as well as the perceptions of self and others that grow out of school experiences. Finally, we may find affect in such places as statements of goals, in classroom processes, and in the relative frequency and power of standardized tests as measures of what is implied to be important learning. Again, the appearance of affect in these areas may be explicit or implicit, intentional or accidental. But it is there nonetheless. Obviously the school is affect-loaded and hence there is a need for a very broad definition such as the one I have proposed.

The definition and examples may seem imposing, because they encompass a wide range of other concepts, each of which has its own definition and history in the education field. But we must remember that affect refers to a major dimension of humanness and, in the end, the one that gives education its legitimate meaning in the school context. After all, we are concerned not simply with cognition and psychomotorics; neither one alone nor the two together contribute adequately to the improvement of human experience. It is the affective dimension, in all of its complexity, that finally serves the crucial personal and social ends of schooling. Definitions of affect and its place in the curriculum that fall short of the one I have proposed are problematic in two ways. While we should not perhaps say that they are wrong, we can confidently say that they are partial or incomplete with regard to a full and accurate explanation of humanness. Moreover, they lead to school programs that are not necessarily worthless but rather are partial and incomplete versions of how we should think about the purpose of schools.

To adequately think about affect in the curriculum, we must consider how affective dimensions of young people might influence curriculum planning and how the school interacts with those dimensions and relates to affective issues in the culture of the young and society as a whole. We must be concerned with all aspects of the definition of affect insofar as they already reside within the individual, are determined by or for the individual, and extend into relations with others from primary to distant. We must be concerned with how affective issues arise, what they mean for personal-social development, and how they are actualized in personal-social decisions. We must be concerned with how to balance personal and social interests as well as dependence and autonomy. And we must consider the implications of these concerns for self- and social idealization.

Furthermore, the concept of placing affect in the curriculum, as I have described it, includes all attempts to do so regardless of stated purpose, program form, suggested methodology, or view of the nature and resolution of affective issues in the larger society. Religious fundamentalists; advocates of character education, moral education, values education, psychological education, and democratic schools; and other voices heard on the contemporary scene are all placed within the definition. No matter how much they differ, in the end all present versions of the same idea: emphasizing affect in the curriculum. In this way, the definition becomes part of a coherent framework for thinking and acting in that area and a common ground from which proposals and their validity claims may begin to be analyzed.

TOWARD A COHERENT FRAMEWORK
FOR PLACING AFFECT IN THE CURRICULUM

One of the major problems in thinking about affect in the curriculum is the lack of a coherent and reasonably complete framework for developing proposals in this area. This creates the further problem of how to evaluate proposals and the claims they make about specific kinds of affective outcomes, methodologies, or issues proposed in relation to the curriculum. To resolve this dilemma, I suggest that such proposals ought to follow several guidelines. Taken together, these guidelines also form a framework for analysis, which will become particularly important when we examine the many versions of affect in the curriculum that emerged in the twentieth century and continue at present. This framework will also guide the development of my own claims made in succeeding chapters. Specifically, I believe that any proposal regarding affect in the curriculum should:

1. Define what is meant by "affect" and its relations with other dimensions of humanness.
2. Be attached to a particular culture or society.
3. Articulate a philosophic basis that names the sources of its views of and positions on affect, affective issues, and the curriculum.
4. Articulate a psychological theory that explains how affect develops and is influenced.
5. Define what is meant by personal development, social development, and the relations between the two.

6. Articulate the view of relations it implies between public and private values.
7. Review the history, if any, of its form.
8. Clearly define its curriculum intentions.
9. Define its relations with other existing aspects of the school program.
10. Describe a process by which discourse about it may proceed.

In sum, these ten guidelines provide a coherent and reasonably complete framework for constructing proposals to place affect in the curriculum and for evaluating their claims. The absence of such a framework has been partly responsible for the confusion about affect as an aspect of the means and ends of schools. Typically proposals have attended to only a few of the components suggested here, and rarely has any attempted to meet all of them. If the present confusion is to be resolved and progress made, we must obligate ourselves to considering the complete framework. Anything less will only perpetuate the confusion and the controversy that surrounds affect in the curriculum.

SUMMARY

The place and role of affect in the school have come to be defined in a narrow and restrictive way. Associated as it is with such terms as *affective education*, affect is most often used to refer to young people's personal feelings and emotions about themselves and their school experiences. While it is partly that, a more complete view of affect involves a much broader definition and a more powerful place in the curriculum.

Affect is a dimension of human thought and behavior that is based on preferences and choices tied to beliefs, aspirations, attitudes, and appreciations found in both personal and social activity. Each of these involves purposeful action that engages some degree and kind of thinking about what is desired and/or desirable; in other words, the simultaneous and integrated functioning of affect *and* cognition. Thus affect involves not only self-perceptions, but values, morals, and ethics that come into play in both personal development and social interactions. In this sense, affect in the curriculum is not simply a matter of its place in learning, but also includes the self-perceptions, values, morals, and ethics that adults, both inside and outside the school, desire and/or consider desirable and deliberately attempt to promote in young people. These aspects may be found in everyday social interactions, curriculum plans, teaching-learning situations, and institutional features that are explicit or implicit, intentional or accidental.

The affect that the school promotes, and that permeates everyday life in the school, grows out of interpretations of affective issues in the larger society and their relation to what is believed to be desired and/ or desirable for the personal development of young people and the common good. However, such issues are interpreted in different ways by different people, and hence there are competing views of what is right and appropriate for affect in the curriculum. As a result, this area is the subject of continuing tension, contradiction, and confusion both inside and outside the school. The way out of this situation depends partly on the development of a coherent and reasonably complete framework within which proposals about affect in the curriculum can be made and their claims evaluated. My suggested framework includes a definition of affect, a specified cultural context, explication of philosophical and psychological grounds, a definition of personal and social development and their relations, articulation of relations between private and public values, exploration of historical antecedents, a statement of curriculum intentions, explanation of relations to existing curriculum forms, and ways in which discourse about affect might proceed. Clearly the topic of affect in the curriculum is not simple, nor is its exploration likely to be easy.

2

The Routes of Affect in the Curriculum

The meanings and versions attached to how we place affect in the curriculum today did not spring on the scene suddenly or recently. Almost without exception they have emerged from a history of invention and refinement shaded by interpretations of several issues: definitions of affect, enduring and contemporary affective issues, the meaning of personal and social development, relations between the school and society, and the ends and means of affect in the curriculum. Within the schools themselves, such theoretical work has, in turn, been interpreted in the context of political relations with the public, various degrees of loyalty to existing curriculum forms, differing views of the needs and interests of young people, varying degrees of confidence in the validity of claims made by competing theories, and the exigencies of everyday life in the schools.

This chapter will describe the historical routes that various meanings and versions of affect in the curriculum have taken in the United States. While this sketch will begin much earlier, our primary concern will be with the twentieth century, when the competition among versions of affect in the curriculum became particularly heated. Over the course of this century the country has experienced wide swings in politics (from the progressive views of the Roosevelt years to the conservative ideas of the Reagan administration), several wars, large-scale immigration, landmark legal decisions, economic swings, industrialization, urbanization (and suburbanization), the advance of technology, and struggles over workers' rights, civil rights, and women's rights. To suggest that the flow of theory and practice regarding affect in the curriculum was isolated from these historical moments is to seriously underestimate the reality of the relations between school and society. Thought and action interpreted each event in its time, as well as the implications for young people, school, and society.

Moreover, it was during this century that the curriculum field itself emerged as an area of inquiry and study. The work of such people as Dewey, Bobbitt, Charters, Kilpatrick, Rugg, Bode, Tyler, Taba, Miel, and the many who followed interpreted the flow of events in society and suggested how affect should be placed in the curriculum. Developments in philosophy, sociology, and psychology, all viewed as foundations of curriculum study, had tremendous impact on curriculum thinking, as did new discoveries and interpretations in the many subject fields on which established school programs were based.

Writing historical accounts is always difficult, even more so when multiple meanings and interpretations coexist over time. Such is the case in reviewing the historical routes affect in the curriculum has taken. Nevertheless, it is crucial to our personal work that we have some sense of how various meanings and versions emerged and evolved. This account does not intend to treat events and episodes fully; that is left to the several excellent curriculum histories that I refer to frequently. Instead, the purpose here is to watch them through a particular lens, namely, one that detects affective concerns and related curriculum proposals. Moreover, we will look primarily at theoretical strands that clearly captured the attention of those responsible for curriculum practice in schools.

IN THE BEGINNING

In 1647 the Commonwealth of Massachusetts passed a law that set the stage for what would be the dominant version of affect in the curriculum until the twentieth century and one that is still popular today. Based on the belief that "Satan thrived where ignorance existed," the "Old Deluder Act," as the law was known, established common grammar schools to expand religious teachings in the lives of young people. Not only was intellectual ignorance to be eradicated through the school, but moral ignorance as well. In a society in which Calvinism was an ascendant feature, children were viewed as innately evil and their bad behavior, or "sins," as a step on the road to death and damnation. Moreover, children were seen as miniature adults who, regardless of age or development, were to assume adult morality codes and conduct themselves accordingly, or suffer the consequences. That morality was religious morality, and it was as deeply etched in the life of the school as in the community. The legendary New England Primer taught children letters through religious morality lessons, the Bible was regularly read, and catechism recitations were regular fare in the classroom. This was evident not only in grammar schools but in the growth of secondary "academies," which surfaced in the 1700s. The Phillips Academy of Andover, Massachusetts, for example, was based on the idea that "the first and principal object of this Institution is the promotion of true Piety and Virtue" (quoted in Krug, 1960, p. 21).

As early as 1749, Benjamin Franklin proposed breaking away from the religious and classical bases of schools, suggesting instead a secular and practical foundation (Tanner & Tanner, 1980). In the particular context of the academies, the time for this idea had obviously not yet come, but it would eventually serve as a historical claim for establishing the twentieth-century public high school program. By the mid-1880s the large flow of immigrants had introduced religious diversity into society, and gradually sectarian instruction in religious morality gave way to moral education reflecting common Christian precepts. This transition was not always peaceful. In Philadelphia, for example, violent riots erupted as immigrant Catholics sought to have their children taught through a version of the Bible that reflected their own views, rather than the dominant King James version favored by Protestants (Feldberg, 1975). Whatever the form, though, catechism instruction and Bible reading were still popular.

Meanwhile, a new and powerful concern emerged. In rapidly growing urban centers, the economic conditions of poor, immigrant groups were perceived by the dominant Anglo society as a source of potential unrest; and their cultural traditions, as a threat to the "American" way of life (Kaestle, 1983, 1984). Political rhetoric increasingly spoke to the need for a common moral code to dissipate cultural diversification and reduce the growing cases of street crime that were attributed to moral "deficiencies" among immigrants (Butts & Cremin, 1953). Not surprisingly, a primary agency in this effort was to be the common public schools whose establishment was supported mainly for this purpose. Nostalgia may conjure up images of "readin', 'ritin', and 'rithmetic," but school accounts of the times have much more to do with "moralizin'."

This drift toward common, rather than sectarian, religious morality was joined in the schools by the emerging popularity of mental discipline rooted in Faculty Psychology. Through the mental discipline theory, natural science began to find a place in the school program, but even this was promoted as a means to "elevation of the moral being of children" (Russell, 1830). This was the earliest form of the view of the mind as muscle in need of exercise, a theory of "learning" that still drives the ideas of some educators. Moreover, this mind-muscle consisted of separate powers in need of separate exercise, and thus separate lessons on morality and virtue were deemed necessary to address those distinct functions. Ironically, this concept of differentiation rooted in mental discipline and actualized in direct instruction would emerge nearly a century later in isolated "affective education" programs whose advocates treated the theory of Faculty Psychology as a joke.

By the early twentieth century religious-based moral instruction in public schools had seriously diminished. One later investigation of moral and religious content in American school readers reported that such content characterized 100 percent of them in 1776–86, but that it had dwindled to about five percent by 1916–20 (McKown, 1935). By the late 1890s the customary practice of opening the school day with prayer and Bible reading had come into question as states moved legally to enact the separation of church and school. Nevertheless, the relation of morality and religion remained much in the minds of educators, serving as an important ingredient in some versions of the moral education that was to emerge in the first third of the twentieth century (Chapman, 1969).

THE GREAT DEBATE: CHILD OR CURRICULUM?

The late 1800s were marked educationally by the rise of classical humanism, so named because of its infatuation with academic disciplines tied mainly to the language, literature, and cultural themes associated with classical views of the "ideal state." Not that mathematics and science had no place in the school program; indeed they did, but their power in comparison to that of the humanities was a matter of considerable debate and their place continued to be tied to moral instruction.

Two reports were particularly important in developing this view. The first, published in 1893, was that of the Committee of Ten, appointed by the National Education Association. This group laid out a collection of several academic areas, including an equalized place for the humanities and sciences, through which cultural ideals would be presented. Of importance in our understanding of this version of what I have called affect in the curriculum was the idea that all students would study the same areas in the same way. This implied that induction into the high-class culture of academic life (college preparation being partly the charge to the committee) was appropriate preparation for practical living (Tanner & Tanner, 1980). In rejecting as undemocratic the European notion of class sorting by program variations in the school, the Committee of Ten embraced the idea that democratic education should be defined as the same program for all.

However, the idea of offering differentiated courses in the name of equality of educational opportunity had already found its way into school programs, especially with the introduction of "manual training." Its presence and its advocates, driven by the idea that responsiveness to individual and social needs promoted democracy, would help to dissipate and finally undo the standardized curriculum of the Committee of Ten. This differentiated program of studies and the theory behind it were part of the evolving movement toward tracking in the schools. Though secondary schools were largely populated by white students at the time, results of this idea would later be felt in the cultural affect of schools in which such tracks would reflect racial and socioeconomic divisions in the larger society. Indeed, the controversy over standardized versus differentiated programs and their relation to racial, ethnic, and socioeconomic distinctions remains with us today.

The second report, issued in 1895, was authored by the Committee of Fifteen, also appointed by the National Education Association, but intended to address elementary education (National Education Association, 1895a). This group, chaired by William Torrey Harris, defined 16 branches for study in the elementary school as well as the number of minutes a week that each was to be addressed. Though direct moral instruction was not among the branches, the report was filled with ideas about and implications for affect. First, it spoke to the need for "rigid isolation of the elements of each branch" (National Education Association, 1895b), a view that would lead advocates of moral instruction to seek an additional branch for its direct teaching. Second, the report reflected the Harris view that the individual was subordinate to the prevailing social institutions and economic system, a status quo that schools were to help preserve and that individuals could participate in through knowledge of the cultural heritage (Harris, 1896).

Ironically, just as classical humanism was in its heyday in the late 1800s, many U.S. educators had begun to pay serious attention to theory and pedagogy flowing from Europe, chiefly that of Pestalozzi, Froebel, and Herbart. One can easily imagine the stark contrast between school practices in this country, as I have described them, and the idea of reformulating the curriculum based on the characteristics and instincts of children as described in the European work.

One of the earliest interpreters of that work was Francis W. Parker, who, as superintendent of schools in Quincy, Massachusetts, in 1875 set out to reorganize the school program around the principles of natural child development and learning as well as to promote freedom of thought as a democratic principle. With regard to the placement of affect in the curriculum, it seems reasonable to say that it was Parker's work in the schools that opened the door for a version that differed from the widely held view associated with mental discipline, transmission, and classical humanism.

The public door to the Progressive education movement was opened in 1893 by Joseph Mayer Rice, who visited schools across the country and reported his observations in a magazine named *The Forum* and then in book form (Rice, 1893). What he had seen was a dull and lifeless institution in which children engaged in rote learning based on the lecture-recitation method. As Herbert Kliebard (1986) has reported, Rice was attacked by defensive educators for his scathing analysis of their schools. We can perhaps understand the strength of resistance to calls for reform by comparing the tone and content of Rice's writing to those of the accusations that would be made by some analysts of school affect three-quarters of a century later (Silberman, 1970).

However, the strongest resistance to the rigid academic interests of classical humanism was the child-centered movement that had already attracted attention with its concern for the natural development of children and youngsters as a source for the curriculum. The most prominent advocate of this view was G. Stanley Hall, whose research on child and adolescent development was to mark a turning point in curriculum theory (Hall, 1901, 1909). His "scientific" studies of growth and development and his emphasis on spontaneous interest arising from age-related developmental characteristics would become a hallmark of one of the strongest wings of the Progressive movement; in fact, the child study method and its application to curriculum can be traced throughout the largely affective child-centered movement across the first half of the century. Later episodes, like the activity movement, the open classroom, and much of the humanistic approach to personal development have their conceptual roots largely in the child-centered approach. The term itself is still strongly associated with the developmental version of education in general and its application to individual affect in particular.

Many modern advocates of the child-centered approach might be surprised to know, however, that Hall's work eventually turned toward a sad paradox. While it is taken as the initial voice for the interests of young people, heredity was to be seen as the main determinant of intelligence and the main purpose of child study would be to identify "gifted" children who would receive the largest share of support in the schools. Moreover, his laissez-faire individualism ignored conditions in the larger society that not only detracted from the quality of living for young people, but suggested that the differences he found among them might not have been so "natural" after all (for example, Curti, 1935). Apparently many modern developmentalists have missed this point about individualism in their own work.

While most child development enthusiasts generally left the fragmented, specialized subjects alone, one group, the Herbartians, took this on as their cause. Though it is questionable whether they really cared about the specific theories of J. F. Herbart, the Herbartians pursued the general concept of correlation of subject areas (Tanner & Tanner, 1980). They eventually settled on the use of "cultural epochs" as organizing centers, using the highly questionable child development theory that "ontogeny recapitulates philogeny," a concept to which Hall's work was also attached. Behind this theory was the idea that development of young people reenacted the development of civilization; that is, people progressed from the "primitive" stage of dependence on the environment to a series of stages in which they gained increasing control over their own fate. Given this theory, it is not surprising that the curriculum emphasized historical epochs that would presumably match the child's stage of development and reveal appropriate lessons for moral development. In this way, according to Charles DeGarmo (1896), children would develop the ideals, dispositions, and habits thought to be necessary for social morality in the twentieth century. Though these theories would hold little sway in school practice, the idea of correlating curriculum with affect had been proposed. It would show up again in the 1950s and 1960s in reform proposals supporting use of the social problems and emerging youth-needs approaches to curriculum organization that spoke directly to personal and social development.

As debate raged over whether the curriculum should follow the "natural" instincts of children or the intellectual interests of adults, its resolution was suggested by John Dewey. In what would be his persistent method of repositioning arguments, Dewey proposed that the issue was not the child *or* the curriculum, but the child *and* the curriculum (Dewey, 1902). As he put it, the "old education" viewed the interests of children as "something to be got away from as soon as possible and as much as possible," while the "new education" viewed

those interests as "something finally significant in themselves." Instead he argued that the concern of the teacher should be with

> the subject-matter . . . as representing a given stage and phase of the
> development of experience . . . of inducing a vital and personal expe-
> riencing. Hence what concerns him, as teacher, is the ways in which that
> subject may become a part of experience; what there is in the child's
> present that is usable with reference to it . . . how his own knowledge of
> the subject-matter may assist in interpreting the child's needs and do-
> ings. . . . He is concerned, not with the subject-matter as such, but with
> the subject-matter as a related factor in a total and growing experience.
> (p. 91)

Important as this controversy was, and as sensible as Dewey's
arguments were as a resolution, it was left unsettled and is still with
us today. Part of the reason is that just around the corner was a new
issue that would attract the attention of those inside and outside the
schools and would speak directly to a particular version of affect in
the curriculum. As we shall see, it was one of those cases where larger
social concerns set aside debates over curriculum within the school.

FROM MORAL INSTRUCTION TO CHARACTER EDUCATION

The place of religion in the public school had largely diminished by
the end of the nineteenth century and had been replaced by what was
called "moral instruction." Though increasingly secular-based, in
some places moral instruction was often a euphemism for religious
instruction; in much the same way, human growth and development
has frequently become a euphemism for sex education in our own
times. As is sometimes the case, educational claims, particularly those
involving affect-loaded issues, are more likely to avoid scrutiny if they
are couched in acceptable terms and popular forms. Such was to be
the case in the early versions of a new affective twist called "character
education."

The main theme of early character educators was to break from
the "moral idea" approach of the classical humanist version of moral
education and take direct aim at the actual conduct of children and
adolescents. Over the second and third decades of this century, character education received widespread attention and appeared in different forms: as a substitute for religious instruction, as part of the

"Americanization" program for immigrants, as a school contribution to the larger social efficiency movement, and as one thread in the Progressive education movement (Chapman, 1969; Yulish, 1980). As we shall see, the last three of these were tied together by perceptions of the expanding industrial age. First, though, we need to see how "character education" emerged as "moral training" and gradually replaced direct religious instruction.

Though the courts may move to separate church and state (and school), we must never underestimate the degree to which many people in our society look to religion for moral guidance in thought and behavior in private and public life. Hence, it is not at all surprising that as religious instruction dissipated in public schools at the turn of the century, it was replaced by moral training that continued the main themes of its predecessor. Among many sources that illuminate this idea, *Moral Training in the School and Home* (Sneath & Hodges, 1914) is particularly instructive.

According to the authors, "morality lies at the foundations of social structure, and it is the essential condition of its perpetuity" (p. 1). Among their important recommendations were that ethical reasoning not be encouraged in the elementary school, but instead an insistence on virtues related to habits of will and forms of conduct or character; that surveys of teachers be conducted to determine what virtues and vices should be addressed at each grade level; and that an indirect method be used through stories and fables, myths, biographies, and history as told by teachers. In stories, they stated, "punishment is swift and reward immediate" (p. 10).

Most of the book was devoted to a detailed explanation of virtues to be emphasized. Though too numerous to list here completely, they included physical cleanliness, industry, perseverance, self-reliance, honesty, wise use of knowledge, obedience, good manners, loyalty, public spirit, justice, courage, and love of beauty in nature, art, *conduct, and character* (italics mine). These and more were related to the "desirable" intellectual, social, economic, political, and aesthetic life. In the end, though, religion entered the picture as the "Divine sanction of morality" and the basis for right living or character. Religion, according to the authors, runs through all cultures and is a natural human inclination. Children should know that "God watches" their behavior just as other people do. However, the authors added that "nothing anti-Jewish, anti-Catholic, or anti-Protestant may be permitted to enter into our public schools" (p. 214). Therefore, while Bible reading was to be done, only sections that did not offend any of these groups were to be selected. Readers were to be prepared in the same way, and school authorities were to grant time for religious instruction.

This review of Sneath and Hodges' book is crucial to our understanding of an important strand of character education that blended the new and the old. The focus on behavior, the use of surveys to identify methods, the separation of child and adult expectations, and the use of indirect instruction were all relatively novel concepts based on work only recently done at that time in psychology and pedagogy. On the other hand, the tradition of religion as the ultimate basis for morality and character entered powerfully onto the scene. In a sense, the newly emerging concepts were already being reinterpreted to provide a place for religion. In the end, this strand of "character education" was a euphemism for religious instruction.

A second variation on the idea of character education emerged in the curriculum as civics courses related to the "Americanization" of immigrants. Though this concept had several variations ranging from nationalistic to multicultural views, most prominent was the "assimilation" mode that held character virtues as a set of behaviors that immigrants should assume on the path to the American way of life (for example, Higham, 1970). For immigrant adults, a major source of such "learning" was the Settlement Houses, but for young people, the major role in the cultural induction process was to be played by the schools.

As we look back on these Americanization programs, they are revealed as a case of serious ethnocentrism on the part of dominant figures in society who had perhaps forgotten their own immigrant roots. Surely, the conduct modes that character educators sought were frequently already a part of the cultures immigrants brought with them. That fact, as well as the belief that public school participation would increase the economic chances for the young, may help explain why resistance to this form of affect in the curriculum was relatively mild.[1] Of much greater concern to immigrant groups were attempts to inhibit native languages and religions, as well as the economic and working conditions of the labor class in which so many were placed. Often obscured behind these issues were proposals, by those who saw immigrant youngsters as destined by class and culture to carry out the manual work of the industrial age, to limit their learning to the "hows" of labor rather than the "whys" (Franklin, 1986).

The concern for formation of proper work habits among young people was not limited to the immigrant population. In fact, that was only one aspect of a larger strand of character education that was beginning to take hold. In 1907, Arthur Twining Hadley, then president of Yale University, suggested that business leaders play a role in solving social problems as a way to protect their vested interests through means that included the identification of morals to be taught in schools (Hadley, 1907). The idea that schools ought to follow the lead of business and industry was to become the basis for the widespread social efficiency movement that would affect curriculum organization, school practices, and school administration (Callahan, 1962; Kliebard, 1986). While many educators embraced this approach, its leading spokesperson was Franklin Bobbitt (1918, 1924), who sought to apply to schools the industrial efficiency ideas of Frederick Taylor (1911).

In the social efficiency view, education was seen as production, and learners as raw material who would eventually become "educated" products. Standards were to be set for learners just as they were set for products in industry, and for teachers just as they were set for production workers. Schools could then show measured results to justify their expenditures. Moreover, social efficiency experts believed that schools were failing to prepare young people for making a living in terms of both job skills and the virtues desirable for the work force. To remedy this problem, they sought to implement a curriculum based on job analysis and the conduct of successful workers. This was accomplished by adding the "scientific method" through surveys and analyses of workers and the breakdown of various work tasks into literally thousands of skill objectives that could then be taught to students (National Education Association, 1919). There was also a clear flavor of class distinction in this movement, whose advocates differentiated those who would "do" from those who had the ability to "lead and appreciate" (Snedden, 1921).

Although the social efficiency movement became very popular in the schools, it was around this notion of the schools' role in class-labor distinctions that a noteworthy resistance movement was formed. According to Kenneth Teitelbaum, socialists of the times recognized the tremendous importance of public schools in theory, but became increasingly critical of the dominant emphasis on capitalism in the curriculum (Teitelbaum, 1987). To offer their children an alternative view of economic and social possibilities, they established "Sunday schools" (so named only because they met on that day) in cities and towns throughout the country. Curriculum themes included labor issues, the place of the working class in history, and distribution of wealth, power, and justice. Though their popularity was to diminish within two decades, these grass-roots efforts remind us that no matter how dominant particular forms of affect in the curriculum may appear to be, there are always those who resist them, not only in theory but in action as well.

While early advocates of social efficiency had spoken to aspects of living other than work, these other aspects were relatively less emphasized until 1918. In that year, one of the most important and revered documents in curriculum history appeared, namely, the *Cardinal Principles of Secondary Education: A Report of the Commission on the Reorganization of Secondary Education* (National Education Association, 1918). Its main feature was a list of seven principles that would guide the curriculum: Health, Command of the Fundamental Processes, Worthy Home-Membership, Vocation, Citizenship, Worthy Use of Leisure Time, and Ethical Character. Since that time countless thousands of education students have been made to memorize these so-called "Seven Cardinal Principles." They have generally been seen, correctly, as a landmark break from the view that subjects themselves are the ends of education rather than some of the means to accomplish goals related to broad areas of living. However, the fact remains that the report itself was one of many documents in its time that reflected the social efficiency movement; indeed, the commission itself was headed by Charles Kingsley, a student of David Snedden, whose role in that movement has already been noted.

Each of the principles represented an area of daily living for a curriculum that was to become an instrument of efficient learning. Reflecting the social efficiency point of view, the report attached the curriculum to existing living conditions. However, the report endorsed comprehensive high schools based on common experiences for all young people as an example of democratic education. As might be expected, this was a position that most efficiency advocates, such as Snedden, argued against. Their interests were chiefly in differentiating the educational experiences of various groups of young people depending on the type of work for which they were "destined" (Kliebard, 1986).

The social efficiency movement is crucial to understanding the evolution of affect in the curriculum in U.S. schools. Not only did it have enormous affective implications, but it served as a backdrop for the burgeoning character education movement of the time. Regarding the efficiency movement, it is important to see that youth were viewed as cogs in the wheel of industrial society and its needs. The "school as factory," an appropriate metaphor, was to be the social instrument for shaping the characteristics of young people as desired for that society, just as it is today (Foshay, 1980). Moreover, young people were to be differentiated according to their perceived potential as leaders or workers. Curriculum, teaching, and administration were to be mechanized along the lines of efficient industrial practices. As Raymond Callahan (1962) noted, "doubtless many educators who had devoted years of study and thought to the aims and purposes of education were surprised to learn that they had misunderstood their function . . . they were to be mechanics, not philosophers" (p. 49). The methods of efficiency were also to be applied to roles and responsibilities that would provide stability in the home, community, and workplace, including gender expectations that worked their way into curriculum mechanization: Those tasks involving the home fell almost entirely to women and became the substance of domestic science and home economics courses (Charters, 1926).

What all this meant was that the school would be reduced to teaching mechanical skills and virtues associated with living in an industrial society. As morality became embedded in behaviors identified by supposedly value-neutral "scientific" methods, it was distanced from the idea of moral development through critical and conscious thought.[2] Further, given existing social conditions, it meant that differentiation of students according to their "potential" would also follow lines of race, ethnicity, gender, and class evident in the larger society. It is crucial to remember that at this time the intelligence testing movement, with its deep ties to eugenics, was in ascendance (Selden, 1985). As present theorists celebrate this movement for its introduction of scientific principles and areas of living to the curriculum, these other, powerful meanings are often obscured. Indeed, we might well want to remember what W. E. B. Du Bois (1902) saw in the relations between job-skill training and the differentiation of labor by race: "The ideals of education, whether men are taught to teach or to plow, to weave or to write must not be allowed to sink to sordid utilitarianism. Education must keep broad ideals before it, and never forget that it is dealing with Souls and not with Dollars" (p. 82).

In the 1920s character education became an accepted approach to educators of many persuasions and the subject of much discussion. Numerous groups, both connected with and separate from the schools, were formed to promote character education, and several contests were held, with cash awards, to solicit moral and character codes (McKown, 1935). Theoretical developments were proposed by George Albert Coe (1917), an influential figure in the Religious Education Association; W. W. Charters (1927), an early curriculum theorist; and many others, including school officials. Discussion ranged over questions such as whether character was a state or a trait, how character became integrated into the personality, and which educational methods were best for building character (Chapman, 1969; Yulish, 1980). A good deal of that talk had to do with the relationship between character and religion; a major focus was on the individual and primary social relations, with very little attention to implications for larger social conditions.

Even some advocates of "progressive" methods cornered part of the character education market. This is not surprising, because one strand of the Progressive education movement focused almost solely on the individual's adaptation to prevailing conditions. For example, Germane and Germane (1929) defined character education as "a process through which the child learns to make wholesome social adjustments to his many perplexing life situations" (p. 10). They listed 33 "traits" of desirable character in terms that replicated the "virtues" of Sneath and Hodges cited above. Basically Germane and Germane were after the same thing, but by less indoctrinaire means and without the ultimate religious overtone. They emphasized methods for promoting character, such as participatory governance, and for responding to character problems, such as the case method, as well as correlation of subjects around real-life moral issues in the school and community, and the use of "homeroom" for direct character instruction. This "progressive" approach to character education was to show up frequently as participants in the Progressive movement evidently felt the need to reinterpret their positions in light of what had become the prevalent version of moral education. As we shall see later, this version of character education has also emerged in our own times.

In the end, the 1920s were to see both good news and bad news for character education. We have reviewed the former. The latter was to come at the end of the decade in the form of a research project on the effects of character education on the actual behavior of young people. In a startling three-volume report by the Character Education Inquiry at Teachers College, Columbia University, Hugh Hartshorne and Mark May (1928, 1929, 1930) demonstrated that character education had little effect on some of the virtues cherished by its advocates. Among the findings were that moral lessons taught in school largely dissipated under the ambiguities and demands of real-life situations, that school life itself often contradicted the very moral lessons that were taught, and that didactic moral lessons ignored the need for experience in their application, including within the school.

The force of these findings on then popular theory can hardly be overestimated. After all, things had been going along nicely in terms of philosophy and proposed methodology, and suddenly the whole movement was subjected to "scientific" analysis, itself a perceived ally from the social efficiency movement. On the other hand, as is often the case, the research at hand had relatively little effect on the practice of character education in schools. Indeed the view of virtue and conduct, the use of behavior codes, story lessons, and even the ties to religious morality continued for many years, especially outside metropolitan areas in schools where secular character education was (and still is) supplemented by daily prayers, holiday ceremonies, and other religion-based rituals. These practices have resurfaced in recent years in a new character education movement that shares most of the rhetoric and applications of the earlier one.

There are some aspects of Hartshorne and May's study that are not usually mentioned. Hartshorne was, in fact, a teacher at Union Theological Seminary in New York and a leader in religious education. May had been a student of Hartshorne's at the Seminary and later of Edward Thorndike at Columbia. According to May (Chapman, 1969), when Thorndike received a grant to do the character studies, he called in his former student, who in turn brought Hartshorne into the project. By this time Thorndike had debunked the transfer theory of the mental disciplinarians and was deeply involved in the intelligence testing scene, where his work was partly driven by the eugenics theory that attributed intelligence and most behaviors to heredity.

In light of these connections, certain recommendations in the study are not at all surprising. For example, the largest finding was that character as taught did not transfer to real-life situations because of inconsistencies between the two; if done properly, the school would have to become a social environment in which such inconsistencies would not exist. This is as near to Thorndike's transfer theory as one can get. Another example in the report deals with similarities between siblings' responses with regard to self-control and service: "These resemblances cannot be accounted for by reference to the influence of such home background features as we have measured and may represent, in part at least, inherited biological factors" (Volume II, p. 448). Even assuming Thorndike did not actually write this statement, it would have appealed to the eugenic streak he favored in his own work. Hartshorne must have been at least mildly disturbed at the poor showing made by religious activity as a correlate of character virtues. In the end we are left mostly with an explanation rooted in Thorndike's transfer theory and the inference of inherited character. However, character education was on the ropes in terms of theoretical respectability.

THE RISE OF "PROGRESSIVE" EDUCATION

While social efficiency and character education had ascended to a dominant position in the curriculum, they were not the only force at work in the schools. As we have seen, turn-of-the-century theorists expressed interest in developmental aspects of childhood and adolescence and in experimentation with "psychologized" methods of teaching. These interests were to serve as the grounds for an emerging "progressive education" movement that was deeply concerned with affective aspects of schooling. The term *progressive* is certainly problematic, because it included a number of different threads. We have already seen its appearance within the framework of character education; here we will add other threads such as child-centered schools, democratic schools, and the search for alternative curriculum approaches. Cluttered as this scene may appear to be, it is here that we will see how the earlier interests, though on the margins of the curriculum for almost three decades, rose to prominence in the late 1920s and into the 1930s.

One can hardly begin to look at this era without first noting the influence of John Dewey. Dewey's early attachment to the Herbartians, a group with which he soon became disenchanted, and his experimental efforts in the legendary University of Chicago Laboratory School (the "Dewey School") were followed by an unbelievable record of publications that explored nearly every aspect of education and schooling. Space prohibits a full accounting of the connections to later work by others, but a few examples suffice regarding affect in the curriculum as I have defined it. *Democracy and Education* (1916) formed the basis for the movement to create schools as democratic communities. *Theory of the Moral Life* (1908), *Moral Principles in Education* (1909), and *How We Think* (1910) showed up later in both the language and theory of cognitive-developmental moral education. Finally, *Theory of Valuation* (1939) set the precedent for the values education movement, particularly as it clearly spoke to the connection between affect and cognition.

A less obvious, but equally important, contribution was Dewey's lifelong battle against "either/or" propositions that set up as oppositional, ideas that were actually related. Connections, rather than oppositions, between the child and the curriculum, democracy and education, for example, forged the way for similar later efforts to make sense out of what otherwise would have been thought oxymora (such as humanistic schools). At the same time Dewey was critical of many interpretations of the so-called "progressive" movement, claiming, for example, that some of its advocates were overly romantic about child development, not attentive enough to the need for reflective thinking, and too little concerned with emerging issues in the industrial society. Though he was often misinterpreted and roundly criticized, Dewey's long shadow is clearly cast across "progressive" claims for affect in the curriculum in both advocacy and disagreement.

The focus on developmental characteristics of young people, "psychologizing" of subject matter, and experimental pedagogy that marked the work of Hall, Parker, Dewey, and others had its most prominent life in what came to be called "child-centered schools." Their connection to affect in the curriculum arises chiefly from the recognition of the need to consider personal development and experiences in curriculum planning. In the first two decades of the century, the child-centered movement was most prominent in private schools, either associated with universities or established by parents (Rugg & Shumaker, 1928). However, with the publication of William Kilpatrick's *The Project Method* in 1918, public school educators increasingly turned their attention in this direction. Experimental programs centered on this idea soon began to appear in schools around the country.

The project method and related efforts were mainly concerned with the *process* of teaching and learning. So prominent was this emphasis that it soon became clear that "process" was to replace or become the "content" of learning, a concept that would deeply influence proposals for affect in the curriculum over several decades. It mattered little that such a notion was quite different from what Dewey, Parker, and others had in mind; what was important was that educators *perceived* that their work was responsive to the needs and interests of young people. By the 1930s, the emphasis on process emerged in the form of the "activities movement," while continuing research on development largely framed the "youth-needs" curriculum approach. Although this movement had been found mostly in elementary schools, its force would be felt in the secondary schools as well.

By the later 1930s, the "progressive education" movement was in full swing. Spurred on by the larger spirit of social experimentation in the Roosevelt era, the many meanings of progressivism were found in schools throughout the country. At the height of this activity the Progressive Education Association sponsored and then published the results of an eight-year study of the effects of experimentation in secondary schools (Aiken, 1941). With the aid of curriculum consultants, 30 high schools developed experimental program forms such as "correlated" studies. The results on the whole suggested that the more experimental the school program, the better its graduates did in college, even when those programs varied widely from the usual subject-centered approach. Here, as in the case of the "life adjustment" movement that would follow, the developmental concerns of the curriculum experiments must be weighed against the quantitative research methods that reflected the social efficiency position. However, the spirit of experimentation and the frequent use of the social problems approach tend to make this study a landmark work in considering affect in the curriculum.

One important contribution of the study was the attempt to identify means for measuring affective outcomes, an effort that was largely original. In fact, many of the devices used were later identified by Krathwohl and associates (1964) as appropriate for the framework of a taxonomy of objectives in the affective domain. In the end, though, what would have been a near-fatal blow to classical humanist views of the curriculum hardly made a dent in the education field. As it turned out, the study was published in the early 1940s when the country had far more pressing matters on its mind than the possibilities of curriculum reform.

As these events unfolded, another aspect of "progressive" concern had also emerged. As we have seen, concern for the relation of democracy to education had been expressed before the turn of the century in many ways, ranging from the standardized curriculum of the classical humanists to the curriculum experimentation encouraged by Parker. Dewey also spoke compellingly to this issue, especially in his classic work, *Democracy and Education* (1916). Yet it was the fact that interest in democracy would be claimed from quite different viewpoints that makes it so problematic as an aspect of affect in the curriculum. In this sense, we need to explore two different conceptions of the relation between democracy and education: one constructed from the view of the school in promoting more democratic conditions in society and the second concerned with the use of "democratic" means within the school.

The first of these conceptions emerged in what came to be called "social reconstructionism." Advocates of this concept, among whom George Counts (1932) and Harold Rugg (1939, 1947) were the best known, saw the school as a primary force in solving the numerous social problems that had beset the country during the industrial age. The school was to become a highly politicized institution with teachers as the critical agents of reform. Through active community

expression and teaching about social problems, the "reconstructionists" would press for reforms of many kinds, particularly the democ-
ratization of all aspects of life.

On this particular point the reconstructionist position departed
from Dewey's in that he continually expressed a faith in democratic
discourse as a method for applying human intelligence to social problems rather than naming solutions. Similarly, Boyd Bode (1935), a
fellow "progressive," objected to this position, saying that "the remedy
for shortcomings of the progressive education movement is not to
proscribe beliefs but to specify the areas in which reconstruction or
reinterpretation is an urgent need" (p. 22). Despite such criticism,
this movement laid the foundation for the continuing efforts to create
democratic schools pointed at social issues, an approach that was
particularly popular in the late 1960s and early 1970s. Moreover, it
represented a major departure not only from the status quo advocates
of the social efficiency and character education movement, but from
the individualistic tendencies of the developmental approach as well.

The second conception of democracy and education was decidedly
less controversial, but presented a serious problem. Advocates of
progressive methods within the school had heeded the call for more
democratic means. However, divorced from a clearly articulated view
of democracy in the larger society, the meaning of democratic "methods" became a source of considerable contradiction. To understand
this concept we will turn to a fascinating account of one definition of
democracy in the curriculum that partially explains some of the
contradictions found in various versions of affect in the curriculum,
especially the curious use of similar methods. According to William
Graebner (1988), this particular variation is understood as "the engineering of consent."

Though the understanding of this concept is not new, the strength
of Graebner's account is in naming it and tracing its chronology. As
he tells it:

> Means replaced ends. Methods replaced goals. Embedded within these
> changes was a new structure or system of authority, democratic in form
> if not always in substance . . . those whose attitudes were to be changed,
> or whose behavior was to be modified, had to be part of the process, to
> participate or be made to *feel* that they had participated. (pp. 3–4)

The method that Graebner defines begins with the decline in traditional Protestant church affiliation in the late 1800s and the subse-

quent shift from individual "soul-saving" to the social gospel and group process techniques in Bible study classes, YMCAS, and Christian Clubs.

Eventually this emphasis on group process and participation would extend into Settlement Houses, scouting groups, school clubs, war efforts, foreman's clubs, golden age clubs, and the various government-sponsored programs (WPA, CCC, NYC) intended to assuage economic problems during the Depression—virtually everywhere that people were brought together to participate in "democratic" decision making and problem solving. That the use of the word *democracy* was powerful in legitimating this method was, according to Graebner, nowhere more clearly demonstrated than in Woodrow Wilson's famous phase, "the world must be made safe for democracy," which would be used to justify the entry of the United States into World War I. If it could be used there, it certainly could be used to legitimate school programs.

Put plainly, the "engineering of consent" names the process by which people are led to believe that they are genuinely involved in making decisions when, in fact, their participation is only an illusion of involvement, aimed at leading them toward a preconceived decision or, at least, a general consensus within which specific preconceived decisions would nicely fit. Understood this way, democracy as social authority appears to be an agreeable compromise between autocratic insistence on compliance and the open-ended democracy of reconstructionism with its perceived possibility for threatening the status quo. It has the ring of autonomy and efficacy, but the assurance of order and conformity—a most seductive combination. Yet its appearance and its means should be understood for what they really are: a method of securing and solidifying the interests of those in power.

Here, then, we may begin to sense an explanation for some of the contradictions in various versions of affect in the curriculum. Why, for example, would some "progressives" find a place in the social efficiency and character education movements, a version that so clearly emphasized compliance with externally imposed conduct rules? Perhaps, because while disagreeing with its autocratic means, they did not necessarily disagree with the behavior ends it sought; "democratic" participation (and child-centered methods) would simply offer a more agreeable way of pursuing those ends. Why would many "progressives" criticize the reconstructionist movement whose members came from their own ranks? Perhaps, in some cases, because the reconstructionists had broken from the emphasis on means and called the ends of education into question. Why would many school officials accept the call for "democratic participation" of young people in school government and curriculum planning? Probably, in many cases, because they saw in its explanation an opportunity to gain compliance under the guise of "commitment."

If the motives behind democratic social engineering were so transparent, why did so many people agreeably participate in it? As Graebner points out, the idea of democracy had emerged as the American "religion"—mere mention of the term apparently was enough to justify almost any project. Resistance, on the other hand, would leave one open to accusations of being "undemocratic" or "un-American." No doubt many people, including those not in dominant positions, also agreed with the ends sought by social authorities—less delinquency, less social conflict, greater social order. Furthermore, we should not underestimate the skill of group leaders who, equipped with the latest in group dynamics techniques, were able to engineer consent without revealing their real agenda.

Yet there was resistance to this method. Many young people refused to participate in student government and satirized the power-lessness of student councils. Many Japanese-American citizens placed in internment camps during World War II refused to participate in group decision-making activities. Some floor supervisors left fore-man's clubs, and unions continued to resist efforts to co-opt their consent. Despite these cases, democratic social engineering defined a powerful current in the progressive movement, including its role in affect in the curriculum.

In naming and understanding this thread of "democratic" partic-ipation, we must be careful not to let it obscure other, more genuine attempts to support democracy in the schools. For example, the involvement of young people in curriculum planning described by L. Thomas Hopkins (1941), Harold Alberty (1953), and others was clearly intended for quite different reasons. Here curriculum deci-sions were purposely left open so that teachers and learners could mutually determine the topics they would study and the methods of doing so. Also, while Graebner names Dewey as one of the people who influenced the "group process" movement, we should not forget how widely Dewey's work was misused or his abiding faith in the demo-cratic way of life as a means of engaging people in discourse around structural problems in the society and the school's role in promoting that discourse. Obviously, though, when it comes to discussing the relations between democracy and affect in the curriculum, we must always ask how "democracy" itself is defined.

LIFE ADJUSTMENT
AND THE REVIVAL OF CLASSICAL HUMANISM

In the 1930s, as we have seen, character education continued in the schools, but it coexisted with the various strands of "progressive" education and initiatives growing out of economic problems created by the Depression. While the latter were meant only as temporary measures, these programs were often cast in language that tied them to resolution of larger socioeconomic issues. However, the work aspects of these programs reflected the virtues associated with character education: industry, perseverance, self-reliance, and so on.

Once the United States became involved in World War II, a new kind of affect entered schools. Much of the study in traditional subject areas and in vocational education reminded young people of their patriotic duties in support of the war effort. Assembly programs and other ceremonies emphasized a nationalistic fervor. Often overt, but sometimes hidden, were pointed reminders of the presence of immigrants and their descendants from countries that were at war with the United States. Many students were immigrants or from immigrant families, and peer tension along nationalistic lines frequently resulted. This version of affect, characteristic of periods of foreign conflict, interpreted affective interests of young people as a matter of national interest. The transmission of nationalistic ideology thus became a major expectation of the school. As we shall see later, this may also be the case when international competition in technology or economics, rather than actual war, are seen as threats to national "security."

During the Depression school enrollments had grown dramatically, particularly at the secondary level, in part aided by the work-study programs that were intended to keep young people, as well as first- and second-generation immigrants who would previously have ended their formal schooling at the elementary level, away from the overcrowded employment market. This meant that schools had been populated by large numbers of students for whom the usual college preparatory program was believed to be inappropriate. The dramatic increase in the number of dropouts during and after the war served to support this belief and was the rallying point for rethinking the curriculum.

The response came in the form of what was called "life-adjustment education." A major event in shaping this movement was publication in 1944 of *Education for ALL American Youth*, by the Educational Policies Commission. Casting its thinking in the social efficiency mode, the commission stated a list of 10 "Imperative Needs of Youth." In actuality, they were the Seven Cardinal Principles with the addition of intelligent consumerism, aesthetic appreciation, and knowledge of the scientific method. First among the 10 was the development of a "salable" skill that might be used to enter the world of work, an obvious hint of what the authors thought was a means for keeping young people in school. As a collection, the 10 needs were seen as functional areas of living for which the school should efficiently prepare young people by adapting the program to individual differences. The academic program, so long entrenched in secondary schools, was not to be dropped; rather it remained as the route for those intending to go on to college.

Meanwhile, in 1945 a group of faculty from Harvard University published a report entitled *General Education in a Free Society*. This group called for a general education consisting of traditional subject areas with the addition of vocational education, raising again the controversy between social efficiency and classical humanism. In this case the protagonist of the late 1800s (classical humanism) had become the antagonist of the mid-1900s. In setting up the traditionalists of classical humanism against an opposing view of the curriculum, the latter was given the ever-convenient label of "progressive education." Ironically, the Progressive Education Association was already in its last days and would be disbanded within a few years.

This point is pertinent to the version of affect in the curriculum that grew out of "life-adjustment education." The movement was widely supported and involved many theorists prominently associated with curriculum reform and reorganization in terms of personal and social needs. Adaptation of the curriculum to individual differences and use of the areas-of-living approach as general education—two hallmarks of the movement—as well as its preference for "progressive" and "democratic" methods, certainly contributed to both the support and involvement. Indeed, these were to be continued as a major theme in the curriculum field itself (for example, see Alberty, 1953; Krug, 1950).

However, as we think about affective meanings, it is important to consider the possible consequences of this kind of thinking. At the very center of "life adjustment" was the concept of adapting young people to the existing conditions in society. This overshadowed the possibility of questions being raised about nonconformity on an individual level or the possibility that social conditions might be in serious need of reform. Curriculum adjustment and democratic methodology aside, there was no organized view of the developmental possibilities of young people or society. Moreover, the ever-growing curriculum tracking system, "democratic" in the sense of recognizing individual differences, often resulted in a most questionable version of affect in terms of democratic principles. That is, the tracking of students across academic areas or into vocational strands frequently paralleled distinctions among race and socioeconomic class, and within tracks reflected gender stereotypes found in work, home, and social relations in the larger society.

While the Harvard report represented a token statement reflecting the classical humanist position, it was not long before other academics and their public allies launched an all-out attack on "life adjustment." By the late 1940s public criticism accused "life adjustment" of "godlessness" and "ethical relativism," evidence that the critics saw the approach as the old progressivism with a new name (for example, see Bell, 1949; Smith, 1949). In the era of Joseph McCarthy such accusations were to be taken seriously, especially in the schools themselves. These public critics were soon joined by professional academics in the classical tradition. Best known among these was Arthur Bestor (1953, 1956), a historian from the University of Illinois, who rejected the whole of life-adjustment theory and pedagogy in favor of a renewal of the intellectual tradition of classical humanism. The way to college and to morality was through disciplined intellect, and its possibility could be guaranteed in no other place but the schools.

As if such academic logic was not enough, the launching of Sputnik in 1957 added fuel to the fire. With that event, the public and the profession discovered a new version of affect in the curriculum. It was that the interests, needs, values, and aspirations of the young should be centered on scientific and mathematical competition with the Russians. So defined, the affective dimensions of young people became a matter of national security, prominence, and pride. Those subjects, which were construed to be "value-neutral," also offered a safe hiding place from the political hunt for evidence of communist ideas. The vehement expressions of people like Hyman Rickover (1959) became the rhetoric of federal support and enthusiasm for this meaning of affect. The message in this version has not been lost on observers of the present scene who see a striking similarity in the current concern over the place of the United States in the world marketplace.

During this period also, renewed consideration was given to the place of religion in the curriculum, as the courts moved once again to reaffirm the separation of the Church from state-run schools. In 1943, the Supreme Court had ruled that children could be excused from pledging allegiance to the flag. While the case was seen as having to do with state indoctrination, it was specifically argued on the grounds that the pledge could be interpreted as a violation of religious freedom (*West Virginia State Board of Education* v. *Barnette*). When, in 1963, the Court ruled against the use of prayer in school, what seemed like the final blow was struck against the presence of religion in public school life (*Abington School District* v. *Schempp*). Many people correctly foresaw the possibility that teachers would eventually become reluctant to even touch on religion in the classroom, for fear of crossing the constitutional line, even though the text of the actual case encouraged such study. Curriculum thinkers, however, urged such study and further suggested that the moral affect of the school reflect the spiritual values of the Judeo-Christian heritage, which they felt ran deep in the national culture (e.g., Krug, 1960; Phenix, 1961). Despite these urgings, explicit reference to religion was to become a forbidden topic in many public schools over the next two decades (ASCD Panel on Religion, 1987).

THE POPULAR RISE OF PSYCHO-EDUCATION

Given the desire to avoid value expressions during the 1950s and early 1960s, it is not surprising that psychology, with its claims for value-neutrality in social "science," rose to prominence. For the most part, this was the heyday of behaviorism as a psycho-educational theory. Growing out of the work of Thorndike and the social efficiency movement, this way of thinking was promoted by B. F. Skinner (1968) and others. The underlying theory was that behavior was simply a response to a stimulus and thus if educators could find the right stimuli they could shape students toward desired behaviors. First, however, the desired behaviors would have to be carefully stated, along with the appropriate stimuli. This was done through development of behavioral objectives that reduced desired learnings to small units of task and time. Not at all unlike the job analysis and adaptation theory of the social efficiency experts, this view had widespread influence on the curriculum and would soon affect administrative behavior as well. Affect in the schools frequently became mechanized and routinized, and restricted to the lowest possible levels of behavioral shaping.

At that time also, many educators were infatuated with the recently published *Taxonomy of Educational Objectives, Handbook I: Cognitive Domain* (Bloom, 1956). This popularity was mostly due to its explication of levels of thinking processes, its focus on behavioral objectives, and the relation of these to post-Sputnik work on curriculum in subject areas, as well as the interest in "scientific" management of schools then (and still) in vogue. Eight years later, a second volume appeared entitled *Taxonomy of Educational Objectives, Handbook II: Affective Domain* (Krathwohl, Bloom, & Masia, 1964). It was, according to the authors, the much requested sequel to the first volume. The booklet included a restatement of the domain theory, an explanation of the affective domain, a description of the latter's relation to the cognitive domain, and a definition of the language used to describe affect and its choice in the committee's work. The largest part of the book was devoted to laying out a taxonomy with sample objectives and measurement devices. The levels in the taxonomy began with willingness to receive and respond to information and proceeded through identification of values, their organization into value "sets," and action based on them.

Several questions might be raised about the content and development of the taxonomy. One is its distinctively behavioristic tone suggested by the emphasis on behavioral outcomes and their measurement, ignoring the possibility that some affective states at some levels might reside in thought alone. The same issue suggests a second point which relates to the fact that this volume (in common with its predecessor) was ultimately more concerned with evaluation than development. A third is the implication that affective development results from repeated input from external sources, thus leaving the possible role of intuition out of the picture. A fourth has to do with the fact that categories selected for inclusion in the domain were suggested by reviewing sources of objectives from schools and colleges, thus leaving open the question of whether they represented a complete or desirable theoretical set.

These reactions notwithstanding, in formulating the taxonomy, the authors made important contributions to serious thought about the affect domain.

1. In defining affect in terms of "interests, attitudes, appreciations, values, and emotional sets or biases" (p. 7), they properly located it beyond the more common view of simple representations of inner feeling and tone.
2. Their arguments for connecting affect and cognition in both theory and practice are as compelling today as they were then.

3. They correctly argued that schools are responsible for individual development at least as much as for socialization, and reflected this logic in the emphasis on internalization of values across the taxonomy, as well as the need for autonomous thought about affective issues rather than compliant behavior.
4. They revealed the fallacy of reductionist arguments for the school as an exclusively passive-academic-intellectual agency.
5. They brought the idea of affect to the attention of educators and suggested that the enthusiasm for the cognitive domain ought to be applied to this domain as well.

Today, much of the confusion about cognition–affect relations stems from the misguided, yet popular, attempt to define intellectual or cognitive activity in terms of the classical academic tradition and to maintain its dominant place in school programs. This attempt has been unwittingly reinforced by those who promote affective learning as a separate course or experience apart from the academic purposes of the school and who pass the affective dimension off as a collection of personal development activities. I use the term "unwittingly" here to give this version the benefit of the doubt; it is not clear whether some of its proponents actually object to the academic-separatist position and merely want their side of the story added onto the curriculum, with the additional plea that academic teachers be "nice" to young people. Whatever the case, work in the area of affect defined this way is left open to claims that it lacks intellectual rigor and thus must be only peripherally related to intellectual activity in academic subjects. As a result, schools continue to operate on the theory that "cognitive" and "academic" are synonymous and both are apart from affect. For example, recent rhetoric tied to promoting higher-order thinking has focused on particular subject areas with little, if any, reference to affective dimensions. More than a little of that rhetoric has involved a revival of interest in the cognitive domain taxonomy.

In retrospect it seems clear that part of the problem of separation has to do with the historical moment when the idea of cognitive and affective domains became popularized in educational thinking. The publication of the cognitive taxonomy (1956) preceded that for the affective domain (1964) by several years. That first "handbook" was widely read and discussed, particularly in the flood of workshops on stating subject objectives in behavioral terms. The second book was, by all accounts, neither as widely read or understood, departing as it did from the intellectual view of schooling. Further, the connection between the domains so clearly explicated in the second volume was separated in time from the first volume, and work following from the first was already well under way before the second volume appeared. We can only wonder what the effect of this work would have been if both domains had been covered together in one volume, with the explanation of their relations.

However, behavioral psychology was not to monopolize the influence of psychology for long. Ironically, as the Progressive Education Association was formally disbanding in the early 1950s, a new, person-centered theory was emerging. Called "third force" or "humanistic" psychology, and set against behaviorism (Patterson, 1977), this theory proposed that individuals constructed versions of their experience through personal perceptions that in turn influenced their view of the world and their actions within it (e.g., Moustakas, 1956; Rogers, 1969; Snygg & Combs, 1949). Thus the development of clear self-concept and positive self-esteem was recognized as a crucial aspect of a fulfilling life. Though most of the early advocates of humanistic psychology worked from the viewpoint of therapists, they soon turned their attention to how their theory might help the larger population. Inevitably, they focused on the school. Albert Alschuler put it this way in 1969:

> At the frontier of psychology and education a new movement is emerging that attempts to promote psychological growth directly through educational courses. Psychologists are shifting their attention away from help for the mentally ill to the goal of enhanced human potential in normal individuals. Educators, on the other hand, are beginning to accept these courses along with the unique content and pedagogy as appropriate for schools. (p. 1)

Critical of institutional demands for conformity and curriculum impersonalness, the humanists claimed that self-concept should be at the center of education, and its development the primary goal of schools (Combs, 1962). This platform gathered momentum through the 1960s and 1970s, buoyed by the self-fulfillment movement in the larger society; it served as the foundation for many efforts, including several of the self-esteem programs available today. While the "self-actualization" described by the humanists was much more complex and serious than the "self-fulfillment" implied by popular psychology in the 1970s, the latter certainly created a climate in which the former could find its way into the curriculum.

One offshoot in particular was to make an important contribution, albeit eventually a most troublesome one. Contrary to some popular beliefs, the early humanistic proponents did not restrict their idea of self-concept to individualized self-fulfillment. Rather they saw it as the center from which flowed relations to others; unless a healthy self-concept was in place, the alienated and problematic state of human relations would never improve. Indeed, one of the characteristics of the so-called "fully functioning person" was that "he sees his stake in others" (Kelley, 1962, p. 18). This idea was at the basis of the human relations and sensitivity training programs that gained popularity in industry during the 1960s, carried out through special workshops and retreats often framed as a response to the racial issues raised in the civil rights movement. By the late 1960s these types of programs had found their way into schools and so was born the idea of separate courses focused on self-concept and human relations, many of which would come to be labeled as "affective education" (Gumaer, 1975, 1976; Stillwell, 1976).

In a most instructive essay on this development, Max Birnbaum (1969) explains that Leland Bradford, Director of the Adult Education Division of the National Education Association, along with Ronald Lippitt and Kenneth Benne, developed an early "sensitivity training" lab at Bethel, Maine, and that Bradford was instrumental in bringing the idea to schools. Supposedly the heightened awareness of the need for improved race relations, following both nonviolent and violent episodes, was to serve as a primary focus for these programs in schools. Birnbaum defended the need for such programs in schools, but issued severe warnings about how the method might be misused. Interestingly, industry-based sensitivity training involved management personnel, but rarely the workers who were supposedly the objects of sensitivity awareness. School-based training programs involved teachers who were, in turn, supposed to carry out programs with young people. Perhaps these arrangements might partially be understood by noting that Graebner (1988) placed Bradford, Lippitt, and Benne within the group process movement that he claimed was the main method for the "engineering of consent." In retrospect, it is fairly clear that these efforts had little, if any, enduring effects in school except in encouraging the idea of separate programs for "affective education."

Not long after, these efforts were joined by direct psychological education that involved similar goals, but also included direct teaching of psychology as a subject (Mosher & Sprinthall, 1970). I will explain later how this view and its contemporary version have narrowed the meaning of affect in the curriculum and left it open to justified criticism. For the moment, though, I will simply note that while such direct teaching may have a legitimate place in the curriculum, this distorted definition has plagued the field since its formulation. Many people continue to believe that anything that has the faint ring of affect requires a new school program, and anything outside such programs is not subject to affective analysis.

VALUES AND MORAL EDUCATION

At the same time that the humanistic psychology movement was gaining momentum, two other versions of affect in the curriculum emerged and claimed widespread attention. While I will discuss these more fully in Chapter 4, their ascendance is an important part of this historical sketch. Early in the 1960s, Louis Raths had begun to frame a theory of values development based on Dewey's concepts of valuing and thinking. Publication of the book, *Values and Teaching*, represented a landmark in the movement away from transmission or indoctrination of values toward a cognitive, reflective approach (Raths, Harmin, & Simon, 1966). Raths' technique of questioning, the nonjudgmental tone of the book, and the description of valuing on which both were based became known as "values clarification." Widely accepted in schools, the original work was followed by a steady stream of "how to" manuals that consisted of activities teachers could use to initiate the approach. Gradually the major focus in popular use was on the suggested activities rather than on using the "clarifying" responses across the curriculum. By the 1980s this apparently value-free or ethical-relative approach had come under criticism from moral education theorists as well as fundamentalist groups and others who sought to revive the transmission of absolute values.

The other program that gained widespread attention was Lawrence Kohlberg's cognitive-developmental approach to moral education (Kohlberg & Mayer, 1972). Following the work of Dewey and Piaget, Kohlberg argued that moral reasoning could be described as a series of predictive stages that were related to age, to stages of cognitive development, and to increasingly complex concepts of justice. Like values clarification, this approach was based on reasoning, but added the feature of content by explicating what Kohlberg believed to be types of reasoning and their grounds at each stage. Further, he suggested ways that teachers might elevate moral reasoning through use of moral dilemmas and described their relation to school structure in what was called a "just community" approach. Unlike the values clarification approach, Kohlberg's theory was more widely accepted than was the suggested application. After all, it was one thing to describe children's moral reasoning, but quite another to tamper with the structural aspects of schools, especially those having to do with the just distribution of power.

Despite its differences from values clarification, Kohlberg's theory was not to escape criticism. In 1977, Carol Gilligan, a research colleague of his, published a paper claiming that Kohlberg had defined moral reasoning from a distinctly male perspective, thus ignoring the fact that women tended to use "caring" instead of "justice" in such reasoning (Gilligan, 1977). Though people in schools paid even less attention to this argument than to Kohlberg's, it was to form the basis for powerful work on feminist moral theory, whose full impact is yet to be felt. Indeed, if schools should ever take the idea of "caring" seriously, affect in the curriculum would be profoundly influenced.

RECENT DEVELOPMENTS AND STRUGGLES FOR ASCENDANCE

Other cognitive approaches to values and moral education appeared in the 1970s, but none captured the attention that those of Raths and Kohlberg did. For example, the "values analysis" approach (Fraenkel, 1980) involved young people in examining the application of existing value positions to various issues, a less open-ended and individualistic method than values clarification was perceived to be. Moreover, during these years the use of analysis and reflection was applied to traditional subjects, especially social studies. Controversial issues usually entered the curriculum in the form of mini-courses and electives, as the social discourse of the civil rights and Vietnam eras spilled over into the schools. Gerald Weinstein and Mario Fantini (1970) put the case this way:

> The pervasive emphasis on cognition and its separation from affect poses a threat to our society in that our educational institutions may produce cold, detached individuals, uncommitted to humanitarian goals. . . . For example, we may know all about injustice to minorities in our society, but until we feel strongly about it we will take little action. (p. 27)

Courses on human growth and development, usually a euphemism for sex education, as well as on drug abuse, also began to focus more on questions of values and morals than on mere dissemination of information. The school as an institution came under attack for its supposedly dehumanizing and undemocratic features (Glasser, 1969; Haubrich, 1971). While some of these criticisms were not always labeled as such, the conceptual stamp of the reconstructionist view was clearly on them. That stamp was most evident in the work on critical curriculum theory, such as that of Michael Apple (1979) and Henry Giroux (1981); influential thinkers outside the United States, such as Paulo Freire (1970) and Jurgen Habermas (1971); and the widely disseminated 1975 Yearbook of the Association for Supervision and Curriculum Development, *Schools in Search of Meaning* (Macdonald & Zaret, 1975).

Like the early progressive movement, these later versions of affect in the curriculum, with their mix of analysis, reflection, development, and reconstruction, were a product of their times. The examination of personal, social, institutional, and political values was the parlor game of the two decades in which they were in ascendance. However, the connection between society and school meant that these versions would be subject to redefinition if the larger social climate changed. The general lack of understanding of the theory underlying the developmental view would also make it particularly vulnerable to validity questions. Indeed, this proved to be the case as the New Right emerged in the 1980s. Confronted with conservative-fundamentalist rhetoric as well as a social streak of hedonism, the more individualistic versions, in both their theoretical and practical forms, were left in an apparently defenseless position. It is hard to underestimate the damage done by the ahistorical and atheoretical curriculum practice of these forms and the subsequent association of anything nonindoctrinaire with the hedonistic ethics of self-fulfillment. Those who attacked the modern approaches to values and moral education were enormously bolstered by the intersection of these two factors.

Tired of criticism, stressed by what were seen as unrealistic expectations that it alone solve social problems, and itself reflective in many ways of the new conservatism, the education profession was not overly inclined to resist. A few defenders persisted (Beane, 1985/1986), and some schools continued programs, but even the area of self-esteem was focused mainly on its relation to academic achievement and the problem of "at-risk" students, and structural problems in the school were tied to academic excellence. By the late 1980s the new "progressive" versions of affect in the curriculum had clearly fallen on hard times.

While the versions of affect in the curriculum based on humanistic psychology, values clarification, and moral reasoning gained ascendance in the 1960s and most of the 1970s, those associated with classical humanism, social efficiency, and character education had their day once again in the 1980s. Caught in the spirit of conservatism and economic concern, the time was ripe for a new round. In the 1970s, growing concern was expressed over what was perceived as a decline in basic skill achievement among youth. The "back to the basics" movement worked quickly to strip the elementary schools of programs not directly related to reading and mathematics achievement, and as might be expected, the first casualty was anything having the faintest ring of affect, which had by then frequently been placed in separate courses or units. This movement also promoted a return to what were perceived to have been stricter disciplinary policies, such as the use of corporal punishment. As already pointed out, this attack on affect was really misplaced—actually, it amounted to replacing one form of it with another.

If the elementary schools were to be returned to the "basics," the high schools could not be far behind. In fact, from the mid-1970s on, there was a steady erosion of electives, social issues units, student participation in decision making, and a variety of other programs that had come of age in the late 1960s and early 1970s (Tubbs & Beane, 1981). These were gradually replaced by a new movement to tighten academic requirements and standards. That movement would itself come of age within a few years and would make those arrangements part of the "null" curriculum; that is, they would begin to constitute the curriculum that is not addressed (Eisner, 1979).

During these years, middle level education was being reconstructed in the middle school movement, which had as its basis the characteristics of early adolescents, personal and social development, and interdisciplinary curriculum plans. The fact that this movement was contained within a particular level of schooling and was not attached to a larger social movement may partially explain its relatively uncontested growth. However, even the strength of this growing phenomenon was not to be untouched by mandates for higher academic standards and requirements.

As the 1980s came to a close, the place of affect in the curriculum became a growing concern. I will discuss this more fully in analyzing the current scene in a later chapter and will only touch on it here. Throughout the Reagan administration, the place of religion was a highlight of the educational agenda. Congress was asked several times to legislate the return of prayer to public schools, though the Supreme Court continued to show its reluctance toward this idea. The Reagan agenda was integrated with that of powerful religious fundamentalists who began legal and legislative initiatives to remove something called "secular humanism" from the schools and to reinstitute Christian principles. Discouraged by the results, these groups created their own movement in private Christian schools while maintaining pressure on public schools through the courts.

Meanwhile, then Education Secretary William Bennett repeatedly emphasized the concepts of content and character in the curriculum, recapitulating the themes of classical humanism and character education to promote moral development (Bennett, 1986). Academicians and the public increasingly interpreted self-destructive behaviors and perceived declines in academic achievement among young people as symptoms of individual moral decay and hedonism. As might be expected, this interpretation brought back interest in the version of character education that emerged in the first three decades of the century. The growth of this movement may be seen in the substance abuse and AIDS education recommendations of the federal administration, which are based on self-reliance and self-control; that is, "just say no." In this age of discontinuity and ambiguity many people seek security and stability. One place these may be found is in the perceived innocence of the recollected past. When the clock is turned back, one eventually finds the morality and virtue that made up the character education version described earlier. As the 1980s came to a close, this view of affect in the curriculum was clearly in ascendance again.

SUMMARY

The purpose of this chapter was to sketch out the main versions of affect in the curriculum that have clearly captured the attention of those responsible for curriculum practice in U.S. schools and to show the routes they traveled over time. This account has been presented in terms of claims made by educational leaders, and while I have made some remarks about the popularity of claims and resistance to them, I do not pretend to tell the complete story as it might be informed by the lived experiences of those in schools and their surrounding communities. One thing that is clear, though, is that efforts to treat affect in the curriculum have touched some of the deepest sensibilities in the larger society. While resistance to various versions has not always been obvious, at other times it has been loud and vehement. Whichever version was in ascendance at any particular time surely offended some portion of the population.

Classical humanism certainly ignored the more practical interests of those not enamored of the high culture world of the intellectual academician. Most variations on the early character education movement related to "Americanization" ignored or degraded the cultures that immigrants brought to this country, as well as those of other nondominant groups. They also must have offended church–state separatists, who saw through the euphemistic attempt to maintain religious instruction in the public schools. Most social efficiency experts, past and present, have typically ignored pressing social issues, particularly those situated in lower socioeconomic classes and racial and ethnic minorities. The eugenic streak in this movement eventually offended anyone who cared deeply about human dignity.

The child-centered advocates offended those who preferred to have children act like miniature adults, particularly those interested in efficient organization of youth-related institutions. The reconstructionists clearly threatened the vested interests of the wealthy and powerful and offended their perceptions of personal and property rights. The humanistic developmentalists offended those who believed the resolution of social problems was inhibited by overemphasis on individualism. Virtually all of the versions ignored gender issues, a result no doubt of the male dominance of educational theory sources. And it is quite possible that young people, subjected to various versions in their times, were at least partially offended by all of them.

Ironically, virtually every version claimed attachment to the idea of deepening "democracy" in society and the "best interests" of the people. This was the case of those who argued for religion as a deeply rooted basis for American democracy, just as much as it was of those who argued for education in the interests of individual rights, adapting schools to the needs of young people, or the reconstruction of the society. Indeed, there has always been ambiguity about the meaning of democracy and its relation to personal-social development in schools and the larger society. This ambiguity has led to tremendous disarray in what I have defined as affect in the curriculum.

Informed by our history, we are still left with many questions, particularly how the guidelines described in Chapter 1 might be used to work toward an adequate and appropriate way to place affect in the curriculum. However, a sense of history will likely prove helpful because it reveals meanings and consequences associated with any claims in relation to that topic. Chapter 4 will look at how the many versions sketched in this chapter appear in the schools at present. First, however, we need to look at some themes that ostensibly support personal and social efficacy in our society and that, therefore, ought to be given serious attention in framing proposals regarding affect in the curriculum.

3

Foundations of Affect:
Democracy, Dignity, and Diversity

Proposals regarding how affect should be placed in the curriculum do not arise in a vacuum. Rather they emerge from (1) particular ways of interpreting the meaning of affect, (2) defining the conditions for personal and social efficacy and the ways in which those may best be developed, and (3) evaluating political, social, cultural, and economic conditions and their implications. All proposals do not necessarily consider all of these elements, nor are they always given equal treatment in particular versions. In fact, most often proposals do not address one or more of these elements or treat them inadequately.

To imagine how affect might properly be placed in the curriculum, we must return to the components of a coherent framework outlined at the end of Chapter 1. This chapter will focus on those that represent the foundations of affect in the curriculum, namely, philosophical and psychological concepts as well as sociocultural trends in contemporary life. As we begin to work our way out of the conflict and contradiction portrayed in Chapter 2, our question is whether there is some lens through which we *ought* to look at affective issues and affect in the curriculum. I will suggest that there is and that it is shaped and shaded by deep themes that are supposed to support personal and social efficacy in our society.

I will limit the focus to public schools in the United States, which, legally constituted, publicly supported, and almost universally attended, serve as the main ground upon which versions of affect in the curriculum are made and contested. Moreover, the political, cultural, social, economic, and legal forces that drive schools are uniquely configured in particular societies and countries, even though certain aspects of them may be commonly shared. To argue a case within the cultural pluralism of the United States is difficult enough. To go beyond would be virtually impossible short of a large dose of arrogant ethnocentrism.

In making these claims I do not want to suggest that the way in which I define particular themes is the "final word" about them in an absolutist sense. Instead I mean to enter my voice as one among the many that ought to be carrying out discourse about affect in the curriculum. As that discourse is expanded (a topic I will take up later), the ideas described here deserve serious attention as continuing themes in our work.

THE DEMOCRATIC WAY OF LIFE

The United States was founded as a democracy and continues to claim the right to democratic self-governance as its fundamental identifying characteristic. While most of us were made to memorize the events that led up to the American Revolution, it is not as likely that we were taught that the democratic form of self-government was an extension of the Enlightenment tradition, which earlier had gained increasing attention in Western social and political philosophy. The key concept underlying that tradition continues to be human emancipation or the drive to grow and develop beyond conditions that have limited or devalued participation in self-determination, or what Habermas (1971, p. 310) characterized as "ideologically frozen relations of dependence." In this sense, democracy is more than simply a form of political governance or a set of procedures for carrying out such a form. Rather it is a disposition or, more broadly, a way of life in which people define and seek personal and social efficacy through full participation (as opposed to being subjected to the interests or whims of others) and in which each person sees all others as having the right to self-governance.

All of this is not to say that the "democracy" framed in the early days of the United States presented a "golden age" of full participation in self-determination. In fact, the reality of that version extended participation rights only to white, male property owners. While one may argue sympathetically that such a view was in step with perceptions of entitlement at that historical time, the fact is that it created a privileged democracy that necessitated a long and continuing struggle for extension of democratic rights to the larger, more diverse population (Zinn, 1980). In part this task has fallen not only on the disenfranchised people themselves, but on the many social institutions and agencies that are maintained by society and expected to contribute to its improvement. Among these, of course, is the public school. As we shall see, this role places the school in a contradictory position.

As only one among many institutions and agencies, the school is not solely responsible for development of the democratic way of life, but clearly it has a large part to play. There are several reasons why this is so. First, as an institution, the public schools are located within an ostensibly democratic society and ought to reflect the democratic way of life. Second, the public schools have long avowed democratic purposes with regard to both individual and collective learning, as articulated in many of the goal statements developed by groups referred to in Chapter 2. Third, the public schools are the common ground that virtually all people experience, and therefore they represent one of the best opportunities to demonstrate and promote the democratic way of life. Fourth, public schools often are, or can be made, small enough to allow for the kind of full participation that is central to democracy but often difficult to achieve in other social institutions. Finally, public schools are, for the most part, locally governed and thus represent one of the few places where the many voices of interested parties may be heard directly.

This role has obviously been difficult for schools to play, because it subjects them to serious contradictions. Not the least of these is that when schools assume the democratic concept of equality, there is conflict with unequal aspects of the larger society, such as race and gender bias and inequitable distribution of wealth. Another contradiction, which is most evident in currently competing claims for affect in the curriculum, is the conflict between critical thinking as a mode of inquiry and unquestioning compliance with imposed political, economic, religious, and other values desired by special interests both inside and outside the school.

The call for undemocratic (or antidemocratic) action in the name of expedience or specialized interests poses a particular problem for public schools. My argument here, as in the other foundation areas discussed later, is that the public schools have a responsibility larger than mere acquiescence to or comfortable compromise with prevailing norms or special interests. Rather the schools represent a kind of repository of "public trust," of which the continuing search for extended democracy is one aspect. As Maxine Greene (1985) argues, "Surely it is an obligation of education in a democracy to empower the young to become members of the public, to participate, and play articulate roles in the public space" (p. 4). That underlying focus of the school, cast as it is in a present state of ambiguity, requires that we think again about the meaning of democracy and its implications for the school.

In its idealized form, democracy calls for the *full* participation of *all* people in making decisions that affect them (Beyer & Wood, 1985). Partly because of such variables as size, distance, and time, the concept of a republic, or representative system of self-government, was attached to democracy in the United States in order to make participation and consent possible. However, this arrangement does not preclude the idealized sense of full participation, which is the critical idea in understanding democracy, not just as a form of government but as a way of life. In fact, as fewer people participate directly and more people are simply "represented" by others, the possibility that some voices will not be heard increases—and so does the possible erosion of interest in expanding democracy.

Moreover, the drift of decision making toward "representative" bodies, even when their members are elected, brings governance to the edge of centralization of power and encourages a network of "governing elites" who have the resources to get elected in the first place. Such an arrangement, in turn, tends to create a narrow definition of democracy in which benevolent protection is asserted as a version of maintaining the common good, and participation is reduced to the simple act of voting, regardless of whether those up for election really represent the interests of those who will be governed. The loss of interest in participation is often attributed to this more limited conception of "protectionist" democracy (Wood, 1984), in which political elites elected in expensive campaigns determine the issues that will be addressed and marginalize the interests or concerns of politically and economically disenfranchised groups.

The idealized form of democracy and its characteristic self-governance depend on certain conditions. These conditions are held in high regard not because they are required by law or contribute to self-gain, but rather because they are necessary to expand and extend the possibilities for democracy. Among the conditions are the following:

1. Faith in the individual and collective capacity to create and critically evaluate proposed solutions for human problems

2. The willingness of people to seek the common good by maximizing equality and individual dignity

3. Faith that people, as a matter of public and self-interest, will choose the democratic way of life and reject policies and procedures that contradict it

4. Belief that the common good can be consensually defined on the basis of central values and moral principles that do not interfere with autonomy or personal efficacy and, in fact, extend them

5. The possibility that all voices and views may be heard and seriously examined regardless of their popularity or position in society (Dewey, 1908; Habermas, 1979)

6. The realization that universal agreement is rarely reached, that decisions are not permanent, and that democracy is an evolving concept

7. Willingness to pursue consensus and, short of universal consent, to accept broadly formulated consensus (Oliver & Shaver, 1966)

8. Individual and collective willingness to continue to engage in democratic processes, so that the capacity to participate will be continuously improved

9. Faith that people exposed to and experienced in democracy will seek to extend empowerment to others rather than "pull the ladder of self-governance up behind them"

10. Where representation is necessary, representatives who seek full participation or, at least, consult broadly with those they represent without regard for wealth, power, or position, and regardless of the representatives' own self-interests

11. The arrangement of institutions, organizations, and agencies in ways that maintain, carry out, and extend democracy

It is important to understand that these are not independent or linear conditions, but rather a set of interrelated, systematically defined propositions, so that all are necessary and none alone is sufficient for extending democracy. Each depends on the others for its full realization, and any action, positive or negative, in one affects the others. For example, if institutions do not function in democratic ways, then experience in democratic processes cannot be gained. Likewise, if equal and full access to the process of governance is denied to some, then they are no longer self-governed no matter how beneficial the actions of others may be for them.

Most people who review the conditions described above will immediately think of many examples where democracy has not been and
is not being realized in the United States. If this is the case, a part of
my purpose is achieved. On the one hand, these conditions are stated
to conceptualize what is necessary for the "idealized" democracy that
our society is presumed to pursue. Its possibility—aside from questions of probability or reality—constitutes the "democratic faith"
(Dewey, 1934, 1944, 1946). On the other hand, the statement of these
conditions is intended to remind us of the idea of democracy as it
ought to be portrayed and pursued in the life of the school.

CENTRAL VALUES AND MORAL PRINCIPLES

If a democratic society was a collection of individuals whose self-interests never conflicted in the ongoing conduct of social affairs, we could
limit our discussion of affect in the curriculum to personal development
and efficacy. However, the ongoing experience of humankind demonstrates clearly that this is not the case. In fact, the histories of relations
between the governing and the governed, between majorities and minorities, and between dominant and less dominant groups offers a
seemingly endless array of examples in which the good of a few is
gained at the expense of many, and in which particular persons and
ideas are marginalized in political, social, and economic affairs. Hence
a particular problem arises, namely, the relationship between self and
social interests in a sense of the "common good" that meets the conditions of collective needs and individual autonomy.

This problem has given rise to a troubling dualism in which
personal and social interests are seen as always competing—one must
automatically be given up if the other is to be achieved. During the
1980s, substantial political and educational rhetoric was directed at
social or group interests, at least partly in response to what was
perceived, in retrospect, as almost exclusive emphasis on individual
rights and interests in the preceding several decades. Assuming that
this perception was true, we might expect collective interests to take
precedence for a time until they too are seen to be excessive, and then
attention to turn again to individual interests—a reenactment of the
"swinging pendulum" metaphor that supposedly describes the history
of educational and social innovation.

However, the accuracy of the perception that individualistic self-
interest thoroughly dominated society and the schools is open to ques-

tion. Much of the rhetoric of the "excellence" reform movement in education, as it related to morality, claimed to be overcoming the individualism and relativism that supposedly began in the 1960s. Yet apart from the singular experiences and isolated examples that critics offer, there is no substantial evidence that the individual self-interests of young people gained a dominant position in schools. Moreover, those examples have usually been taken from versions of affect such as values clarification and cognitive-moral development, both of which have been seriously misunderstood and misused. Research evidence used to support the perception of widespread selfish individualism in the society at large, such as that of Robert Bellah and his colleagues (1986), is likewise problematic in its focus on white, upper middle class populations. In contrast, evidence regarding the self-concepts of nonwhites (Euch, 1987; Nobles, 1976) and moral reasoning among women (Gilligan, 1977, 1982) indicates the salience of such features as interdependence, cooperation, and social responsibility, while studies of Native American cultures reveal an emphasis on cooperative economics, resource sharing, and interpersonal harmony.

Clearly, a visible streak of individualism and hedonism can be observed in some portions of the young population. But to say that this is the first generation of youth to exhibit these characteristics is silly. In fact, accounts of the youth culture of the "serene" 1950s usually give more than a little attention to James Dean as the "rebel without a cause," in marked contrast to the social activism of the 1960s, precisely the period in which selfish individualism is supposedly rooted. Moreover, to blame the schools for whatever degree of hedonism presently appears among young people is likewise irresponsible. It would be more accurate to look closely at the commercial interests reflected, for example, in mass advertising aimed at young people (Henry, 1963) and the ethic of individualistic competition that is suggested to them as the way to "get ahead." (The implied assumptions about economic resources and opportunities may, of course, also say something about the discrepancy between self-interests among middle-class whites and social interests among nonwhites and women.)

These powerful messages in the larger society place schools in the same kind of contradictory position we saw in considering their role in extending democracy. In this case it is a problem posed by pursuing individual and social development that conflicts with special interests served by competitive individualism and hedonism. We should not lose sight of the ambiguity this creates for young people themselves, who are, after all, subjected to the ambivalent curriculum affect that arises from these contradictions.

The way out of such confusion is to consider the possibility that self- and social interests might be integrated, but not by sacrificing one or the other and not by simply promoting enlightened self-interest that either obscures self-gain or depends solely on recognition that what is good for many is also good for the individual. Rather the integration of self- and social interests ought to be attempted in light of the possibility that central values and moral principles might be defined so that they simultaneously support both personal and social efficacy, and so that they serve as referents for identifying desirable actions both within and between the two.

Typically any attempt to articulate shared values or moral principles is met with extreme skepticism, because it is immediately assumed that anything "shared" will necessarily interfere with individual rights or represent only those of a particular group. As we saw in Chapter 2, this assumption has often been borne out across the history of proposals to place affect in the curriculum, as in versions of morality that expressed the interests of religious sects, "high" culture, and corporate efficiency. However, the historical existence of such claims does not mean that they represent all that are possible. Instead we must consider the possibility that shared values and moral principles might be defined that are worth considering because they extend the efficacy of individuals and groups regardless of their positions and histories in society.

The possibility of defining shared values and moral principles in this way arises from two sources. One is the concept underlying the "inalienable rights" that were posited as "self-evident" by the original framers of American democracy on the grounds that those rights (theoretically) accrued to all people by virtue of their common position within the broad definition of humanity. The other source is found in the implications for human efficacy of the human principles democracy itself suggests and is intended to protect. Of particular importance here is the related implication that shared values and moral principles developed upon these grounds define the "common good" in a particular way: not as the good of the many or the majority, but rather as the good of all, both individually and collectively.

Having thus established the conditions for articulating shared values and moral principles, we face a new problem. There are many particular values or moral principles that might simply be listed and defended, each on its own merits: caring, justice, freedom, integrity, and so on. However, often such principles lead to serious contradictions when applied singularly in specific situations. For example, should the principle of truthfulness always apply even if the truth will certainly hurt someone, as might be the case if one is asked to comment on another's taste in clothing? And is truthfulness in this kind of situation to be regarded in the same way and at the same level as truthfulness in statements about government activities by elected or appointed officials?

Frustration with these kinds of contradictions is apparently what leads some to assume completely relativist positions in which values or moral principles are completely open to question depending on particular situations where they might apply, while leading others, such as religious fundamentalists and character educators, to rhetorically insist that particular values or moral principles always apply and to ignore situations in which contradictions arise. Both of these positions present problems, the first because thorough relativity may ultimately be used to defend individual self-gain apart from social interests and the differential treatment of particular individuals and groups, and the second because it fails to address the ambiguities of real-life situations.

To simply reject commonly used versions of values and morals debases those who have defined them and their sincere efforts to suggest what is desirable for personal and social efficacy. Instead, I want to reexamine those values and moral principles and suggest that we ought to think about them at different levels. The first or primary level consists of human dignity, the idea that all people, as belonging to humanity, are worthy and have a right to self-respect.[1] In this sense human dignity is an underlying and central concept from which other values and moral principles may be derived and to which they may contribute (Oliver & Shaver, 1966).

Human dignity serves as the central or overriding concept for several reasons. First, genuine personal and social efficacy is ultimately dependent on the degree to which people feel they have dignity and are regarded as such by others. Self-esteem in its most authentic form cannot be achieved short of personal dignity, nor can humane and democratic social relations be realized unless dignity is accorded to others. Second, human dignity is the fundamental entitlement of people, as suggested by the broad concept of "belonging to humanity." It is an entitlement that is characteristic of rather than dependent on the conditions and outcomes of particular situations. Third, and related to the other two, is the idea that human dignity may be posited as so fundamental and central that other values and moral principles may be derived from it and, in turn, it may serve as a referent for discourse about the contradictions among the others. We can thus understand human dignity, or the "inalienable" entitlement of worth and self-respect, as a consistent and necessary concept from which to proceed in deliberating values and moral principles.

Using human dignity as the "first" among possibilities for shared values and moral principles, what may be suggested as a second level in which its meaning is clarified and extended? The answer to this question lies in determining what human dignity implies and what is necessary and sufficient to support it. Here I would argue for a minimum of four related values and moral principles.

1. *Freedom.* When people are free, that is, when they can pursue self-determination and self-governance without the threat of tyranny or oppression, they not only may have a sense of personal dignity, but are likely to respect the dignity of others (Combs, 1962). Lacking freedom, people can hardly be expected to have a sense of self-dignity and are thus liable to seek only personal gain, either to protect themselves or to maintain and extend their own position in relation to others. In a democracy, the personal freedom to *do* (to speak, to assemble, and so on) is balanced by the right to freedom *from* (from oppression, from imposition, and so forth). To sustain what I called "the democratic faith," this kind of reasoning must be seen not only in terms of legal rights, but in the context of more personal, everyday relations as well. For example, racial or ethnic slurs, often considered to be protected by legal rights to free speech, are unacceptable in terms of their obvious impingement on personal dignity (even when they are legally protected).

Moreover, we must recognize that to some extent the freedoms ordinarily associated with democracy are also limited by the realities of particular conditions in our society, such as economic standing. For example, in the United States all people are supposedly free to speak in print by publishing their own newspaper, but economic realities mean that only some can speak in this way because only a few can afford to do so. Thus the freedoms of those few and the power they hold are conditioned by their obligation to honor the rights of others: to hear competing points of view, to be free from slander and invasion of privacy, and so on. Following this line of reasoning, then, freedom is a necessary condition for personal and social efficacy that extends from human dignity but that must be exercised so as to contribute to and protect the dignity of others.

2. *Caring and Justice.* One aspect of the current discourse about what it means to be moral involves the distinction between the disposition to "care" about ourselves and others as human beings and

the development of justice-based rule systems that would "objec-
tively" define desirable grounds for reciprocity in relationships
among people. I want to argue here that a complete theory of human
dignity and its relation to what it means to be moral ought to consider
the possible place of both positions and, more specifically, that justice
presents a particular kind of caring necessary in certain circumstances.

   People come to particular situations, behaviors, and decisions
with feelings, concerns, aspirations, and a history of personally lived
experiences as well as a deeply human need for a sense of well-being.
Human relationships based on respect for human dignity reveal sensitivity to these in both everyday relationships and conflict resolution.
To *care* about others means that we attempt to see beyond the "desira-
bility" (in our terms) of particular feelings or aspirations and to
understand how particular people came to want what they want, to be
who they are, and to behave as they do. It also means that we are
concerned about their sense of well-being and our part in maintaining
or improving it. When we care about others, we do not simply act for
people (on their behalf) as "objects" of our care, but also *with* them as
mutual "subjects" in the human experience. Caring also means that
we are concerned about ourselves and our own sense of well-being.

   When caring forms an ethic that is brought to problematic situations, it leads us to seek more information about those who are involved and the circumstances of the situation. Our attempt is to
become part of the situation with others and to work through its
concrete aspects (Noddings, 1984). We avoid simply analyzing the
situation and searching deductively for some abstract rule that will
tell us what to do. In this sense, the person and human interests are
placed before the law. This does not mean that we ignore reasoning;
rather our reasoning is directed at the human dimensions of the
situation rather than at determining what objective rule might allow
us to resolve the dilemma independent of complete explication of
personal conditions.

   It is quite possible that institutions and even societies might be
filled with people who "care" in these ways and also that we might
help others to learn the ways of "caring." But it is also likely that even
(or until it is) so, we would not know about every human dilemma that
would benefit from care. Thus, one way of extending the concept is to
work for rules that would make caring a prior condition of human
relationships in, for example, institutions or societies. While this
would not represent caring in its authentic sense, it would nonetheless
suggest that concern for humanness ought to be a condition of our

relationships. It is here that I place distributive justice as a particular kind of caring that offers a possible alternative in situations where care in the larger sense cannot be directly offered.

Justice involves recognition of the reciprocity of rights among people; that is, people have rights and are entitled to be treated in accordance with those rights. One of the most frequent ways in which the concept of justice has been used is in relation to legal rights as defined by the Constitution, the courts, and other legal authorities. Adherence to and recognition of such rights is typically seen as a moral principle in and of itself. However, to avoid reducing such rights to contractual agreements, we must also consider that people have human and civil rights that derive only partly from legal opinion. Human dignity, and the concept of justice that follows from it, assigns rights such as equality and freedom that are much larger and more powerful than the economic ones most often regulated by contract law (e.g., Rawls, 1971). In fact, by comparison, economic rights become highly problematic in the sense that it is hard to argue broad examples of their meaning, because they have been denied to so many individuals and groups. Thus, the concept of human dignity suggests the need for justice as a mediating principle in social interactions so that relationships may be based on concepts of individual and reciprocal realization of human rights. Conversely, justice contributes to human dignity by defining and mediating ways in which such rights may be preserved and extended.

The concept of justice just described is often construed in ways that attempt to objectify the reciprocal relations among people (Kohlberg, 1966; Rawls, 1971). That is, obligations are interpreted according to laws or rights that apply independent of the personal affect that is involved in particular situations. In this sense, it is seen as quite different from a theory of caring that recognizes that because people are human, their experiences cannot be totally objectified and must be considered as "subjective" as well.

Before leaving this concept, however, we need to ask why versions of morality have been so dominated by justice, while caring has played a far lesser role. There are at least two reasons for this, and they are connected. One is that typical justice-based rule making appeals to the dominant tendency to rationalize human thought and behavior into abstract systems that seem, at least, to be more efficient than subjective sensitivity. "Systematic" rules of justice appeal to the interest in social efficiency and the distinction between cognitive and affective. The second reason is that the concept of caring has been articulated largely by women, whose place in theoretical deliberation on many subjects, including morality, has been marginalized in a largely male-dominated society (Gilligan, 1977, 1982; Stocker, 1987; Tronto, 1987). The connection between these two reasons is this: In an efficiency-oriented, rationalized discourse dominated by males, the voices of subjectivity are silenced, particularly when those voices are largely of women. Yet, the overriding issue here is ultimately not one of gender, but rather the need for a genuine ethic of caring, including justice, as part of a larger effort to support and extend human dignity.

3. *Equality.*   Human dignity, in the sense of personal and social efficacy, implies the necessity for equality among people; that is, that all people have an equal right to dignity regardless of what differences may exist among them. This conception of equality means more than equal opportunity, although this is one aspect of it (Beyer & Wood, 1985). Once access is gained to an opportunity, such as an institution, equality in the broader sense means that people have a right to have their work within it dignified and that their rights to happiness, justice, care, peace, and freedom continue so long as they do not threaten or violate the dignity of others. This latter argument sets a condition on the continuing right to equality and may appear to be inconsistent with happiness and freedom. However, as John Rawls (1971) points out, if the concept of equality is to be more than simply an "original position" in human relationships, it must function on a continuing basis in which, for example, one person cannot gain some advantage unless that gain also improves the state of things for others, particularly the least advantaged. If we recall the idea that caring means acting with, rather than simply for, other people, then this meaning of equality may be understood as more than an aspect of justice. Beyond that, it recognizes the possibilities of a sense of interdependence and intersubjectivity among people for personal and social efficacy.

4. *Peace.*   Actual or potential threats to human life do not define all of the possible intrusions on human dignity that may arise in conflict situations. They do, however, imply the general nature of such intrusions that can be characterized as "violent." When dialogue about disagreements is reduced to physical or verbal violence, both parties experience loss of self-esteem as well as social efficacy. The same may be said for acts of "symbolic" violence, such as those in institutions when, for example, people are labeled, stereotyped, and

sorted in ways that debilitate their dignity (Apple, 1982a). The extension of human dignity requires that we attend to these kinds of "violence" through reasoned interaction that creates a truly humane discourse around problematic situations. Here again, of course, we see the contribution of feminist moral theory developed around the notion of caring, described earlier. Both psychologically and philosophically, the use of nonviolent discourse, particularly one that emphasizes "care," is not only implied by human dignity but contributes to it as well.

Such a conception of central values is necessarily broad, because it seeks to recommend conditions for personal and social efficacy at the most general level of humanity rather than within the context of factors that might otherwise divide people: race, class, gender, geography, ethnic heritage, and so on. To define the possibilities for central values and moral principles in a lesser or reduced form risks violating the central concept of human dignity by dislocating or depriving particular individuals or groups. For example, some current proposals regarding character education define "morality" by listing behavior rules such as respect for authority, compliance with rules, and patriotism. Upon close examination, however, these rules are more accurately defined as social conventions that operate in the best interests of those who are in power in various relationships and who have historically been white, male, and middle class. Here we might ask:

- Should young people respect the "authority" of adults when some of those adults abuse them?
- Are people required to comply with rules that reduce their right to equal access to institutions?
- Should those who have been historically marginalized in political, economic, and social aspects of our society be expected to demonstrate patriotic loyalty to it?

The answers may best be found by asking whether to do so would detract from people's sense of dignity as human beings, a question that is larger than their "obligations" as children, students, or citizens. While some adults argue for behavior rules as "moral education" on the grounds that the issues involved in the above questions are confusing to young people, research in this area demonstrates that even young children are quite capable of dealing with them and do so on a regular basis (Nucci, 1987).

Thus, the fundamental concept of human dignity is intended to be the central right to which all people are entitled because they belong to humanity. The related values and moral principles that follow from and support it are no less important, but may be interpreted and applied in various ways as particular policies or practices are seen to extend or detract from human dignity.

For those unaccustomed to thinking on the basis of values or moral principles, such reasoning may appear overly complicated and cumbersome. Indeed it is quite different from methods that are aimed only at efficiency or that depend on the arbitrary use of authority, power, and oppression. Yet it is a way of thinking and acting that leads to the preservation of human dignity and the actualization of central values and moral principles, whereas the alternatives do not. As it involves the balance of self- and social interests, as it considers human dignity as central to personal and social efficacy, and as it describes a discourse that uses nonviolent, caring, and reasoned deliberation, it reflects the democratic way of life as previously described.

A question arises concerning the source of such central values and moral principles, namely, whether religious or secular interests serve as their ultimate basis. Put simply, the answer is that both may do so, but if affect claims are made for *public* schools, the secular sources must be used, because they represent the *public* sense of personal and social efficacy. This does not mean that the religious heritage of the nation is ignored or rejected; rather it is not the appropriate source for speaking to moral issues in light of the constitutional separation of church and state and in recognition that religious observance is not universally shared in our diverse culture. Nor does this mean that those who make affect claims about public schools, or work in and attend public schools, must reject their personal religious beliefs or the lived experiences in which they may blend those sources. That would deny their right to dignity and freedom and also incorrectly imply that the matters of values and moral principles can be completely objectified. Rather they must set religious beliefs aside in discussions of moral and value issues in the public school context, except to point out that those beliefs may be one source of principles to which some people turn.

As harsh as this might sound, it is the proper way to pursue the possibility of shared values and moral principles in public, democratic life. The apparent harshness is perhaps somewhat alleviated by the fact that the values and moral principles described are characteristic of many, and probably most, religious groups. Thus the public and private views of many people may coincide to a large degree on these issues. In the public school context, however, the secular sources must take precedence. Moreover, if we are to extend dignity, freedom, equality, and so on to *all* people, the secular sources must take precedence, even where a large majority of a particular community share the same religious views.

The central values and moral principles serve not only as the theoretical concepts underlying personal and social efficacy, but as the starting point for how those might be consciously pursued or might come to life in social settings, including the school. The values and moral principles themselves are central to our discourse because they articulate rights of all people as participants in humanity. Whether human dignity should be valued or accorded to individuals is not a matter for debate or discussion. How it is defined and how it might become a unifying theme that permeates our personal and social lives is an appropriate and important topic. Indeed, moral discourse of this kind is desperately needed.

If we now turn back to the present perception of the imbalance between self- and social interests as well as the contradictory position of schools, we may see these in a way quite different from the rhetoric of recent school "reform." Consistent emphasis on dignity and the related central values and moral principles described here is not easy to find in the larger society. Thus, whatever individualistic or hedonistic behaviors we observe among young people, as well as their own contradictory behaviors, may be seen as reflections of the tendency toward indignity, injustice, inequality, lack of caring, and so on, that is so visible in the larger society. Yet it is exactly the opposite of these tendencies that formed several of the versions of affect in the curriculum that gained popularity in the past three decades and that are criticized today for undermining morality among the young.

Seen this way those versions and most of the programs associated with them were not grossly relativistic—indeed they stood for precisely the ideas we ought to pursue. The claim by critics that these versions were (and are) relativistic and valueless, as well as the implied message that the critics have the only version of central, common values and moral principles, is simply false. Once again, though, it is the difficult responsibility of the schools to see beyond this popular rhetoric and articulate the deeper (and less simplistic) ideas I have described. Reducing affect in the curriculum to the moralizing and reductionist slogan systems of the critics is the real threat to the personal and social efficacy of young people.

THE RIGHTS OF CITIZENSHIP

The concept of democracy and the central values and moral principles allied with it are not matters of easy or universal consent. Indeed they are contested every day in the lived experiences of many individuals and groups, particularly those that are marginalized in the political, economic, and social structures that define power and authority in our society. Thus the meaning of those principles is defined and theoretically protected by the U.S. Constitution and other legal authority.

A review of "guaranteed" and "protected" constitutional rights may seem condescending, as if most of us had not already been made to memorize them early in our own school experiences. However, there are some adults who apparently have forgotten that "all persons born or naturalized in the United States, and subject to the jurisdiction thereof, are citizens of the United States" (Article XIV). This provision does not specify the exclusion of young people nor does it suggest that their rights as citizens do not apply to their time in school. Indeed, in dealing with one right, free, symbolic speech, the Supreme Court suggested exactly this point by saying, "It can hardly be argued that either teachers or students shed their constitutional rights to freedom of speech or expression at the schoolhouse gate." Of course, the fact that educational authorities have contested students' rights on constitutional grounds is itself evidence that they believe the Constitution applies to young people in school.

The relevance of democracy and central values and moral principles may seem more obvious when discussing how affect should be placed in the curriculum than is the consideration of constitutional rights. Yet the public (and private) schools are legally constituted institutions that are attended on a compulsory basis by legal mandate. Furthermore, as representatives of the state authorized to maintain the institution, educational authorities establish rules and regulations that govern the lives of young citizens while in school. The concepts of citizenship and law are closely related to the very existence of schools, and thus the making of such rules and regulations without concern for constitutional rights represents a serious gap in educational policy (Wise & Manley-Casimir, 1971). When we understand that such rules and the procedures that follow from them partly constitute the hidden curriculum, the absence of constitutional provision is unthinkable; that is, it is fair to presume that the concept of constitutional rights as an everyday experience ought to be among the powerful learnings taught by the hidden curriculum.

It is true that while very young children are certainly protected by the Constitution, they are not reasonably in a position to exercise all of the rights extended by it or to meet the obligations attached to those rights. Indeed, the courts have often restricted the rights of young people on these grounds. However, the schools are among the major agencies by which the "learning" of rights and responsibilities is supposed to be carried out. Thus, discourse about affect in the curriculum ought to be concerned with how expeditiously those rights and responsibilities might be expanded in the lives of young people within the school. Here, as in the case of democracy, I would argue that the answer should be, "as soon as possible."

It is often argued that schools and the states that govern them would be better off without the intrusion of legal authority, particularly from the federal level. From the viewpoint of those concerned with the "right" to local expedience or prejudice, this may seem to be a good point. However, looked at through the lens of personal and social efficacy related to human dignity, democracy, and citizens' rights, the case may be seen quite differently. Were it not for such "intrusion," racial segregation could still be locally enforced, sectarian religious interests promoted, and handicapped persons denied access to schooling. On the other hand, rulings on matters such as corporal punishment and freedom of the student press have served local interests and obviously not expanded students' rights. Thus the "intrusion" of legal authority on behalf of the constitutional rights of young people has been part of the continuing tension in how values are represented and expressed in the life of the school. While those rights have frequently been clarified and extended, they have at times also been restricted, such as in the case of the right of school authorities to control student newspapers.

Moreover, in many cases, the court rulings themselves are only a small part of the legal process of extending or restricting rights. Following a ruling there is still the issue of full local compliance, which depends on many factors: administrative support, the views of state and local school boards as well as community political elites, whether local groups demand implementation, the clarity and specificity of the ruling, attitudes toward the court's role in educational policy, and whether individuals agree with the ruling and are willing to abide by it (Lufler, 1986).

We will now look briefly at several pertinent constitutional points and return to them later in considering how affect should be placed in the curriculum. The Constitution is expressly intended to secure for people—including the young—justice, tranquility, and liberty. The first of these we have already directly explored as a moral principle. Tranquility also is related to the moral principle of peace and implies the right to be free from violent intrusion, while liberty suggests the concept of freedom and the right to self-determination. Within this context other rights are similarly extended. Among these are:

1. The "rule of law" and the right to due process that guarantee that actions of authorities will be deliberative rather than arbitrary
2. Representation and informed consent, which relate to the matter of self-governance
3. Freedom of religious expression and from religious intrusion, the grounds on which the separation of church and state are established
4. Protection of personal effects against unreasonable search and seizure, which is ordinarily interpreted to include personal effects brought into the school
5. Protection against cruel and unusual punishment

The matter of specific interpretation of these rights has been a source of many legal cases arising out of particular situations in particular places and is the subject of considerable study, a review of which is beyond the scope of this work. What is of major concern in considering affect in the curriculum is the "spirit" of the Constitution as it should apply to young people in school. Consideration of the possibilities begins with the idea that they are entitled to rights, rather than how such rights might be limited or circumvented. It is hardly to the credit of school authorities that over the past several decades crucial cases involving fundamental rights related to democracy and dignity have had to be brought against those authorities by the very "clients" they are meant to serve. If the school is meant to extend and expand democracy and dignity, it would seem that cases regarding segregation, corporal punishment, censorship, and due process, for example, should never have arisen. Surely many educators have been active in behalf of democracy and dignity, but the fact that such cases have been brought to the courts is a sad commentary that reflects poorly on our whole profession.

Moreover, just because something is within the bounds of legality does not necessarily mean that it is also moral, as in the case of corporal punishment in the school. Indeed, the odd juxtaposition of these cases with others in which the school has properly been the defendant against sectarian interests is one more example of the contradictory nature of institutional values. When affect based on democracy and dignity is deliberately situated in the curriculum, the school plays quite a different role. In this instance, school authorities engage in a continuous effort to expand the rights of young people and the democratic interests of the curriculum beyond what has been established by the courts. Challenges to this role emerge only when special interests groups outside the school are opposed to the expansion of democracy and dignity, and correctly see the school positioned on the side of those concepts. In other words, as affect is placed in the curriculum, the issue should be how constitutional rights might be brought to life and expanded in the lived experiences of young people in the context of the school.

A DEVELOPMENTAL VIEW

The discussion so far has centered on philosophical and legal issues. We will now turn to the possibilities for a psychological view that is also necessary for a complete and coherent approach to affect in the curriculum. That is, in addition to suggesting the idealized conditions for personal and social efficacy, we must also consider how people come to seek, learn about, and pursue those conditions.

The need here is not to restate the content of various views of psychology, but rather to question which is the most appropriate for the conditions of democracy and dignity. There are, of course, many different views of the psychological aspect of affective development, all of which are supported to some degree by their own sets of empirical evidence. For example, there are substantial data to support the idea that the behavioristic method of shaping by reward and punishment can produce certain types of desired behavior. Similarly, ample evidence may be supplied to argue the case for a nondirective, humanistic approach.

Given these multiple realities, it is no wonder that many people who work in schools have tended to contest psychological methods for so long without any resolution. Argued on a "what works" basis, almost any position can be defended. The problem here is that such arguments substitute psychology for philosophy, and habit for preference; that is, the fact that some approach works does not necessarily answer the question of whether it is a desirable method. When psychology is attached to philosophy, a new question emerges: Do the means or methods used reflect and represent the ends that are both desired and desirable? In other words, which psychological approach presents a view of means and ends that is most congruent with the concepts of democracy and dignity?

In this regard, the case for a developmental approach to affect in the curriculum is both persuasive and compelling. The developmental approach suggests that self-views, attitudes, values, morals, and other aspects of personal and social affect are informed by prior experiences, social and cultural contexts, personal characteristics, and reflective thinking, as well as other factors that have both objective and subjective influences. These are personally arranged as a matter of individual differences, and their content is perceived in different ways by individuals in the same or different situations. Depending on how these factors are configured at any particular time, people construct views of themselves and others and the meanings of their knowledge and experience. These, in turn, are the grounds on which they attempt to develop toward what is desired and desirable in their personal and social life.

Understood this way, self-perceptions are a central feature in the human personality from which flow thought and actions regarding self and others; the environment, in turn, acts in powerful ways to inform self-perceptions (Beane & Lipka, 1986). This last point is particularly important because it has implications for both personal and collective discourse. Individuals and groups alike represent some configuration of the factors previously mentioned, and it is from this view that they proceed to develop ways to pursue personal and social efficacy. In this sense, we might speak not only of self-identity and actualization, but of group or community identity and actualization. Thus understood, the developmental approach may be taken as both a psychological theory of individual learning and a theory of collective social development.

Another aspect of the developmental approach is its attention to basic human needs and the ways in which they are met. Such needs range from survival (food, clothing, shelter) to interpersonal and intrapersonal needs such as belonging, achievement, self-concept and respect, economic security, and so on (Raths, 1972). These are not seen simply as base, irrational "emotions" that are to be shaped according to some external version of desired conduct. Rather they are an integral part of what it means to be human and are met or frustrated through ongoing interaction with the environment. Furthermore, their realization is constructed from that experience in ways that reflect and contribute to personal and social efficacy, a process that depends on the maintenance of dignity based on choice and thoughtful reflection. For example, the development, maintenance, and change of self-concept combine feelings about the self interrelated with reflection about them and the experiences by which they are influenced (Beane & Lipka, 1986). The same holds for relations with others and the interactions by which such relations are developed. In this way the developmental view rejects the incorrect separation of affect and cognition and instead integrates them in an accurate theory of authentic humanness.

Using that description of the developmental approach, we now turn back to the concepts of democracy and dignity to ask whether those conditions are satisfied. The developmental view recognizes that both personal and social configurations of affect emerge from the ongoing lived experiences and perceived meanings and feelings derived from them. In this sense, while the conditions of an idealized society may be imagined, their actualization in everyday life may involve ambiguity and tension. Preferences and choices are not determined by simplistic and intransigent virtues demanded by external authority; rather they are continuing attempts to identify ways of pursuing personal and social efficacy (Dewey, 1929, 1939). Moreover, since the factors that influence them may be configured in various ways, individuals are likely to perceive meanings and possibilities in different ways. Such differences are not construed as inconveniences to be overcome by shaping conformity. Instead they represent the rich diversity that characterizes humanity in general and the pluralism of our culture in particular. It is out of this diversity that a range of alternative courses of action is most likely to emerge (e.g., Oliver & Shaver, 1966).

It is these basic tenets of the developmental approach that position it most closely to the concepts of democracy and dignity. It recognizes and prizes diversity, a fundamental condition of human dignity; it acknowledges the continuous struggle to seek meaning and direction from lived experiences rather than external and absolutist authority; it recognizes and accommodates the variety of lived experiences rather than the illusion of a single, universal experience for all people; and it values the contributions that varied experiences and perceptions may make to the possibility of discourse about alternatives. Furthermore, the developmental view, properly understood as both psychology and philosophy, recognizes the search for personal efficacy or self-esteem and the pursuit of social efficacy as both an expression of the common good and as a powerful influence on the personal perceptions of individuals (Patterson, 1977; Phenix, 1977).

It is here, then, that we see the psychological version of democracy and dignity and the possibility for integrating self- and social interests toward freedom, autonomy, caring, justice, and equality. Neither the individual nor the environment taken alone offers a sufficient explanation for what determines the course of personal and social events. Instead it is the interaction of both and the consequent tensions and contradictions that account for the full description of experience and the necessary grounds for democratizing and dignifying the personal and collective future.

Set against this portrait of the developmental view, other psychological theories are incomplete and inappropriate. For example, the behavioristic approach to shaping behavior denies democracy by externally defining and imposing a version of what is right and good for all people. In this sense it violates the right to self-determination, suppresses diversity, and devalues human dignity. Nor does the romantic notion that people inherently seek social efficacy and the common good suffice in this regard. On the one hand, the history of marginalization of minority groups, women, and poor people tells quite a different story, even in a country such as ours where the concepts of democracy and dignity are espoused. On the other hand, the social and cultural environment is powerful and informs self-perceptions in serious ways. To imagine that individuals can simply choose to transcend the realities of that environment is not only wishful thinking but an unfair and unjust expectation. More likely, many people are so dislocated and paralyzed by inequity and injustice that they are literally unable to fend for themselves in the social, political, and economic configuration of society. Of course, many are subject to pervasive prejudice and bias, which simply prevent their participation. When we speak of affect in the curriculum today, such conditions deserve special attention in light of the portrait that emerges from the current social scene.

THE EMERGING SOCIAL SCENE

School is not the only situation in which various factors inform the personal and social affect of young persons, nor is it the only one in which self-views, values, morals, ethics, and the like are applied. Young people interact with a whole range of individuals, agencies, institutions, and networks that are at least as powerful and likely more so than the school. Affect is also informed by prior experiences and personal characteristics—race, gender, ethnicity, socioeconomic position, physical characteristics, language, religious beliefs, and so on—that the individual carries through those interactions. Thus, the realities of young persons' lived experiences reflect a complex and systemic interplay of personal characteristics, prior experiences, social networks, and institutional contexts that are interrelated and enormously powerful.

In the room where, for many years, I met most of my classes there was a chalkboard on which we usually worked out ideas about what did or could happen within schools. Surrounding the board was a "yellow wall" that we used to understand the relationship between life inside and outside the school. The yellow wall—larger conditions in society—was not only around the chalkboard, but behind it as well. It was only a small leap in our thinking to imagine that the wall came through our board. The board could not stand freely; it was riveted to the wall and could not be separated from it. Nothing we did on the chalkboard could be thought of as independent from the yellow wall. It was only when we understood this that we could fully appreciate the need to look at affect not only inside the school but outside as well.

Furthermore, schools are maintained not simply to exist as a part of society, but to contribute to both individual and collective well-being. Obviously there are many versions of what counts for personal and social well-being, but the fact remains that they are at the very center of the school's purpose. Because the larger society informs affect and serves as the real-life stage on which it is played out and because the school is supposed to be connected to that society, consideration of how affect ought to be placed in the curriculum requires that we explore the contemporary society as well as probable and possible trends that might be part of its future. Given the broad definition of the term *affect*, the themes of this unfolding portrait may properly be called "affective issues."

The United States is currently experiencing a shift toward a postindustrial age. Such an occurrence is unprecedented—the industrial age itself was a novel development, as was the agrarian age that preceded and partially continued throughout it. The use of the term *postindustrial* is not meant to imply that the shift is a matter of economics and methods of production alone. Instead it refers to the apparent change in the real and/or perceived characteristics of the industrial period, including composition of the population, acceptable distribution of wealth, relative homogeneity of values, accepted social roles, loyalties to institutions, stability of knowledge, continuity in relationships, certainty of occupational possibilities, access to affluence, and so on. Such factors were assumed to be stable in the industrial era and partially formed the basis for policy making as well as the foundation for individual goal setting and institutional programs, such as the school curriculum. Thrown into the realm of uncertainty, they now appear in the form of affective tensions and contradictions in individual lives and social configurations. They are part of what makes this the age of discontinuity and disbelief, of ambiguity and ambivalence.

The shifts in real and perceived characteristics of society are not simply objective events that are happening to us as a result of some unseen force outside of human experience. Rather they are the result of individual and group efforts to shape and reshape, protect or expand, and refine or change their lives and positions in the political, cultural, economic, and social contexts in which they live. Such shifts portray the real-life efforts of people to improve the quality of their personal and social lives. The difference in opinion about what such improvement means to particular individuals and groups and its effects on others underlies much of the current confusion about values that creates tension and contradiction across society, including within the schools (McNeil, 1986). Some examples of how this takes place may clarify, but not resolve, the current dilemma. Without pretending to portray a complete picture, I will touch upon five representative trends—technology and work, cultural diversity, emerging gender issues, wealth and its distribution, and family structure. From the discussion, they will be seen not only as distinct trends, but in terms of their cumulative effects for particular people.

Technology and Work

Hardly any of us could possibly have failed to notice the rapid expansion of technology in virtually all areas of life. At one level it has enhanced the quality of life in areas such as medical treatment, communications, transportation, and access to knowledge. However, technology has also created affective problems for many individuals and groups. It has presented enormous moral and value problems as the ethics of nuclear armament, access to personal information, genetic engineering, life extension, surrogate parenting, and other potential applications are pursued and their meanings confronted or ignored. As the workplace (industrial, agrarian, and service) becomes increasingly technicized and centralized, some workers find themselves displaced (a euphemism for unemployed), while others experience a deskilling of their work or the need for reskilling to maintain their jobs (Baran, 1986).

These dilemmas raise critical questions about whose interests technology does and should serve. As a result, the schools are presented with a whole range of ambiguities, such as whether or how to address the moral dilemmas of technological "progress," its implications for occupational instability, the uncertainty of knowledge, equitable access to technological tools, and the deskilling and reskilling of those who work in schools (Apple, 1986). Obviously these themes are filled with affective meanings, not the least of which are their relations with the dignity of work and the extent to which being employed is deeply engrained in the social values that press upon self-esteem in our society.

Cultural Diversity

Another trend is the shifting population distribution that presently characterizes the United States. Hodgkinson and others have described the nature of this shift as it relates to changing birthrates among particular groups and immigration patterns. First, present birthrates are higher among minority groups situated in lower socioeconomic groups than among upper-class, white groups (Hodgkinson, 1985). Second, 80 percent of immigrants are from Latin American and Asian countries. Taken together, these factors mean that the traditional white "majority" is not as pronounced as it once was, while in some regions the "minority" is rapidly becoming the majority.[2] Furthermore, the majority of people in those groups are positioned in the lower socioeconomic class along with other "minorities" (including Native Americans and African Americans) as well as those displaced by work reduction, disabilities, and so on; together they make up a large and growing underclass in society.

Policy decision makers, including those in education, have traditionally worked with an assumed portrait of society that was almost totally "white" and presumably reflected a certain pattern of values, aspirations, and histories. Those who were nonwhite and not middle class were given some recognition, but their numbers, along with powerful class and race bias, were enough to marginalize their place in social, political, and economic policy. The ongoing shift in population characteristics now creates a new set of conditions or, perhaps more accurately, makes previously disregarded conditions more obvious.

It is clear that the United States can no longer continue to function as though the population were white and middle class, and thus marginalize people not fitting that description. Moreover, if we return to the themes of democracy, dignity, equality, caring, justice, and the like, it is immoral for such a view to continue. As indigenous

and immigrant "minority" persons seek their economic, political, social, and legal entitlement, current tensions will only be exacerbated
by clinging to the old view. While we may seek agreement about
values and moral principles across society, it is clear that we are and
will continue to be a culturally diverse population. The possibilities
for truly democratic discourse as well as human dignity will depend
in large part on our willingness to take seriously the rights and
contributions of culturally diverse people and groups.

Gender Issues

The issue of equality and the search for equity do not involve
groups defined by race or ethnicity alone. A third trend in the shift
from assumptions characteristic of the industrial age is found in the
changing place of women in society that has grown out of the several
threads of the women's movement (Banks, 1987). Frustration over
traditional stereotyping and patriarchal relations that defy democracy, dignity, and citizens' rights, along with economic necessity
caused by other changes, has led women to organize and reposition
themselves in a number of important ways. Perhaps the most obvious
is the tremendous growth in the number of women who have entered
the paid work force. While some have assumed what have traditionally been seen as male-reserved positions in the organizational hierar-
chy, most occupy low-status and low-paying positions that are most
vulnerable to displacement and deskilling. Moreover, the changing
place of women in the paid workplace has had implications for change
in other areas, such as an increase in the numbers of women in higher
education progams, the expanding need for child care services, the
beginnings of consideration of women's concerns in political and commercial campaigns, and the need for legal action to protect women
against discrimination.

Less obvious, but equally important, has been the ongoing effort
to recapture the hidden histories of women, both individual and collective, in the events of politics, economics, social improvement projects, the arts, and other areas, including education, which traditionally were told with only male characters (for example, see Donovan,
1985; Laird, 1988; Schneir, 1972; Spender, 1981). If we add to this the
fact that almost all the male characters have been white, an important intersection of issues related to equality and equity begins to
emerge. That is, the sometimes fragmented picture of nonwhite minorities on the one hand and women on the other blends into one in
which these struggles have a vivid meaning for a particular group,

namely, women of color. When taken seriously, intersections such as this make the combined and accumulating picture of work, cultural diversity, and gender even more complex and its consideration clearly more urgent.

Distribution of Wealth

A fourth trend in the most recent phase of the transition out of the industrial age is the positioning of wealth within and across society. In the industrial-age version, the distribution of wealth was pictured as a bell curve in which the extremes of affluence and poverty were experienced by portions of the population that were relatively small compared with the central, large group of middle-class persons. In reality, there were far fewer at the upper level compared with the lower level, and that level controlled a much larger proportion of the wealth. It was the large middle class that was portrayed as one of the distinguishing characteristics of the United States as compared with other countries, and to which particular values and morals were attributed and institutional programs aimed, including the school curriculum (e.g., Alberty & Alberty, 1962; Krug, 1950, 1957; Saylor & Alexander, 1954).

In the 1980s this picture was dramatically contradicted as an increasingly bimodal distribution of wealth emerged in which the numbers of people at the upper and lower extremes increased and those in the middle decreased (Carnoy, Shearer, & Rumberger, 1983; Cohen & Rogers, 1983). While this observation has been made in many places, a second level of analysis has not; namely, that the numbers in the lower economic group are increasing much more rapidly than those at the upper level. In other words, while the distribution is becoming more bimodal, the two peaks are not necessarily twins; instead they are unequal and becoming even more so. Thus the much publicized increasing gap between the "haves" and the "have nots" is made even more dramatic.

To understand this we must return to the shifting trends previously described. As the workplace becomes more technicized and less human-dependent, jobs are eliminated, and people become unemployed, particularly those who are "last hired"—minorities and women. Reskilled jobs are filled by those already employed in relatively higher positions, and new jobs emerge primarily in the lower-paying clerical and service sectors. Many of these jobs are part-time, because technology has reduced the need for full-time workers, and hence the related benefits are no longer available. The reduction in actual jobs and the lesser cost of part-time workers combine to increase the profit margin for those who are in the upper economic class by virtue of their ownership or control of business and industry. Meanwhile, more and more workers are living on the edges of economic existence, and when they become unemployed or reduced to part-time jobs, the plunge to poverty is precipitous. Added to this growing population are retired persons who increasingly experience economic dislocation as their sheer numbers place a strain on the social security and health care systems, both of which were constructed on the assumed stability of age and wealth distribution.

As these trends emerge, the picture of economic class differences is made clearer. A growing but relatively smaller portion of the population captures increased wealth and power. Meanwhile a growing and much larger portion, consisting largely of women, minorities, and the aging, constitutes a rapidly expanding underclass of unemployed, nonemployed, and marginally employed persons. Moreover, the old assumption that these people will be aided by the state has become precarious. On the one hand, "welfare" support has not grown in comparison with the cost of living or the size of the group in need of assistance; in fact, it has actually decreased in both cases. On the other hand, cutbacks in federal employment (partly through "privatization" of public services)—which had been a major source of jobs for marginalized people—have themselves added to the unemployed sector (Carnoy, Shearer, & Rumberger, 1983). In the end, we come to an economic picture that is made up of increasing technicization, shifting demographics, the struggle for gender equity, and a widening gap between the "haves" and "have nots." We begin to see that each factor is an important event alone, but taken together they constitute a sheer drama in the transition out of the industrial age.

Family Structure

The fifth and final trend has to do with what many take to be the most fundamental institution in society, the family. The industrial picture of the family consisted of two natural parents living together with their children in a unit defined by clear roles: The father worked at paid labor outside the home, the mother managed the home (unpaid) and took primary responsibility for child rearing, while the children attended school. Over the past two decades, this picture has become blurred as new and varied forms of family structure have emerged. In fact, the traditional description just given now constitutes only about 7 percent of all families in the United States (Hodgkinson, 1985). Thus it is much more common to encounter single-parent homes, families in which both parents work, blended families made up of natural parents and stepparents, and other forms of "family." Furthermore, geographic mobility has transformed the centrally located extended family which included grandparents and other near relatives. This transformation of the family is the result of interpersonal problems, the rejection of sex-role stereotypes, economic necessity and difficulty, and other very real circumstances.

Furthermore, the change in family structures has not taken place without a cost to those involved. Single parents (overwhelmingly women) often experience a loss of economic status and social acceptance. To maintain economic support they often must enter the bureaucracy of "welfare" assistance; if they are working, they have to negotiate the maze of child care services. Less severe, but also problematic, is the case for families where both parents work. Energy is dissipated, less time may be spent with children, participation expectations by other institutions (such as the school) cannot be met, and child care services must be found and supported. Blended families may face these same conditions in addition to the need for reconstructing interpersonal ties; addressing tensions arising from the mix of natural parents, stepparents, and siblings; and the juggling of legal obligations to previous families.

In these ways the family structure has become part of the ambiguity and ambivalence of the postindustrial age and both a source of and ground for tension and contradiction. This trend too is not necessarily removed from the other trends. If the discontinuity of a family involves crossing the line into poverty or if it was already existing at that level, the consequences may be dire indeed. Should the loss of economic sustenance lead to the loss of home or if assistance is insufficient to maintain a home, the parent(s) and children are likely to head down what is becoming the well-worn path to homelessness. Again, by accumulating the previous trends, we may discover that this represents a particular problem for women and minorities who have the least access to work and who are already most likely to be living on the economic margins. The fate of such people, when they enter the "land" of homelessness, is vividly and depressingly described by Jonathan Kozol (1987) in his study of families living in welfare hotels. Clearly, and by any stretch of the social or political imagination, these are not places in which to "raise a family."

Implications of Trends

To really understand the meaning of these five trends, we must recognize that they do not simply involve nameless and faceless people constructed by statistical manipulation and objectified by group descriptors. Instead they are real people, living out the realities of the late twentieth century. No description such as the one I have given here can possibly begin to portray the actual tensions and frustration, the desperation and despair, or the sense of ambiguity and uncertainty that sweeps across all segments of society. Nor can this description be considered complete, because we have not touched upon matters such as changing lifestyles, increasing individualism, commercial manipulation and seduction, political and corporate malfeasance, and environmental destruction—let alone increasing global tensions and interdependence. All of these as well are important to our sense of how the perceptions and assumptions of stability in the industrial age are rapidly giving way to new trends, problems, and issues.

In my description of trends I have paid particular attention to people who have been marginalized because of certain personal characteristics or socioeconomic position. This is not to say that the effects of trends are felt only by these people, though these people certainly feel them more severely than others. Such others, including whites in the middle and upper classes, have also experienced ambiguity in direct and indirect ways. The effects of technicization on work, the dissipation of the middle class, the emergence of gender issues, and the change in family structure have all directly involved the lives of such people. Those same events, and certainly the increasing diversity of culture, have contributed to the need to reexamine and reconstruct important self-perceptions related to the meaning of "majority," privileged access to work and property, gender roles and relations, and others. While the children of the privileged may not be economically, politically, or socially threatened in the same way as those of the nonprivileged, the widening gaps in these areas nonetheless detract from the collective, social efficacy to which their lives are inextricably related.

This sketch is crucial to understanding the relationship between the trends described and the issue of affect in the curriculum. Very often, proposals regarding such affect are constructed from a within-school view. By this I mean that they tend to portray the school as a significant influence on self-perceptions, values, morals, and so on, and to cast the school's role in terms of sensitivity to young people within the school structure and curriculum. Such sensitivity is, of course, terribly important, and where it emerges, it is a major breakthrough in the impersonal tradition of the institution. However, even when this is so, it is altogether too easy to forget that young people live under the conditions previously described. They are the children of the technologically displaced, participants in "minority" cultures, the girls and young women who are stereotyped, the hungry children of the poor, and the younger "guests" in the welfare hotels. They are objects of seductive advertising, consumers of the video culture, adolescent parents of their own children, enrollees in day care programs, subjects of custody battles, initiators and victims of crime. In short, these same young people who come to our schools are living participants in the larger world on the outside. To imagine that such lived experiences do not inform self- and social perceptions in powerful ways is simply foolish. To think that those ways are not more powerful than the school influence is terribly naive.

In the end, we must come to the realization that these trends and meanings constitute affective issues on a large scale, and that they permeate affect in the curriculum, whether we like it or not. They enter the personal histories of young people as antecedents to school experiences, as mediators of school transactions, and as critical variables in even the most well-intentioned school outcomes. These trends and meanings are constantly on the minds of young people and always with them; they cannot be cast aside conveniently while attention is turned to long division with remainders and to diagramming complex sentences. And try though the school might to affect self-esteem and social predispositions through carefully designed and well-meant programs, the effects (if there are any) are likely to be washed away by realities of life on the outside.

The temptation, already embraced by some, may be to turn hopelessly away from such conditions and cleanse the curriculum in a bath of academic dominance. Yet we have already noted that students are human beings and that the personal and social affect created by those conditions cannot be eluded. The only possible effects of such myopia are that school success will once again come down to survival of the socially privileged, and the school will experience further contradictions created by the attempt to isolate itself from the "yellow wall."

Instead of turning away from these issues, we must realize that the picture of the school rendered insignificant by conditions in the larger society is only an interpretation. A second possibility is not nearly so bleak or dangerous. In this interpretation the trends and their meanings are not only "facts" in the lives of young people that inform their personal affect and to which we must be sensitive. They are also affective issues that, when cast in terms of democracy, dignity, and diversity, become themes for reflection and action in the curriculum. I will have much more to say about this possibility in a later chapter.

SUMMARY

In this chapter I have addressed those components of a coherent and reasonably complete framework that have to do with philosophical, psychological, and sociocultural foundations. In doing so I have suggested that there are deep themes that are supposed to enhance personal and social efficacy in our society and that therefore ought to be included in any proposal or version of affect in the curriculum of the public schools.

At the core of any appropriate and defensible proposal must rest the idea of democracy, which is claimed as a founding and continuing principle in the United States. In its proper sense, the democratic way of life encourages and depends on free expression, reasoned consent, full participation, willingness to pursue the common good, and faith in human capacity to create and evaluate solutions to human problems. Second, and related to that, is the central concept of human dignity as the entitlement of all persons by virtue of their belonging to humanity. Following from human dignity are four values and moral principles that transcend the special interests of particular groups and present a vision of the common good while simultaneously enhancing personal efficacy: equality, caring and justice, freedom, and peace.

Third, I have suggested that any proposal for affect in the curriculum ought to pay attention to the rights of young people as citizens that are extended and protected by the Constitution and other legal authority. Fourth, I have proposed that in considering the psychological aspects of affect in the curriculum, the case for a developmental approach is compelling. In its recognition of dynamic interaction of the individual and the environment and the premium it places on personal thought and efficacy, this approach is certainly more appropriate in relation to democracy and dignity than behavioristic approaches that favor shaped compliance with externally imposed conduct.

Finally, in the analysis of emerging sociocultural trends, we have seen the urgent need to recall the themes of democracy, dignity, and diversity. Surely there is much that detracts from the realization of these themes in the everyday lives of people: technicization of work, the devaluing of cultural diversity, gender stereotyping and inequity, inequitable distribution of wealth and power, and the exigencies of family life in the present political and economic climate. Such conditions weigh most heavily on those who are least advantaged in our society, yet they threaten us all in the sense that we are all inextricably bound by the fate of the common good. And they are the very conditions under which the young people who come to our schools must live out their lives and envision their future.

In the end, these themes present a picture of both realities and possibilities in our society. For this reason they are the proper grounds from which to proceed in making and evaluating proposals for affect in the curriculum. In the next chapter we will return to the many versions described in Chapter 2 to see how they appear in our own times and how they stand in relation to democracy, dignity, and diversity.

Affect in the Curriculum: The Present Scene

In this chapter we join up again with the many versions of affect in the curriculum whose historical routes were traced in Chapter 2. However, here we will be concerned with the form they have taken in the present scene in schools and how they stand in relation to the themes developed in Chapter 3. Three points in particular should become evident in this analysis. First, all of the historical versions that have emerged may still be found in the curriculum in some form or another. With little effort one may find in the curriculum affective claims concerning religion, the high culture of classical humanism, character, social efficiency, life adjustment, social reconstruction, self-actualization, and more. Second, their coexistence is not as peaceful as it may have been at some other times, especially because the issues in the larger society to which they are related have become more complex and pronounced. Third, conflicts and contradictions may be found not only across versions, but within them as well, because over time some have drifted from their original formulation while others have evolved as variations on a particular proposal.

As we apply the themes developed in the last chapter, however, an even more important issue emerges. Virtually all of the versions of affect in the curriculum are either incomplete in important ways or inappropriate for public schools in the United States. This does not mean that they should all be rejected. As we shall see, several involve very important claims insofar as those themes are concerned. In working out a coherent and appropriate approach to placing affect in the curriculum, we can learn much from them for both theory and practice. The critical analysis of all of them is an important part of the reasoned and deliberate discourse that can lead us out of the present confusion and contradiction.

CLAIMS FOR RELIGION IN THE CURRICULUM

In Chapter 2, I showed how religion served as the main theme for affect in the curriculum until late in the nineteenth century and that even thereafter some versions of character education were largely euphemisms for religious instruction. While the courts have persistently maintained the separation of religion from the life of the school, it is only in the relatively recent past that observers have noted a truly conspicuous absence of religious concepts and practices (see, for example, Davis, 1985; Jenkinson, 1979). After all, the content of court cases shows that for much of this century, and even to the present, public schools have allowed the distribution of Bibles to students, released time for religious instruction, and prayer and religious music in the context of various ceremonies. While it is true that religion does not have the obvious place it once held, we ought not assume that it is so thoroughly removed as some might suggest.

During the 1980s, increasing attention was given to the place of religion in the public schools, primarily as a result of the tremendous growth in radical fundamentalist Christian groups. Some of this concern came directly from these groups as they sought a larger place for their beliefs in all social institutions; some came from politically driven sources in the New Right that were either sympathetic to or aligned with fundamentalists; and some concern came from those who sought to modify fundamentalism by reviving interest in religious heritage through nonsectarian forms.

To understand the direct claims of the extreme fundamentalist groups, we must understand that their religious views are as hegemonic in their lives as were those of the early Calvinists. In light of this we may also understand not only the absolutist nature of those views but the insistence that they be applied to all aspects of society, including the life of schools (Gabler, 1985). For example, Reverend Jerry Falwell (1979) said: "I hope I live to see the day, when as in the early days of our country, we won't have any public schools. The churches will have taken them over again and Christians will be running them. What a happy day that will be" (p. 53). But the tenacity of fundamentalists is demonstrated only partly by such school claims. More powerful is their attempted use of the courts to carry out their agenda.

Over the course of the twentieth century, the courts have ruled on many cases involving religion in the public schools. Most well known are those regarding the antagonism between proponents of creationism and evolution, and the constitutionality of prayer and religious instruction as part of the school program. Such cases have a long history, and they have appeared again in recent years in episodes in which the courts have reaffirmed their traditional separatist position (for example, *Edwards* v. *Aguillard*, 1987; *Wallace* v. *Jaffree*, 1985). In the 1980s plaintiffs in Tennessee claimed that a particular reading series conflicted with their religious beliefs, and in Alabama another group charged that certain textbooks unconstitutionally advanced what some fundamentalists call "the religion of secular humanism." Presumably informed of the courts' persistent separatist stance, these fundamentalist groups likely sensed the possibilities of a sympathetic public and a new line of reasoning in support of their argument. That line of reasoning came unexpectedly from the very courts that had appeared to be unsympathetic to their cause.

In 1961, the Supreme Court ruled that individuals may refuse to sign loyalty oaths if those oaths conflict with deep religious convictions (*Torcaso* v. *Watkins*, 1961). Having spoken to "mainstream" American religions in the text, a footnote was used to mention as other examples Buddhism, Taoism, Ethical Culture, and Secular Humanism (Footnote 11, p. 495). By the latter, the court apparently meant deeply held convictions that, while not based on religious sources, are nevertheless concerned with deep issues such as the meaning of human existence and experience.

The use of secular humanism as a central theme of the fundamentalist case stems from an argument by John Whitehead and John Conlan that the court had named it as a religion, and further, by implying its religious-like but civil basis, had established it as the *de facto* state religion (Whitehead & Conlan, 1978). Such thinking is meant to suggest, therefore, that if religion is banned from the public schools, then the "religion" of secular humanism should be also. If one believes that society is bedeviled by a state-sponsored conspiracy to abolish religion, an argument like "secular humanism as a (state) religion" can be very seductive. At issue, of course, is whether the court meant to say that secular humanism is actually a religion or used the term simply to suggest that loyalty oath protests need not be attached to mainstream religious beliefs.

Whichever the case, *secular humanism* has become a code word that is applied to many school programs and practices opposed by radical fundamentalist Christian groups. These may include almost anything from attitudinal surveys to contemporary literature, from global interdependence to multicultural education, from values education to substance abuse education (United States Department of

Education, 1984). Such items and themes, of course, largely reflect the approaches to affect in the curriculum that came of age in the 1960s and 1970s and are now seen as rejecting theological sources of problem solving in favor of human reasoning. Interpreted this way, the term *secular humanism* is not as elusive as many educators believe. Rather it is the predictable label for any program or procedure that does not follow the absolutist views of the radical religious fundamentalists.

I do not mean to imply in this discussion that secular humanism is simply a false concept invented by radical fundamentalists as a symbol to resist. Indeed, there are people who name themselves secular humanists and do, in fact, explore value and moral issues without regard for religious sources. Most prominent among these is a group that developed a document entitled *Humanist Manifesto II* (1973). The major points in their platform include respect for human dignity, cultural diversity, and personal autonomy, as well as the need for democratic participation, a sense of global interdependence, and more equitable distribution of wealth, power, and justice. Given the relatively small circulation of the document, it is doubtful that large numbers of school professionals even know about it. Had they read it, the particular philosophy it espouses and its open skepticism of traditional religions would hardly have received the kind of universal assent its critics suggest. Moreover, given the disarray of affect in the curriculum found in schools, it is impossible reasonably to imagine, let alone adequately show, that educators are participants in an organized secular humanist conspiracy to abolish religion from American life (Lockwood, 1989).

Part of the power and tenacity of religious fundamentalist groups is drawn from the fact that they have found a sympathetic ear among political officials, many of whom they have helped to elect. As part of the larger conservative agenda, the Reagan administration and like-minded officials at the federal, state, and local levels repeatedly called for a "return" of religion to the public school program. The revival of school prayer was an explicit part of the Reagan election platform, and the absence of religion in textbooks became a controversial topic fueled by conservative groups (Vitz, 1986).

The most noteworthy example of this political agenda was the refinement of the Hatch Act of 1974 (The General Education Provisions Act). Originally the purpose of this act was to make instructional materials intended for use in federally funded experimental programs available for inspection by parents or guardians. In 1978, the act was amended to protect parent and child privacy rights by

prohibiting required psychological examination, testing, or treatment that intended to reveal political affiliation, sexual behavior, or
attitudes; family behaviors and income; and other "privileged" information (subsection *b*). These provisions were supported by a variety of
professional and public groups, and the media embellished reporting
of the amendment's passage with horror stories of the intimate information revealed on permanent record cards. As it turned out, the
original event was mild compared with what would follow.

In early 1984, the Education Department proposed regulations
for enforcing the Hatch Act and its amendment. In an excellent
review of the events that followed, Bert Greene and Marvin Pasch
(1985/1986) revealed how the proposed regulations were viewed by
radical Christian fundamentalist groups as an opportunity to implement their agenda for schools. According to their account, a former
Education Department employee with prior notification of the regulations informed these groups of upcoming hearings and suggested
they place themselves on the agenda. As a result, virtually all of the
allotted spaces for testimony were taken up by those who supported
the regulations; they attacked almost all secular approaches to affect
in the curriculum, citing as grounds the perceived lack of academic
emphasis and the loss of local control of schools.

This three-pronged approach supported a clear line of reasoning:
first, get rid of secular humanism; if that is not possible, remove any
affective content from the school by limiting the program to factual
academic content and skills; finally, return control to the local level,
where extreme fundamentalists could exercise more power. In addition, these spokespersons ignored the fact that the act applied only to
federally funded programs, and sought to have its provisions applied
to all programs and procedures. So virulent was the attack and its
interpretation widespread, that in February 1985, Senator Hatch
himself called for a "common-sense" and accurate interpretation of
the law (*Education Week*, 1985).

As the fundamentalist agenda has been more vehemently
pursued, the absence of religion in the planned curriculum has also
drawn attention from more moderate sources. Concern has been expressed over the place of religion in the cultural heritage as it is
shared with students, especially in the content of textbooks. The
power of this claim is demonstrated by the fact that the same conclu-
sion has been reached by ordinarily conflicting groups, an intersection of forces that text publishers will likely not ignore (Davis, 1985;
Vitz, 1986). In 1987, the ASCD Panel on Religion in the Curriculum
released a report that captures the essence of this position. The au-

thors argued that any version of history, including one of the United States, is incomplete unless it portrays the role of religion in cultures and historical events. However, the authors claim that misunderstanding about the intent of the Supreme Court rulings has led to "scant" treatment of religion in the planned curriculum. In the end, the panel recommended that local professionals cooperate with community leaders and state agencies in developing a "fair and factual treatment of religion in the curriculum" (p. 35), that textbook publishers portray such treatment, and that the view be nonsectarian and sensitive to individual beliefs.

Moderating as such proposals may seem to be, their implementation poses an issue that promises to be most problematic. In the document just described, which is representative of its kind, the role of religion in culture is portrayed in terms of its effects on salutary events: the formation of the American republic, the founding of public schools, the abolition of slavery, and the emergence of the civil rights movement. Absent, however, are negative examples, such as relations with Native American cultures, cliché stereotypes of nonmainstream religious groups, and the place of religion in extremist groups such as the Ku Klux Klan. While I do not mean to imply that such proposals intentionally ignore these realities, I would suggest that including them in the planned curriculum would alienate those who wish only to portray the salutary version. Moreover, what happens when some people see the positive and negative nature of the examples I have given reversed, particularly when such persons represent a local or regional majority?

The problem here, as in the general case of religion in the curriculum, is that mixing religion and democracy in the public school curriculum is a very complex issue. Religious principles and the groups that promoted them have certainly played an important role in forming the culture(s) of the United States and the moral consciences of its citizens. However, insofar as democratic thinking involves examination of all sides of the issue, anything less than a reasonably complete picture of the positive and negative influences of the wide variety of religious forces in past and present society is inappropriate. Yet the sensibilities of individual groups must also be respected if the Constitution is to be honored. If religious beliefs begin to enter the moral ethos of the school, no matter how nonsectarian, there is the problematic presence of those who find the basis for moral principles in other than religious sources, including those who exercise their constitutional right to believe that no religious content, except perhaps that of historical pertinence, has a place in public institutions.

Thus far the courts have largely inhibited the narrow views of radical fundamentalists from entering the life of the public school, and many of these groups have sought to exercise their beliefs in private schools of their own making. However, the tenacity of these groups has found a sympathetic ear in the conservative political arena. Further, their views have intersected with other groups that object to specific developments, such as sanctioned abortion, surrogate parenting, and genetic engineering, to form coalitions that are a powerful lobbying force in the U.S. government. While moderating forces seek amenable ways to bring religion back into the curriculum, their proposals are unlikely to be easily implemented within the present tension between private religious views and public life. In this context they mostly appear to be attempts at compromise between the obviously irreconcilable values of radical fundamentalism and public school life. I will have more to say about this in the next chapter, but the fact remains that the role of religion persists as one of the most problematic aspects of affect in the curriculum.

THE REVIVAL OF CLASSICAL HUMANISM

When situated as a curriculum form, classical humanism constitutes a subject-centered approach based on the traditional academic disciplines. Since this is the typical way in which the planned curriculum is organized, classical humanism is never far from the scene, no matter what other form may be temporarily popular. As the 1980s unfolded, this proved to be the case just as it had in the past.

As described in Chapter 2, classical humanism seeks to transmit, through the study of history and literature, "great" ideas that have presumably been passed down over time; by studying the past, young people may learn the great moral lessons of antiquity and apply them to the exigencies of modern life. The present argument for classical humanism is based on the perception that in the 1960s schools began to turn toward electives, social issues courses, and contemporary, relativistic literature and thus denied young people access to the great wisdom of the past. This, in turn, supposedly led not only to the dissipation of intellectual excellence in the schools, but to the utilitarian views, hedonism, and self-destructive behaviors believed to permeate the young culture.

As in the past, the impetus for classical humanism has come from university academics. For example, in 1981, Mortimer Adler described "six great ideas" that he claimed presented perennial wisdom:

truth, beauty, goodness, liberty, equality, and justice. One year later these emerged as central themes in *The Paideia Proposal* (1982), a school reform plan that presented a quintessential statement of classical humanism in modern form. More recently, the theme of classical humanism has been sounded by Allan Bloom (1987), E. D. Hirsch (1987), and Diane Ravitch and Chester Finn (1987) in versions of a cultural literacy approach. All three books interpret present events in terms of what the authors see as the inability of young people to engage themselves in an ordered society because they lack the requisite knowledge of the cultural heritage.

While these voices have been loud and popular, none was more powerful than that of former Education Secretary William Bennett. True to the conservative agenda of the Reagan administration, Bennett repeatedly called for a return of classical humanism to the public schools. It is instructive to note that he frequently referred to his version of the ideal school as an "academy," a term that summons up the specter of the classical, high culture school of the eighteenth and nineteenth centuries. Given his position as Education Secretary, Bennett was able to take this seductive message to a wide audience through the media and in speeches before a variety of professional associations.

In the past, the rhetoric of classical humanism was typically offset by the realistic accounts of people with more practical concerns, chiefly those who work in the schools themselves. However, the present case defies this history, at least in textual interpretation. For example, the American Federation of Teachers (1987) issued a report entitled *Education for Democracy* in which the way toward shared democracy and moral order was to be through a nationalistic version of classical humanism. In their view, "history is . . . the integrative subject, upon which the coherence and usefulness of other subjects depend, especially the social sciences but also much of literature and the arts" (p. 17). By "history," the authors mean the story of the United States, told not only as a chronological series of events, but also as a series of salutary moral episodes.

Another group that has drifted from its history of objection to classical humanism is teacher educators, or at least a powerful segment of them. Organized in the mid-1980s, a coalition of representatives from schools of education at large research universities, the so-called "Holmes Group," issued a call for reform of teacher education along the lines of classical humanism (1986). Most revealing in this regard is their recommendation that prospective teachers major in a particular subject area rather than in education. This idea is congruent with the classical view that pedagogy is secondary to strong grounding in content. The fact that this group has adamantly insisted on the need to recruit more "minority" teachers and to improve working conditions of teachers in general should not obscure its high culture view of the curriculum or the contradictions between those aspects of its platform. High culture curriculum versions have historically not done much to improve the conditions of those outside the high culture class or to honor the diversity of cultures.

Caught in an era of increased testing, higher standards, and proliferating requirements, many school officials undoubtedly find the Holmes view seductive, especially when attached to the allure of prestigious higher education institutions. Only the most subject-centered teachers, however, could miss the obvious implication of teacher incompetence and cultural illiteracy. Moreover, the application of the Holmes recommendations to elementary education, with its presumed history of integrated and child-connected studies, is clearly an attempt to impose the academic view of the world represented in secondary schools on the lives of young children as well.

This approach to curriculum in general and to affect in particular represents a world known to and experienced primarily by white male intellectuals for whom the classical tradition is a lived experience, and its perpetuation a condition of stable existence in university departments in which most of them work. Although many modern classical humanists, caught in the reality of universal education, acknowledge the right of all people to their "high" culture, they believe that their own culture is the right and best one. Rarely, if ever, do they speak of the democratic discourse that might address race and class issues in the larger society where these issues are actually located. The "high culture as right culture" view borders on arrogance when applied in a pluralistic society, especially one in which access and understanding to that culture may be inhibited by the material conditions under which many people live. Moreover, as one critic put it, the contempt in which the subculture of youth is held "must be recognized for what it is: the lamentation of aging white males in a declining cultural empire."[1]

As a theory of learning, the idea of intuitive transfer from history and literature to life has been under fire since the early research of Thorndike and Hartshorne and May, reviewed in Chapter 2. As a theory of affect in the curriculum, it represents denial of pluralism, the complexities of real-life situations, and the realities of children's lived experiences. Perhaps the only really redeeming aspect of this position is the insistence that the cultural heritage be taught to all young people, regardless of their individual differences; content problems aside, this at least denies the tracking systems that are largely informed by race and class (Apple, 1986). In the end, though, the classical humanism approach to affect in the curriculum is much too narrow and thoroughly problematic.

REFORM PROPOSALS AND CURRICULUM AFFECT

If, in the end, the 1980s did not turn out to be the decade of actual reform, it will at least be remembered as the decade of reform proposals. I have already mentioned *The Paideia Proposal* (Adler, 1982) and the recommendations of the Holmes Group (1986) for teacher education. These are but two in what turned out to be a dizzying array of reports aimed at the issue of excellence in the schools. Because of their particular content and popularity, I will review two more reports here to indicate how the excellence reform movement addresses affect in the curriculum as I have defined it. Those two are *A Nation at Risk: The Imperative for Educational Reform* (National Commission on Excellence in Education, 1983) and *Action for Excellence: A Comprehensive Plan to Improve Our Nation's Schools* (Task Force on Education for Economic Growth, 1983). These reports are especially noteworthy because they were followed by a stream of state-level reform proposals that honored both their rhetoric and their content.

When these reports were originally issued, many observers commented that they ignored the "affective" aspects of schooling. This turns out to be correct only if one defines affect in terms of the modern developmental versions of self-esteem, values development, and the like. However, this is an excellent illustration of the dangers of incomplete definition. Though the term *affect* was not explicitly used in the proposals, they contained a great deal of implicit affect in the sense of what they proposed to be of value for young people and the larger society.

There have been many content analyses of the reports from a variety of perspectives (Stedman & Smith, 1983; Walberg and Keefe, 1986) and another extensive review is not needed here. The reports amounted to a neo-Sputnik concern for the place of the United States in international affairs, although in this case the central issue was economic competition. Recommendations were aimed at developing scientific and technological competence among young people as a way to revitalize the economy, balance the national trade deficit, and reverse the decline of ailing manufacturing industries. Specific recommendations involved upgrading content, raising standards, and increasing teacher "competence." In their emphasis on academic excellence and economic power, the reports were a curious blend of classical humanism and social efficiency. This feature, along with pithy phrases and powerful metaphors, undoubtedly contributed to the widespread attention they received. These documents were, if nothing else, politically astute.

The most obvious effect of these reform proposals was to project the solution to perceived economic problems onto the schools in general, and specifically onto the people who work in them and the young people who attend them. Moreover, the reports represented a political interpretation of postindustrial economic conditions through the lens of industrial age rationalism. By this I mean the perception that the school could shape young people into economically contributing roles while avoiding questions about larger social or economic forces that might otherwise influence position in society. Thus interpreted, the implications for affect in the curriculum become clear: The personal and social interests of young people and the program of the schools should be based on national economic interests congruent with industrial age virtues embodied in the work ethic.

That such a version of affect ignores the developmental personal-social interests that are a part of childhood and adolescence is an important, but not complete, criticism of the reform reports. An equally serious problem is that the implied values are incongruent with the reality that faces many young people. The content of the proposals having to do with the "need" for scientific and technical competence creates the impression that jobs in those areas will be readily available to any who choose to follow the path toward educational excellence. While the technical aspects of many types of paid labor are intensifying, the greatest number of projected job types is in the service sector, in which technical competence is only a peripherally related skill (Bureau of Labor Statistics, 1982). Further, most of these jobs (building custodian, cashier, salesclerk, food server) require little education. Worse yet, many of those positions and the people who are presently in them are already threatened by technology, though not necessarily in the sense of requiring new skills, but of replacing them as workers (for example, automatic teller machines, robots, and so on).

Thus the proposals place schools in an untenable position; the schools are asked to solve a problem in ways that will not solve it. The work ethic and the promise of work implied in the proposals are contradicted by present realities and future projections. Such conflicting claims create tension in the affective climate of the schools, as teachers and young people attempt to justify curriculum reforms handed down to them. Further, the upgraded standards and proposed increase in school time complicate school affect by intensifying the feeling of many young people that school is an impersonal and burdensome institution.

The most evident result of this condition is the increase in school dropouts as the upgraded standards reduce the marginal space in which those with achievement problems are typically located. Obviously this was either an unanticipated or unimportant consequence for the authors of the reform proposals. The response has been remarkable from an affective point of view. Similar to the projection of the economic problems onto the school, the dropout problem has been projected onto the dropouts themselves. These individuals are seen as personally lacking the perseverance and motivation to complete school, just as those who are caught in the growing socioeconomic underclass are assumed to simply lack the will to rise out of their conditions (Finn, 1987). In this view, current school programs and the reform proposals that led to them are not in question, but rather those individuals who supposedly fail to *choose* to transcend obstacles and conditions in their lives. In keeping with this nightmarish Darwinian view, many schools have implemented efforts to enhance the self-esteem of potential dropouts. To imagine that self-esteem alone is sufficient for school success and the choices it involves, especially as standards rise, is, of course, simply a misguided view. Moreover, not all school dropouts have negative self-esteem (Beane & Lipka, 1986).

In the end, the round of reform proposals in the 1980s implied a version of affect in the curriculum that is misleading and unfair. By projecting economic problems onto the schools, corporate and government officials managed to avoid responsibility for creating or resolving those problems, while placing the school in an impossible position. Further, the implied version of affect places the burden of economic difficulties on young people who did not create them and may eventually become their victims. Finally, the proposed need for self-reliance and motivation simply ignores the powerful socioeconomic conditions that render them useless for many young people. On the other hand, it takes little insight to understand that those who do manage to find their way through the socioeconomic maze will add to the pool of labor from which business and industry might happily draw. In the interest of developing a positive and worthwhile version of affect in the curriculum, one can only wonder how long it will take to undo the damage already done by the reform proposals.

THE RETURN OF CHARACTER EDUCATION

Chapter 2 described character education as the transitional form of
moral instruction as the place of religion in public schools declined.
While some variations of character education euphemistically continued the religious tradition, others took a more secular form, particularly those that were tied to the larger social efficiency movement in
the second and third decades of this century. The version of character
education that has most recently emerged and is gaining popularity is
not so much a modern variation of the latter programs as a reproduction of them.

The use of the term *character* reentered professional language
largely due to its repeated use by former Education Secretary Bennett as part of his slogan for educational excellence. However, character education programs in the 1980s most frequently reflected versions proposed by Edward Wynne, who advocates an indirect
instruction approach, and the American Institute for Character Education, which proposes a direct approach.

Wynne's version (1980, 1985/1986, 1988) is indeed an authentic
reproduction. In his view, self-destructive and "hedonistic" behaviors
of young people are signals of moral disorder and misconduct. To
reverse what he describes as an increase in this phenomenon, Wynne
recommends shaping character (or conduct) to socially acceptable
behavior so that it becomes habitual. Unlike other versions of affect in
the curriculum, this one defines "good" and "bad" conduct and attempts to completely avoid situation relativity. "Good" character
amounts to conduct that consistently demonstrates truthfulness,
promptness, obedience to "authority," diligence, patriotism, and acceptance of responsibility. "Bad" character is revealed in laziness,
rudeness, disrespect, deceit, and disobedience. The former he refers to
as commonsense virtues, while the latter presumably describes the
conduct of too many of today's young people.

Moreover, Wynne claims that the virtues he describes are consistent over centuries and upheld by a tradition of "transmitting" them
to the young by behavior shaping and didactic lessons. In common
with others, he blames the demise of good character among young
people largely on the tendency of schools and other social agencies to
emphasize reasoning about situation relativity rather than insisting
on persistent, habitual conduct. The pedagogy he suggests includes
encouraging participation in club and athletic activities, clear and
strictly enforced discipline codes, cross-age tutoring, school and community service projects, team competitions, use of "great" literature

for morality lessons, and patriotic ceremonies. Like earlier proponents of this approach, Wynne recommends some methods, like community service projects, that were associated with "progressive" education, but rejects others, particularly student participation in school governance.

Remarkably, there has been relatively little published dissent from advocates of other approaches to affect in the curriculum. One notable exception was a response by Alan Lockwood (1985/1986) to an article by Wynne. By citing historically simultaneous and competing views, Lockwood correctly challenged the notion that there is or ever was consensus on codes of conduct. Moreover, he disputed the idea that moral choices in real-life situations can always be clear, the claim that reasoning-based approaches ignore conduct, and the reduction of moral principles to a "bag of [everyday] virtues" (p. 10). I would add to Lockwood's analysis that Wynne's version of character education is yet another case of implying that young people should be made to adapt to present conditions without questioning the morality of the conditions themselves; for example, should young people treat all adults with respect even when some adults abuse them? In shying away from reflective deliberation and personal efficacy, this variation of character education departs from the "democratic" way of life it proposes to promote.

While Wynne's version is relentlessly consistent, the case of the American Institute for Character Education (AICE) is curiously inconsistent, as revealed in a major text and its packaged program. In the volume entitled *The Case for Character Education* (Goble & Brooks, 1983), the authors interpret troubling affective episodes among young people as lawless behavior caused by lack of standards, ethical relativism, and lack of self-control. While avoiding overt religious instruction, they propose that public schools recapture the "American" ethic rooted in Judeo-Christian virtues. Pedagogically they recommend a separate program of direct character instruction to avoid the heavy expense of revising existing programs, although the teaching of morality through literature and history is also proposed. Whether this is a well-reasoned pedagogical theory is unclear. It is unlikely, though, that the developers of a separate, packaged program would recommend only indirect instruction.

The authors' list of virtues is similar to that of Wynne, but they go one step further in pointing out possible excesses in them. For example, industriousness is "good," and laziness "bad," but overachievement is undesirable (Goble & Brooks, 1983, p. 90). The same configuration would hold true for objectivity, which is opposed to inflexibility in opinions, but which should not become emotional; and love, which is better than hate, but should not become indulgence. That this view conforms to traditional views of conventional conduct is revealed plainly in the many references to virtue lists and didactic transmission that the authors claim characterized earlier times.

Meanwhile, the *Character Education Curriculum*, a packaged program distributed by AICE and the Thomas Jefferson Research Center (of which Goble was the founder), matches the rhetoric of the virtues described above in its promotional materials and teacher's guides. However, the program itself engages young people in activities, such as dilemma discussions, that bear a striking resemblance to those used in other approaches to values education that the authors of *The Case for Character Education* strongly criticize. A major difference, of course, is that the teacher is not intended to remain neutral in discussions. But how to account for this curious inconsistency, given the connection between the institute and the research center, remains a mystery. Is it truly that the same means can be used for different ends, or was this a case of unwitting inconsistency? Or is this a contemporary example of the "engineering of consent" in which young people are led to believe that they have discovered the character virtues on their own? Whatever the case, it is quite possible that some who have examined these materials have mistaken them for a quite different version of affect in the curriculum.

RENEWED INTEREST IN SELF-CONCEPT AND ESTEEM

Amid the fever pitch of concern for academic excellence in the 1980s, one ironic twist was the renewed interest in the self-concept and esteem of young people. A possible explanation for this is the connection of self-perceptions to affective issues in society, particularly self-destructive behaviors evidenced by young people, as well as the social conditions, messages, and pressures that influence self-views. One way of interpreting these instances of self-destructive behavior is to recognize that people who are satisfied with themselves and their lives are not likely to be seduced by contrary evidence or to engage in self-destruction. Thus such behaviors might be partially alleviated if efforts were made to enhance self-perceptions.

A second connection is the one between self-perceptions and the school agenda. Research has demonstrated a persistent relationship between self-esteem as learner and such factors as school completion, academic achievement, and success at independent work (Beane &

Lipka, 1986). Moreover, problems with such self-esteem have been linked to the "learned helplessness" that characterizes those with long-term academic achievement problems and likely to be placed in learning disability classes (Bryan & Bryan, 1986). Obviously such correlations would be of interest to both advocates and antagonists of the "excellence" reform movement, either as fuel for the movement's fire or as evidence of the institutional dysfunctions of the school. My own experience in this area suggests that it is actually this correlation with academic achievement and school completion, not some moral imperative, that has driven most of the renewed interest in self-perceptions.

There are several variations on the self-perceptions as affect theme, and one must be careful not to let the familiar rhetoric of concern for mental health obscure the actual content of programs and their claims. For example, Richard Lipka and I (Beane & Lipka, 1986) have argued that self-concept and esteem should not be separated from social relations, including those required for the resolution of social issues. Furthermore, we have deemphasized the separate instruction approach that characterizes individualistic self-fulfillment programs, though we have not totally rejected the possibility for some direct teaching. Instead we have proposed a restructuring of institutional features and curriculum plans that would enhance self-perceptions as well as social relations. Among the recommendations we have made are a humane school climate, participatory governance, heterogeneous grouping, cross-age interactions, community service, cooperative learning, teacher-student planning, curriculum opportunities to discover self and social meanings, and use of projects to extend personal ownership of the planned curriculum. Such a view integrates child and adolescent development, democratic schooling, and social reconstruction platforms. Our work, of course, has not been alone in recommending this variation of enhancing self-perceptions as affect in the curriculum (see also Purkey, 1970; Purkey & Novak, 1978; & Hamachek, 1978).

Another variation on the self-concept and esteem version grows directly out of the "affective education" approach that was popular in the 1970s. In this variation, the matter of self-perceptions is addressed through separate courses during regularly scheduled times in the school day. The national scene is literally cluttered with a variety of these programs, commercially packaged and marketed along with in-service education programs for teachers on how to implement them. In 1970, Gerald Weinstein and Mario Fantini estimated that there were at least 350 such programs known, involving some 3000 "affective exercises and techniques." There is no reason to believe that the number of self-esteem "programs" presently available is any less, although only about 30 are widely known and used on a national level (e.g., Kaiser-Carlso, 1986). Most of these programs claim that if young people are involved in them for one period a day or every other day for a semester or year, drug use, crime, adolescent pregnancies, attempted suicides, and, of course, academic "underachievement" will be reduced.

Such claims are highly seductive to school people who are desperately seeking ways to respond to the problems of youth. The problem here is that the success stories of these programs are based almost entirely on the testimony of participants rather than some careful evaluation. The former evidence is not necessarily useless, but the methods used in gathering it as well as the possibility of selective editing raise doubts as to its validity. One exception to this problem was an evaluation study done on the Skills for Living, or Quest, program, a widely popular variation intended mainly for early adolescents and disseminated through Lions Clubs International. This program involves young people in activities centered on eight themes: adolescent development, communications, exploring personal emotions, peer relationships, family relationships, decision making, goal setting, and personal potential (Gerler, 1986). On pre- and posttest measures, program participants outscored control groups on seven of the eight measures used in the study (Crisci, 1986). The lone exception was "feelings about school," which was based on views of the self as a worthwhile member of school classes and as understood by teachers.

There is a serious question as to whether this kind of evaluation and its methods can adequately measure self-perceptions, particularly in light of their complexity in real-life situations. However, even in this study the finding related to school is crucial and might have been expected. The fundamental problem with these kinds of programs as an approach to affect in the school is that they are woefully incomplete. It is one thing to promote self-esteem in one selected segment of the overall program, and quite another to then send young people off to experiences in other parts of the institution (and outside it) that may contradict their new skills or self-perceptions (an exception to this is the program developed by Reasoner, 1982). In a sense this issue recalls the substance of the research done on character education programs in the 1920s by Hartshorne and May and reviewed in Chapter 2. There, as here, the transfer of "taught" attitudes and skills was seen as seriously inhibited by the inconsistencies across the rest of the school and in larger life.

The point is that direct instruction in separate courses alone is not enough to adequately address self-perceptions. Among other things, it recalls the social efficiency movement, in which young people were simply taught to adjust to existing conditions. Moreover, it tends to re-create the reductionist separation of affect from cognition. Nothing less than a restructuring of the dominant institutional features and curriculum plans will finally suffice in this matter. Further, if these programs are to come closer to a complete version of affect in the curriculum in anything like their present form, their advocates must associate themselves with larger social issues that present debilitating conditions under which many young people live. Those conditions pose a continuing threat to whatever progress is made on self-esteem through school efforts.

In a time when so many messages suggest that self-esteem is tied to what one buys (commodification of the self), it is perhaps not surprising that some schools would want to buy packages to improve self-esteem. However, glossy packaging and seductive rhetoric do not and must not obscure the realities faced by so many young people in their lives.

THE MISINTERPRETATION OF VALUES CLARIFICATION

No version of affect in the curriculum has been more widely known or more roundly criticized than the approach called "values clarification." It has been used in literally thousands of settings, and the methodology it involves has been claimed by many programs in counseling and "affective education." On the other hand, it has become a favorite target of religious fundamentalists, classical humanists, character educators, and moral educationists who in one way or another protest what they see as its relativity and aimlessness (e.g., Junell, 1979; Strike, 1982). In the 1980s, values clarification largely became a collection of activities associated with self-fulfillment and realization, and in this form it deserves much of the reasoned criticism it has received. However, I will claim that this was not its intended form, that it has become separated from its origins, and that if it is to be rejected as an approach to affect in the curriculum, values clarification should first be reconsidered in its original form.

As explained in Chapter 2, the theory behind values clarification was originally developed by Louis Raths as an alternative to indoctrination approaches to the teaching of values. Its fundamental claim, that democracy and democratic discourse required development of a valuing process based on reflective thinking, followed from the work of John Dewey (1939). It is instructive to note that at the time Raths was working on the values theory, he also published two related works. One was *Teaching for Learning* (1969), in which clarifying values was listed as one of 10 components of teaching. The other was *Teaching for Thinking* (Raths, Wasserman, Jonas, & Rothstein, 1967), in which he described symptoms of unclear thinking in terms such as apathy, flightiness, uncertainty, overconforming, and overdissenting. The first work is important here because it indicates that values clarification was not seen as a complete pedagogical theory. The second work is also noteworthy because, as it turns out, the symptoms of unclear thinking described by Raths are basically the same as his symptoms of unclear values (Raths, Harmin, & Simon, 1966).

The theory behind values clarification has several elements, of which the following are crucial. First, valuing involves reflective thinking as a method for considering reasons why values are chosen as well as the consequences of those choices. Second, valuing is a learned process that opens up the opportunity for continuous reflection and choosing. Third, if values are to be really prized and representative of the democratic way of life, they must be freely chosen; in this sense, the theory was clearly anti-indoctrination. Fourth, thinking is not the end of the process, because freely chosen, prized values are acted on as expressions of commitment and for reality testing; in other words, the theory was concerned with conduct. Finally, the process of valuing presents a method of discourse that is to be applied not only in everyday personal and social relationships but also to larger social issues. In fact, a close look at examples Raths used reveals a persistent and explicit concern for such issues as bigotry, corruption, and violence.

Raths' intention was to place values clarification in the curriculum in the form of clarifying questions that teachers were to ask as a way to help young people think about their choices, conclusions, and behaviors (Raths et al., 1966). Such questions were to be used across the planned curriculum to encourage thinking and when value dilemmas arose in the course of everyday events. Teachers (or other adults) were to play a nonjudgmental role in responding to value choices, but were to continue asking questions, particularly where, for example, thinking appeared to be dogmatic or overconforming. This process was very close to the democratic discourse described by Dewey (1908) and later by Habermas (1971) as a process for making, examining, and redeeming value claims in the society at large.

By the late 1970s, however, values clarification had taken quite another direction. For one thing, the theory eventually became misused as others began to create artificial value dilemmas rather than using those that emerged in the lived experiences of young people. Furthermore, with the exception of one text, the approach increasingly moved away from the larger school program (Harmin, Kirschenbaum, & Simon, 1973). A growing number of "handbooks" and school-based programs interpreted values clarification as a collection of activities that teachers might use to encourage self-exploration during set-aside time slots. Thus it became separated from the integration theory that Raths had worked out. In the 1980s, many of the activities emerged in self-esteem packages and substance abuse programs, without any explanation of their origins or the theory behind them. At one level the issue of ethical relativity raised by early critics became minor compared with the individualistic self-realization programs that had captured much of the meaning of values clarification.

Clearly Raths and his original co-theorists might have imagined this possibility and explicitly issued warnings about it. Moreover, they might have labeled some of their illustrative activities as examples for teachers and other adults to use in understanding the theory and the process attached to it, and not as suggestions for actual classroom use. Although the theory was concerned mainly with the *means* by which values might be developed, they certainly might have made it more explicit that while teachers were to remain value-neutral in dialogue about choices or conclusions, they were entitled to hold values of their own and to openly promote them insofar as they represented the democracy, dignity, and diversity that were prominent in the theory behind the process. Thus, values clarification was left open to misinterpretation as it became widely disseminated in conferences and workshops, done at times by some of the original theorists themselves. Though some attempt was made to redeem the original claims (Harmin, Kirschenbaum, Jacobs, & Simon, 1977), the die was clearly cast.

As the pattern of misinterpretation emerged, so did several criticisms, mainly from Alan Lockwood, the critic of character education whom we have already discussed. He argued in one paper (1977) that many of the questions and activities being used could violate the privacy rights of children, a point with which Raths would have agreed where participation or public response was not voluntary. In another paper, Lockwood (1978) systematically dissected a large number of studies on the effects of values clarification and concluded that claims about actual effects on behavior of young people were grossly overstated and that many of the studies were poorly constructed. Meanwhile, many teachers became wary of the approach as they saw themselves being asked to play the role of "psychologist"; they were told how to get young people to reveal their thoughts, but felt unqualified or helpless to do anything about serious problems that emerged. This increasingly became a valid point of concern, and I will let Raths (1972) answer it.

> Are you expected to be a clinical psychologist or analyst or psychiatrist? By all means, NO! . . . If you have any reason to suspect that a child has some very deep psychological problems, you do have a responsibility to take the matter up with your school officials. (p. 65)

The point is that most issues that might arise during values discussions are of the sort that are common among young people and not seriously threatening. On the other hand, some young people with serious problems might never get help if someone, perhaps a teacher, does not open up opportunities in which they might surface.

Where, then, does this leave values clarification as a possible version of affect in the curriculum? This discussion has attempted to redeem original claims for the approach. However, it has been not so much an effort to endorse it as to suggest we be certain what it is we are rejecting or accepting. Certainly values clarification is not a complete version of affect in the curriculum, because it does not, for example, adequately address self-perceptions or institutional features of the school. However, the current criticism of it is based largely on a misinterpretation of its intentions, though many both inside and outside the school would no doubt object to the "thinking and freely choosing" aspects of the original theory. So far has the original approach drifted, that some critics discuss the approach mainly on the basis of work by people other than Raths; moreover, they fail to pay attention to other parts of his work that are crucially related to this one (Chazan, 1985; Goble & Brooks, 1983). If we are to consider the possible place of values clarification as I have described it, there is a serious need to reconstruct the original theory. In doing so, the fact that the term itself has become a "red flag" to so many groups suggests that the name might have to be changed to protect the theory.

THE SHIFTING VIEW OF MORAL EDUCATION

The term *moral education* has been with us for centuries, and as we saw in Chapter 2, it has been placed in the curriculum with several meanings. Until relatively recently, those meanings were mostly associated with didactic transmission of character virtues, although Dewey's interpretation was certainly an exception to that. The version to which I want to refer here grew out of the work of Lawrence Kohlberg in the 1960s and 1970s and has dominated much of the meaning of moral education since that time.

Kohlberg began by rejecting the traditional transmission approach and the romantic, idealistic view of natural goodness in young people. Instead he articulated a theory based on cognitive reasoning and developmental psychology rooted largely in the theories of Dewey, Immanuel Kant, and Jean Piaget (Kohlberg & Mayer, 1972). From this view he described six sequential and predictive stages through which individuals supposedly ascended in the development of moral reasoning. The central theme in the stages was an increasingly complex and integrated view of justice as the grounds for reciprocity in social relations where moral reasoning was called for. This theory became enormously popular, especially as it proposed to explain how and why young people make moral decisions the way they do. As experimentation began to reveal ideas about how higher stages of moral reasoning could be promoted, scores of books and journal articles appeared to spread the word. This work was bolstered by empirical research that demonstrated that modeling higher level reasoning while engaging young people in moral dilemma discussions did effect movement to higher stages in Kohlberg's sequence (Leming, 1981a; Lockwood, 1978; Schaefli, Rest, & Thoma, 1985).

This popularity should not be taken to mean that the theory was free from criticism. Jack Fraenkel (1978) claimed that Kohlberg had given insufficient attention to emotion as an aspect of reasoning and suggested the approach be integrated with others that addressed that aspect of affect. Carol Gilligan (1977, 1982), a colleague of Kohlberg's, claimed that the theory was biased against women, because the perspective of interpersonal regard ("caring") from which they reasoned was relegated to a fairly low level in the stages of justice. Habermas (1971) suggested that Kohlberg's theory overemphasized individual reasoning and that the necessity (and reality) of social, communicative discourse about moral issues should be integrated at the higher stages. Moreover, as previously suggested, the recommendation for more equitable distribution of power and justice in the school was enough to make many school officials wince.

In framing the original theory, Kohlberg was heavily influenced by libertarian views of the 1960s, especially in his call for wider ascendance to the highest stage (individual conscience as a basis for ethical reasoning). However, by 1976 he had focused on the fifth stage, social contract reasoning, in the hope of promoting democracy in that context. By 1980, his interest moved to the fourth stage, conforming to social and legal obligations, and he spoke in terms of developing a "good member of a community or a good citizen" (Kohlberg, 1980). This shift, which Lockwood (1982) characterized as "elevating the possible to the desirable," reflected a reaction to his perception of growing individualism and his frustration over efforts to move young people to the higher stages in actual rather than hypothetical moral dilemmas in schools. However, the transition also moved Kohlberg, and some of his followers, increasingly away from Dewey and closer to the views of Emile Durkheim, the conservative French social philosopher. In this realignment, the moral *development* theory more clearly became one of moral *education*.

Durkheim's view of morality was based on three essential concepts (1961). The first, *discipline*, involved regularity of conduct, not simply as a result of restraint, but rather as a condition of clearly stated modes of appropriate conduct and individual goal seeking within those modes. Because modes of conduct were clearly stated, individuals supposedly were not confused or frustrated by a personal search for appropriate conduct. The second concept was *attachment to the collective order*. This meant that morality was found within the norms of social groups to which individuals were attached; the norms defined obligations for the conduct of individuals. The third concept, *autonomy*, recognized self-determination in relation to the first two concepts; that is, the individual's enlightened and reasoned choice to adhere to group norms.

The pedagogy of Durkheim's theory involved the school as the agent of transition from the intimate morality of the home to the impersonal regulations of society. Teachers of young children were free to use authority, including punishment, to impose "moral" conduct, while those of adolescents were to attempt to reason through the bases for social norms and obligations. Those norms, of course, were the "moral" values that society used to regulate individualism and maintain stability. The school and classroom were viewed as a social system in which those values were promoted, tested, supported, and "learned."

Durkheim's views have increasingly caught the attention of many whose work followed Kohlberg's theory. James Leming (1981b), for example, sees Durkheim's approach as resolving the major dilemma posed by moral education research; that is, while the reasoning level of young people may be raised, their conduct has not necessarily followed. Thus Durkheim's social norm and obligation view is presumed to offer a possible substitute for the individual reasoning or monological approach to moral development and is more closely aligned with the transmission approach to shaping conduct. The emphasis on subordinating individual interests to community norms, I believe, is not unlike what we might imagine in Kohlberg's fourth stage, in which moral reasoning was based on laws or regulations and the need for social order. This shift also partially explains the vehement opposition among many moral development advocates to the present version of values clarification with its adherence to individual reasoning.

One of the curious sidelights has been the emerging interchangeability of terms like *moral education, values education,* and *character education.* Michael Silver (1976) and Albert Alschuler (1982) considered moral development among approaches to values education. Barry Chazan (1985) situated values education under moral education. Thomas Lickona (1988) speaks of character education within the framework of moral education. Kevin Ryan (1986) presented a blend of classical humanism, character education, and moral development under moral education. And, *Education Week* (1987) reported the results of a conference on moral education with the curious headline, "Values Education Accord Elusive."

The resulting confusion is reflected in the following statement made in 1987 by the President of the National School Boards Association in releasing a report entitled *Building Character in the Public Schools:* "character, values, morality—or whatever word we use to define this issue." However, one gets the impression that among theorists, at least, a struggle is going on for the rights to the generic title for affect in the curriculum as I have defined it. Or perhaps this confusion stems from the particular persuasions of individuals that function in the absence of a coherent framework within which affect proposals and claims might be made. I would contend that given the claims that have historically been attached to particular versions and the way in which any one might restrict discourse about the broader theme of affect in the curriculum, our choice of terms is very important.

Clearly, moral development/education has become a collage of versions with increasing support for compliance with social obligations rather than reasoned choices. One excellent reproduction of this ambiguity is *Moral Education in the Life of the School* (ASCD Panel on Moral Education, 1988).[2] The report begins with a tour of young people's problems that has the ring of character education in its implication that these stem from a lack of self-control and motivation.

The second chapter is largely an explanation of Durkheim's theory, with a final description of a "morally mature person" that blends virtually all positions. The third chapter presents a collection of methods for promoting moral growth that honors selections from a variety of versions, including some that clearly contradict the foundations laid in the first two chapters. In the end, the report identifies issues and makes recommendations that, with few exceptions, would be attractive to the most concerned advocates of democratic, progressive education. I do not mean to belittle the report; it represents a well-meant attempt to integrate disparate versions. However, in its internal inconsistencies it reflects not only the current confusion, but the increasingly obvious fact that some aspects of the versions simply do not synthesize well.

I interpret the events described here as a product of the times and the interests of the participants on the moral education scene. The libertarian views of the 1960s and early 1970s emphasized individual rights in opposition to pressures for conformity. By the 1980s, what was libertarian a decade earlier appeared to many as grounds for potential excesses of individualism and an explanation for perceived hedonistic aspects of the youth culture. It is possible that this perception is partially true, but perhaps it is also a case of aging, frustrated theorists and practitioners reenacting the intergenerational conflict that views each new generation of young people as morally "at risk." In the 1960s the concern was overconformity, while in the 1980s it was one of radical individualism and hedonism in the context of discontinuities in social forms in the family, schools, communities, and other settings. Nowhere has this view been more pointedly addressed than in the popular study of value trends by Bellah and associates (1986) mentioned previously. That this work was widely read and favorably cited reveals the support for its interpretation of the scene.

The search for community norms and the desire for individual commitment to them raises some very difficult issues. For example, whose version of norms will be used? How will they be identified? What happens if individuals or groups disagree with the norms on the basis of conflicting, but equally valid, claims? After all, community norms may be democratic and liberating or they may be overzealous in support of order, conformity, and the status quo. This point raises a most troubling issue regarding the shifting view of moral development at a time when economic and political inequities are so common, when demographies are changing, and when new issues are upon us. Clearly this is a most dangerous time to abandon the hope for pursuing with young people the higher-level stages of moral reasoning that

Kohlberg originally described or introducing them to the process of reasoned, democratic discourse. Looking back on the themes in the previous chapter, it is equally clear that there is really no appropriate time to abandon them.

THE UNDERCURRENT OF DEMOCRATIC SCHOOLS

Almost all of the school reform proposals of the 1980s used the slogan of "excellence" to replace the concerns for equality and equity that had characterized reform for much of the previous two decades. I have purposely used the term *undercurrent* in the heading of this section, because this dominant tone of recent reform proposals has obscured, but not eradicated, the themes of a quite different view found in the democratic schools movement where "equality" and "equity" still have a prominent place.

The continuing life of this movement should not be surprising. For one thing, the 1960s and early 1970s, in which the movement had a prominent place, are still "recent" history, and many of its spokespeople are still on the scene. For another, we can expect that in any era of growing economic disparity, changing demographics, social efficiency, and high culture claims, there are bound to be many people who are concerned about the relation of those factors to the broad and enduring themes of democratic principles and process. Moreover, the availability of texts that critically analyze the "excellence" movement in light of democratic concerns is increasing (for example, Battistoni, 1985; Lazerson et al., 1985; Oakes, 1985; Bastian et al., 1986). In this case I will depart from the pattern of analyzing well-known texts and instead use a lesser known, but no less revealing, source. It reflects well the meaning of democratic schools intended by this movement and is authored by people actively engaged in work in public schools.

The source is a journal named *Democratic Schools* (published until 1987 as the *Networker*), which is distributed by the Public Education Information Network, a St. Louis–based organization. The journal uses contributions from several local and regional groups interested in democratic school reform, such as the Boston Women's Teachers Group, the Institute for Democratic Education at Ohio University, and the Rethinking Schools Project in Milwaukee. Titles of articles reveal the flavor of specific issues of concern to these activists: "Peace Education Programs Grow in U.S. Schools," "Black Perspectives on School Reform," "Paying the Price for Democracy," and "Do Educational Standards Require Standardization?" The way in which such work is framed is explained in a document entitled *Equity and Excellence: Toward an Agenda for School Reform* (Public Education Information Network, 1987). Here we find the sense of platform that is guiding the present democratic schools movement.

As the title of the document suggests, the authors believe that equity and excellence are not mutually exclusive if they are interpreted through the lens of democracy. Two ideas present the centerpiece of this reasoning: (1) democratic schools are essential for a democratic nation, and (2) schools should provide the best education for all children, rejecting any notions or practices that suggest potential is limited by heredity, social background, or values. The proposed process for developing democratic schools is participatory management at the local level. The main body of the document is devoted to recommendations for action in several areas.

In the area of social issues and schooling, the authors indicate that contemporary reform proposals have diverted attention from large-scale issues such as the decreasing number of available jobs, inequitable distribution of wealth, social inequality, threat of nuclear war, and centralization of decision making. As an alternative to the main problem of centralized definitions of important problems and proposed solutions, it is recommended that "people in each school community must develop their own agendas and specific programs for reform . . . [and that] priorities and programs for action must be negotiated from the conflicting interests and values of students, teachers, parents, and citizens" (pp. 4–5).

The major pieces of a reformed democratic curriculum are described as the development of the capacity for critical literacy, understanding of histories and cultures of dominant and minority groups, and opportunities for personal and social action based on informed decisions. To support such efforts, the authors recommend that the education of school administrators include an understanding of multiple cultures and the processes of participatory management. The latter point implies a major recommendation: the empowerment of teachers in terms of administrative, curriculum, fiscal, and personnel decisions. Moreover, teacher education would need reform with regard to the quality of coursework, the cultural content of programs, development of closer relationships with those who work in schools, and departure from "prescriptive credentialling and certification regulations" (p. 10).

A major concern of the authors is the increasing emphasis on testing and evaluation, a movement that they see as driving the curriculum and distracting from qualitative learning as well as insensitive to the "enormous potential and range of the human mind and a respect for the diversity and complexity of human cultures" (p. 11). In the latter sense, they insist that current tests ignore issues of gender, race, religious background, and cultural differences. In the area of school discipline, the authors reject current notions of "laxness" in schools and apathy among young people. Instead they believe that concern for control has been a leading item on the school agenda and has, in fact, interfered with self-discipline and interest. Finally, the document recommends that teachers "accept the responsibility for continuing self and peer evaluation of their curriculum, pedagogy, and control practices" supported by "administrators, communities, professional associations, and institutions of higher learning [that] must provide the requisite moral, intellectual and material support" (p. 14).

The clear message of this report is the belief that democratic discourse is a necessary condition for democratic schools and that its use at the local level would provide a better chance for resolving educational problems than does centralized decision making. Such faith in the process apparently overrides the possibility that a local body politic could choose to practice undemocratic procedures or select solutions contrary to those proposed in the document. In that sense, the authors take what might be perceived as a courageous, but dangerous, stance in times that they themselves characterize as decidedly undemocratic. Undoubtedly the faith of the authors is at least partially buoyed by the fact that serious attempts at local discourse do not have a large history that could refute their claims. Also, it might be argued that people are not likely to reject broad participation in decision making, because it expands their own efficacy.

As a whole, this stance is a reproduction of much of the early reconstructionist movement toward democratic schools described in Chapter 2. In addition, the points that the authors raise are crucial to the issue of affect in the curriculum. The extension of democracy has, after all, been the most consistently avowed purpose of the public schools for most of the twentieth century, more powerful than national economic or special interests and partially the test for any version of affect in the curriculum. In the next two chapters I will deal with this issue as it applies to institutional features, curriculum plans, and relationships within the school culture and between the schools and people and issues outside of them. For the time being, it is instructive to know that even in the whirlwind of reform proposals about excellence, the issues of equality and equity are still alive in the context of a continuing democratic schools movement.

MULTICULTURAL EDUCATION

One of the most oustanding characteristics of contemporary society in
the United States is the changing nature of demographies. The
United States is becoming an increasingly pluralistic country, and
the traditional numerics of "majority" and "minority" are rapidly
changing, especially in particular regions (Hodgkinson, 1985). This
trend suggests a need to look carefully at the long-standing issue of
the status of multicultural education in schools in relation to cultural
pluralism in the larger society. Carl Grant and Christine Sleeter
(1985, pp. 98–99) have defined a typology of six approaches to multicultural education, ranging from a minimal view that replicates the
status quo outside of schools, to a social reconstructionist approach.
Here the concept of "cultures" includes ethnicity, race, gender, social
class, and handicap diversity. The approaches include the following:

1. "Business as Usual with Minimal Compliance to Civil Rights
   Laws," in which social stratification is maintained and assimilation encouraged through simply mixing diverse groups in schools.

2. "Teaching the Exceptional or Culturally Different," in which social stratification is maintained, but assimilation is more directly
   addressed through altered instruction and curriculum plans intended to bridge mainstream and nonmainstream cultures.

3. "Human Relations," in which social stratification is maintained
   and assimilation promoted, but students are encouraged to display
   tolerance and humane attitudes toward those who are culturally
   different.

4. "Single Group Studies," in which attempts are made to reduce
   social stratification and assimilation, and promote social, structural change through teaching about the histories, contributions,
   and material conditions of cultural minorities.

5. "Multicultural Education," in which social, structural change is
   promoted through altered curriculum plans, recognition of language diversity, nontraditional staffing patterns, and sensitivity to
   diverse learning styles.

6. "Education That Is Multicultural and Social Reconstructionist," in
   which social stratification is directly confronted by a social issues

curriculum organization, teaching of political skills, and altering the school as in the multicultural approach.

While all of these approaches might be found in schools, the tone of the 1980s concentrated heavily on the first two; that is, cultural differences were (and are) seen as difficulties to be legally tolerated or as objects for assimilation. This attitude was typified in the movement for "English only" instruction and attempts to designate English as the "official" national language. This movement had historical precedence as a reaction to immigrant populations among those who supported the expansion of urban public schools in the mid-1800s and the Americanization programs earlier in the twentieth century. Ironically, the earlier efforts were aimed at immigrant groups from which many who see themselves in the "beleaguered" majority today are, in fact, descended.

Much of the rhetoric of classical humanism and character education is aimed at defining a common culture based on some core of shared values to which people should commit themselves and toward which behavior should be shaped in school settings. There is no doubt that some set of shared beliefs, such as the themes described in Chapter 3, is necessary if society is to avoid selfish individualism. However, the major question is this: What version of values can be shared without offending or eradicating the rich diversity of our pluralistic population?

The high culture version is problematic in that it represents the views of only one group—at that, a portion of the population that is defined largely by economic and political power that has not been accessible to the whole society. Moreover, the definition of the high culture was partly conditioned by its distinction from that of other classes. To propose this version is thus to suggest again that the privileged definition of culture is necessarily the right one. The category of "middle class" values, assuming there ever was such consensus, is also problematic because it too represents only a portion of the population, albeit one whose traditional economic status is in a tenuous position in the current occupational outlook.

Yet these conceptions of shared values represent precisely the version of affect in the curriculum that ascended in the 1980s and found its way into the everyday life of the school, including that of young people who were not part of the dominant Anglo culture. That it was only thinly veiled in many reform proposals was a constant reminder of its continuing place and power in the political arena. The degree to which schools moved to implement those proposals can only suggest the pressure there must be for young people to conform to the classical humanist's definition of what is right and good.

In reviewing the versions described in most of this chapter and Chapter 2, I was more than once struck by the fact that almost all were developed by white, male academics. Certainly some of these versions have been supported by people of other descriptions, and clearly some of the versions have been acutely concerned with cultural pluralism. However, I have often wondered whether even these latter have, in the end, been reflective of or applicable to the lived experiences of those who are characteristically different from the theorists who proposed them.

SUMMARY

This chapter began with three claims about the current scene in relation to affect in the curriculum. One was that the versions traced in Chapter 2 coexist in contemporary theory and practice. The second was that the coexistence is not as peaceful as it might have been at other times. The third claim was that conflicts and contradictions may be found not only across versions, but within them as well. In light of the survey of the current scene, those claims appear to stand as an accurate and appropriate representation of the present condition.

However, the survey has revealed some additional important points. While the various versions are contested in schools mostly on pedagogical grounds, a more powerful struggle is being carried out in relation to perceptions of affective issues in the larger society. For example, the curriculum view of the radical fundamentalists is part of a broader concern about secularization in all aspects of life. The shifting focus of moral development is best understood in the context of perceptions about changing value orientations. The meaning of the "excellence" reform movement is most clearly revealed when related to the ambiguous nature of the emerging postindustrial age and discontinuity in the industrial-economic sector.

In each case we see reenacted what has become a nearly inevitable result of perceptions of affective issues in the larger society. That is, sooner or later attention is focused on the young either as victims of or willing participants in those issues. In either case, the schools, as the common ground for all young people, are seen as the agency with the best chance for helping them to develop the attitudes and skills necessary to meet needs or solve problems in society. At times this process simply projects problems onto the young; at others it reflects the hope that they will do a better job of solving problems than their elders have. In either event, it is in this way that affect gets placed in the curriculum, either explicitly or implicitly.

Another point is that versions of affect are often incomplete with regard to particular aspects or meanings. This characteristic complicates their analysis. In Chapter 1 I proposed questions that ought to be addressed by proposals for placing affect in the curriculum and suggested that they might also be used in examining proposals and their claims. Describing contemporary claims in relation to those questions has frequently been difficult, requiring a tedious search for reasons why particular proposals have been made and what they really imply. In some cases I have chosen to avoid guesswork and instead suggested that one or another version is simply incomplete. Moreover, much of the research on affective development suggests that while the reasoning level of young people may be influenced, the matter of deeply affecting actual behavior remains elusive.

In the end we are left with a most troubling picture of the current condition of affect in the curriculum. First, particular versions are incomplete, some in more important ways than others. Pressed toward completeness, particularly in terms of the themes described in Chapter 3, they might be caught in such internal contradictions as to render them indefensible. For example, some of the popular self-esteem programs fail to suggest how self- and social interests might be integrated; if they did, their comfortable individualism might well unravel in the complicated emergence of social conditions. If the democratic ideas of empowerment and participation were brought into "excellence" reform proposals, the centralized definition of economic "needs" might well disintegrate and with it the claims made on the aspirations and motivations of young people.

Second, across the versions there are some common grounds, but in other cases particular versions are in thorough opposition. This latter observation is especially meaningful in comparing proposals in terms of transmission and developmental theories, sectarian and secular views, centralized and empowering processes, and self- and social interests. It is even more powerful in light of perceptions about the sources of affective issues, the location of social problems, and the placement of responsibility for dealing with them. In many cases, attempts to negotiate compromises would be frustrated by the wide and irreconcilable differences between claims. That schools are forced to deal with such conflicting claims is particularly problematic. How they do so is a remarkable indication of their adaptability and a revealing explanation of their confusion over affect. Whether they can long continue under these conditions and still offer a reasonable education should be a matter for serious reflection.

The picture is also troubling because we ought to be able to do better than this. That present versions of affect in the curriculum are informed by their histories is obvious. That proponents are explicitly aware of particular histories is not nearly so clear. Given the length of time over which claims about affect have been made, the seriousness with which they have been proposed, and the powerful implications they have for young people and society, the absence of reasonable consensus can be explained only by the contradictory demands made by competing interests in the larger society—contradictions that often seem to paralyze the efforts of those in schools to pursue a unified and clearly articulated approach to affect in the curriculum. Moreover, that "paralysis" is understandable in light of the narrowness in which some versions are conceived and the refusal of their proponents to engage in reasoned discourse.

As we look also at institutional features of schools, our concern for the personal affect of young people should be heightened. Large numbers of them are now subject to the affective tension associated with higher standards, more frequent testing, and mechanized approaches to learning and discipline. It is difficult to believe sometimes that the years of concern in research and practice over heavy pressure, anxiety, and tension, as well as findings on healthy growth and development, have come to so little. These features are exacerbated for cultural minorities by other factors, such as ability tracking (Oakes, 1985) and inequitable access to resources (Apple, 1986). Nor should this focus obscure the fact that many adults in schools are experiencing frustration and dissonance as well.

Looking beyond the debate among academics, then, and into the lived experiences of personal affect, we should clearly see that there are conditions in the schools that are in need of serious restructuring. Some of these affect all young people, while others are more problematic for certain groups. Moreover, this description of the current status of personal affect should not be seen as directed at any one group of proponents of any given theoretical version. Personal affect in the curriculum represents the lived experiences of all children and adolescents in schools and therefore should be the concern of all versions and all of those who propose them.

5

Placing Affect in the Curriculum

In this chapter we will consider how affect might be placed in the curriculum in ways that would bring to life the themes of democracy, dignity, and diversity. This will require a careful journey into the everyday workings of the school to see how concepts and conditions may come to life in deliberate and consistent ways. Yet even done in this way, our discussion can only be descriptive and suggestive; before appropriate action can finally take place, actual curriculum forms must be worked out in each local school rather than be handed down in a prescribed, authoritative fashion.

If we bring the themes of Chapter 3 together into an integrated and coherent form, what does that form suggest for schools in general and curriculum in particular? Here three important questions emerge.

1. In what way(s) should we view young people in the school?
2. What should the relationship of the school to the larger society be?
3. How might curriculum plans and institutional features be deliberately organized and developed to reflect and promote the foundational themes?

By exploring these questions we can determine how affect, broadly defined, can be placed in the curriculum. At the same time, we will also examine some of the current policies and practices that contradict such a vision. It is hoped that the examples used here may encourage us to create many more ways of bringing democracy, dignity, and diversity to life in the school.

A VIEW OF YOUNG PEOPLE IN SCHOOL

At any one moment while they are in school, young people are simultaneously involved in several roles. They are:

1. *People* with needs, problems, concerns, interests, desires, aspirations, and individual histories of experiences both inside and outside the school

2. *Young people* engaged in working through various stages of human development and creating meanings in light of their perceptions that help them make sense out of their experiences and their environment

3. *Participants in networks of human relationships* such as the family and the peer group

4. *Citizens* of a society in which the particular rights and responsibilities are accorded by the legislative and legal traditions

5. *Participants in particular cultures* and thus informed by their race, class, gender, age, and other dimensions that may differentiate people's lived experiences

6. *Students* enrolled in a particular school, participating in the interactions, regulations, and demands of life within that institution

7. *Future adults*, not simply in a distant way but already, in an odd temporal sense, partially formed by their past experiences

These roles are not necessarily what young people in school want them to be (though the individuals may be more or less happy with them), but rather what they inevitably are because of the place and time in which the young people are living. As a result, their experiences within the school are partly defined by the conflicting demands the various roles place on them. School life would probably be much easier for young people if they were able to simply differentiate among these roles at particular times; for example, to assume at one moment the exclusive role of student or at another that of social participant. In this way they might be able to negotiate more easily the maze of contradictions that arise as claims are made by the various roles or as demands are made to spontaneously assume one and set the others aside.

However, the realities of humanness function against such momentary differentiation, especially because the "natural" roles (person, young person) conflict with those that are imposed by the institutional expectations related to being a "student." Because one or another role cannot be conveniently cast aside, we must recognize the presence of all of them and seek ways to create opportunities for creatively integrating them; that is, ways of simultaneously paying attention to the various roles and promoting holistic rather than fragmented development (Brown, 1969).

Furthermore, as "young" people, they probably have had little control over their experiences within various roles. Instead their experiences and the conditions under which they have lived have been determined almost entirely by parents or guardians, school officials, and other adults, as well as by social and cultural boundaries (especially with regard to race, class, and gender). True, some young people may have resented or contested those authorities and boundaries, but such feelings or actions have not dramatically changed the larger picture.

Added to this, of course, is the fact that attendance in school is compulsory, a legal requirement that should not be taken lightly, because it imposes the role of "student" on young people and places them under control of school authorities. While federal and state legislatures, courts, and state boards of education have defined limits in many areas, the largest measure of regulation over everyday life in the school (in such matters as school governance, use of time, and discipline policies) is still exercised by local authorities. This control arrangement places school officials, including teachers, in a very powerful position: They are able to choose the way in which power will be distributed within the school and need not necessarily consult with students about it.

Because attendance is compulsory and adults hold prior power, a first principle for a view of young people in school is that we are morally obligated to unconditionally accept all young people in school without regard for the backgrounds or characteristics they bring with them. Such acceptance has posed a considerable problem within public schools historically, particularly as access to them has been extended to nonwhite and nonprivileged young people. Conditional acceptance has been faced at various times by the children of non-Protestant immigrants, who were faced with a largely sectarian curriculum; by working-class children, who were faced with a curriculum based on high culture interests; by children of color, who were segregated from white schools; and by children with physical and mental characteristics that inhibited their full participation in the school program.

Obviously it would be unfair to say that no progress has been made on this theme over the years. Non-Protestant immigrants did succeed in initiating the ongoing efforts to reduce sectarianism in the curriculum. Supreme Court rulings have promoted the desegregation of schools and Public Law 94-142 (1975), though politically problematic (Sleeter, 1987), increased access to schools by children with physically and mentally handicapping conditions. Yet if we view the unconditional acceptance of young people as a moral obligation, it is clear that the moral intentions of legislation have not necessarily found their way into many aspects of the school. While access to schools has increased, there is still compelling evidence that not all young people have equal opportunities to participate fully in school programs or achieve their intended outcomes. For example, Jeannie Oakes (1985) and others have shown that where homogeneous tracking is used in schools, young people who are poor and/or nonwhite occupy the lower tracks in numbers that are seriously disproportionate to their percentages in the overall population.

In these groups they are often subjected to low expectations, slotted into remedial classes, and reminded in many ways that they are less capable than others. While a few occupants of higher tracks may at times, be moved downward, there is rarely upward mobility across tracks. For those in the lower tracks, their placement becomes a "permanent address" not unlike the position in the larger society in which those who are poor and nonwhite are situated. Moreover, as the years go by, these young people are "guided" into more remedial classes as well as vocational courses, where time, expectations, and curriculum plans limit consideration of concepts and themes like democracy, economic systems, comparative cultures, and others that are "affect-loaded."

This line of reasoning suggests how the lack of acceptance of some young people, based on personal characteristics that are theoretically ignored in "public" schools, eventually is played out into problems of access to certain curriculum themes that reflect important issues in personal and social learning. What begins as a problem of conditional acceptance in terms of access to the school itself eventually also becomes one of unequal access to curriculum opportunities and outcomes. Indeed, as we think through how affect is placed in the curriculum, access to the doors of the school is only part of the picture.

The matter of unconditional acceptance has thus been made problematic for two reasons. One has to do with the acceptance of those who are not part of the white, middle-class population, while the other has to do with accepting those who do not easily fit the academic expectations of the school. Anything less than unconditional acceptance immediately raises several difficulties or contradictions. To resent or decry the personal characteristics of some young people is to deny their dignity. To differentiate their opportunities in school is to deny the fundamental concept of equality and reduce their chances for personal efficacy. To resent or disparage their socioeconomic position is to project political and economic inequities onto them; that is, to blame the victims. In short, to place conditions on acceptance in all phases of schooling is to deny the very concepts of democracy, dignity, and diversity that should define how affect is placed in the curriculum.

From this principle of unconditional acceptance let us now turn to some further ideas that would emerge from the themes of democracy, dignity, diversity, and developmentalism. Such a view begins with the notion that young people, as whole beings, are placed at the very center of thinking about what might happen in the school. The various roles in which they find themselves are not inconvenient distractions from school purposes, but rather the result of being human and of living out their lives in particular places, at particular times, and under particular conditions. The actual content of these roles is something over which they and we, as educators, have only limited control. That content more largely depends on such factors as the families they come from, the socioeconomic conditions in which they are placed, their prior experiences in school, socially imposed gender, race, and ethnic boundaries, and so on.

The fact that these contexts are presently beyond the control of young people suggests that their behavior should not always be looked upon as self-controlled. Much concern has been expressed in recent years about the behavior of young people, especially self-destructive behavior such as drug abuse, crime, adolescent pregnancies, and so forth. Obviously these behaviors are to some degree chosen, but they are also influenced by the perceived range of choices, the conditions under which young people live, and their developmental characteristics. In other words, much of what we observe in the behavior of young people can be seen as the consequences of environmental and developmental influences.

For example, educators who work with early adolescents have come to understand that the obsession with peer approval among those young people is part of the developmental need for group acceptance and belonging, while their emotional volatility is largely influenced by the physical aspects of puberty. If we can understand this influenced behavior, then perhaps it is also possible to understand that drug use may often be an apparent way to escape the realities of unhappiness caused by external conditions; pregnancies, a way to receive unconditional love from another human being in an otherwise unloving environment; hedonism, a consequence of ubiquitous commercialism; and the desire for wealth, a result of larger economic greed in society and fear of poverty.

In this sense, then, a fair view of young people must recognize their behavior in the context of an environment that powerfully informs what they do. Thus, to place responsibility solely on young people to eschew certain behaviors is to underestimate the power of the conditions under which they live and of their developmental characteristics. This is not to say that we should not encourage them toward safe behaviors, but rather that in understanding their actions we are compelled to look to their environment and their developmental characteristics for possible explanations. Insofar as behavior in school is concerned, such a look must include not only conditions outside the school, but those on the inside that we ourselves largely create. Somewhere among those we are likely to find an explanation for much of the conflict and contradiction that so often plagues the relations among students and between students and teachers.

Because they are human, and especially because they are young, young people are expanding their view of the world and creating meanings about it. Some of these meanings are liberating in the sense that they extend beyond previously held narrow or restricted attitudes and past behaviors. Others may tend in just the opposite direction. But the process of learning is the process of making mistakes, and it is this process in which young people are engaged. It is remarkable how adults, including educators, often react with alarm to some problem in school, as if missing a concept, forgetting an assignment, or "misbehaving" in class foreshadows a doomed adulthood. So, too, it is odd that panic sets in if a young person is not "up to" reading level in the early years of schooling. After all, in almost all cases, young people are in school for 10 to 13 years, a span that would ordinarily be seen as plenty of time to accomplish almost anything. It is more than twice as long as the "five-year plans" that so often are called "long term." These examples simply illustrate how far we sometimes are from a view of young people as developing human beings and how caught up we have become in a system whose affective dimension is based on a metaphor of efficient machinery.

This issue further suggests that our view of young people should consider how developmental age enters into affect in the curriculum. Only the most romantic of theories could imagine that young children are ready or able to take on affective issues in the same way, for example, that adolescents might be. There is substantial evidence that the thinking young children use in constructing critical views is not as logical as that of adolescents, if we take "logical" to mean the extent to which decisions or judgments involve consideration of abstract, alternative possibilities (Inhelder & Piaget, 1958; Piaget, 1932). However, we should not mistake a difference of this kind to mean that young children in school are incapable of making judgments or identifying moral tensions (Nucci, 1987).

Lipka and I have noted in our self-concept interviews with young children that they often have a great deal to say about themselves. They have a sense of what they like and do not like and are quick to point out teachers and peers who are "nice" and "mean" (Beane & Lipka, 1986). Moreover, they are quite able to give reasons for these judgments. Thus to say that young children are incapable of critical thinking can only be taken to mean that they do not form judgments in ways that (some) adults do or that they do not see in situations the same things that (some) adults do. Yet this is often implied in proposals about affect, particularly those that focus on conditioning or shaping behavior through systematic reward and punishment procedures.

In one sense, the way in which "feelings" enter into the judgments of children might be seen as a fuller and clearer integration of affect and cognition than some theories of critical thinking that use only cold, dispassionate logic. Because young people can think and do have the democratic right to do so, adults (including educators) have the consequent responsibility to encourage such thinking and to extend it as far as possible. This requirement holds not only for critical thinking but for other reflective and creative forms as well (National Association for Education of Young Children [NAEYC], 1988).

Another aspect of this view of young people is the understanding that in many ways they are already "learned." For example, as participants in various cultures within society they have come to know at least one language as well as many customs. In roles as family member, friend, sibling, and others they have developed attitudes and learned a good deal about social interaction. In all these situations they have come to have views of themselves and a sense of how others view them. Such learnings will continue throughout their school years, often in ways that contradict what the school teaches. To say that young people are ignorant or unlearned is a serious mistake. When such a statement is made, we must realize that it is necessarily done in a relative sense; that is, what young people "know" may be different from the language, customs, attitudes, interaction patterns, and self-perceptions that are desired by the school and reflected in curriculum plans. This has been particularly true for immigrant

groups and racial minorities since the public schools began, and it
continues today in our culturally diverse society.

The fact that young people are learned in their own ways indicates that they are also capable of learning. To say that some cannot
learn is again a misstatement that would be more accurately phrased
as "they have trouble learning what the school wants them to learn
and in the ways that they are taught in school." Even those who have
the most difficulty in school seem oddly capable of learning to make
friends, to play games, and to create and live within their own youth
culture. Such cases suggest that rather than being incapable of learning, young people are quite able to learn in their own ways about those
things that matter most to them.

In the end, what young people have learned about themselves and
others is integrated into their self-perceptions and values, which in
turn guide their behavior. What they believe and do may or may not
be congruent with the concepts of democracy, dignity, caring, justice,
freedom, equality, and peace, as I have described these. Like other
concepts these are learned and so are the kinds of behaviors we might
associate with them. Morevoer, they are learned through experience
and prized when they are chosen from among other alternatives.

In recognizing young people as individuals, it is also important
for us to remember that they are thus subject to the same physical and
emotional needs that impinge upon the lives of other human beings.
From a physical standpoint such needs include food, clothing, and
shelter as well as freedom from conditions that are likely to cause
disease or physical harm. From an emotional standpoint such needs
include love and affection, achievement, belonging, self-respect, freedom from intense feelings of guilt and fear, economic security, and
self-concept and understanding (Raths, 1972). When such needs are
met, the chances for positive self-esteem and personal efficacy are
enhanced and, in turn, so are the possibilities for seeing others in a
positive light and caring about them.

It has become increasingly popular among some educators to
question whether the school should have to assume responsibility for
these needs. More than a few feel that other institutions or agencies
such as the family and the church have abdicated their responsibilities in this regard. Given the discontinuities in traditional family
structure as well as the apparently declining participation in mainstream religious organizations, it may well be true that such agencies
are less influential than they are perceived to have been in the past
(Niebuhr, 1984). However, this does not alter the fact that young
people have these needs or that meeting them is a crucial part of

healthy living to which the schools are supposed to contribute. Moreover, the assumption that other institutions are not pulling their weight is not sufficient reason to absolve the schools of their responsibility in this area.

Instead, two kinds of action are called for. First, because educators do exercise a large measure of control over what happens during the school day, they must make every effort possible to ensure that the school itself presents a safe and sane environment in which the personal affect of young people is not at risk. This means that continuing analysis of the school, particularly its institutional features, must have a prominent place on the professional agenda. Second, recognizing that unmet emotional needs often result from conditions outside the school, educators at all levels must become more active in working with parents and guardians, as well as community agencies, as advocates for the young. If it is really true that adults outside the school are creating conditions that work against the emotional needs of young people, then it is incumbent upon educators, who have by virtue of their positions accepted responsibility for helping young people, to work for change in those conditions. The fact that such efforts consume time and energy and are often unsuccessful does not at all lessen the compelling need for this kind of action.

In presenting this way of viewing young people in the school I do not want to imply that it is not already held by many educators. Indeed, it is. Nor do I want to imply that all young people lead grim and unhappy lives. In fact, just the opposite is true. Instead I want to point out that if we begin with the concepts of democracy, dignity, and diversity we are compelled to follow with a view of young people that is consistent with them. This means that educators in local schools must be willing to examine the views that they presently hold to look for consistencies as well as inconsistencies. As they do so, they must be very careful to try to see what the school really looks like through the eyes of young people and to identify how it "feels" to them. Moreover, the amazing outward resilience of young people should not be taken to mean that they do not hurt "on the inside."

If we look back on the complexities of life for young people, the many roles in which they are cast, and the difficulties of negotiating life in the school, it is remarkable that so many do as well as they do. In fact, given those conditions it is quite reasonable to question such labels as "underachiever" or "unmotivated." More likely, if one considers how powerful affective concerns are, a realistic view of young people in school might well include the notion that they are doing the best they can at any given moment.

Are teachers and administrators psychologists? Can school adults successfully replace parents or guardians in the lives of young people? Are the experiences that adults believe are important for young people to be totally set aside if they cause some degree of dissonance for the young? Should the life of the school be totally governed by the perceived interests of young people? The answer to all of these questions is "no." Despite criticisms to the contrary, placing young people as whole human beings at the very center of thinking about the curriculum is not a misguided or romantic concept. Instead it is related to the compelling themes of democracy, dignity, and diversity. As such, it requires difficult and thoughtful reflection that will involve educators in the hard work of restructuring many of the policies and practices that characterize affect in their schools.

THE SCHOOL'S PLACE IN THE LARGER SOCIETY

It is clear from earlier chapters that although proponents of one position or another debated the exact form of affect in the curriculum, all expressed a continuing belief that the school did have a role to play with regard to affective issues in the larger society, a belief that continues in our own times. Therefore, as we consider how democracy, dignity, and diversity might be brought to life in the curriculum, we must consider what such action will mean insofar as the school's relation to the larger society is concerned.

The question of how the school might relate to the larger society opens up three possibilities. One places the school in a conservative posture in which it proceeds very slowly in responding to such issues, even lagging behind larger social trends and clinging to its policy traditions. Here we might say that the curriculum is planned through a "rear-view mirror" as past precedent serves present policy. A second possibility is that the school replicates whatever seems to be the popular interpretation of affective issues—a kind of politically safe position in which the school drifts whichever way "the wind blows." A third possibility is that the school reflects an analysis of affective issues and trends based on some enduring themes. Here affect in the curriculum would be constructed in such a way that whatever issues or trends emerged, they would be considered through the lens of those persistent themes.

The twentieth-century history of affect in the curriculum has mainly been a mix of the first two of those possibilities. As an example of the first, the case for character education was developed partly as a

way to sustain religious virtues without religious language or materials. Likewise the high culture basis of classical humanism has been
a voice of resistance to the perceived threat of "modernism" in both
the school and the larger society. In both examples, and others like
them, the basis for thinking about affect in the curriculum was (and
is) based on a nostalgic view of a past that is perceived to have been
less complicated and more sharply defined. It is almost as if by
replicating the past in the schools, emerging affective issues in the
larger society could be made to simply go away.

On the other hand, by responding to whatever viewpoint seems
most popular or acceptable at any given moment, the school is vulnerable to continuous attack from other viewpoints as well as to the
confusion and contradictions that result from "false equilibrium." As
we have seen, the history of interpretations of affective issues is one of
struggle and debate. While one or another view may seem to hold
sway at a given time, others continue to live in competing theories as
well as in resistance by people in local schools, including the young
people who are the object of particular programs. Thus while the
rhetoric of educational purposes may appear to suggest some kind of
equilibrium (that is, near-universal acceptance of some viewpoint),
the reality within and around schools is more likely to be dissonant
and contradictory. Our own times offer a prime example of this
scenario, namely, the "excellent schools" movement that dominated so
much of educational activity in the 1980s following the reform proposals reviewed in Chapter 4.

In responding to this politically popular version of the curriculum, the school, as is often the case, took on a game it could not
possibly win because the rules were not as simple or narrow as they
appeared to be. The political and economic "payoffs" were accompanied by increased dropout rates and increasingly specific "top-down"
mandates that distanced local educators from important curriculum
decisions. Yet lacking a clear and consistent definition of the grounds
upon which the school ought to function, there appeared to be little
choice but to accept that version of "improved" education. It would be
a mistake to assume that many educators did not believe that such a
role was philosophically correct as well as politically prudent. Indeed,
there were more than a few who did believe it, as would be the case
with almost any external proposal for school reform. However, the
point remains that simply playing by the rules of political popularity
is inevitably a very risky role for the schools.

The third possibility for defining how the school might relate to
affective issues in the larger society extends beyond the desire to

recapture the past or maintain the status quo while also reducing the political vulnerability of the curriculum. Here, thinking about how to respond to such issues is guided by enduring and consensually defined themes that also serve the ongoing work of curriculum planning. In practice this approach would mean that some set of powerful and defensible concepts would enter into any specific situation, either proactive or reactive, that involved affect in the curriculum. While many versions of such concepts have been proposed, I have argued that the enduring themes of democracy, human dignity, and cultural diversity ought to form the basis of the school's claim for affect in the curriculum. Here I am further proposing that these concepts be deliberately articulated and applied to the discourse about the school's relation to the larger society. In other words, whether the question is "what should the curriculum include?" or "how should the school respond to a particular problem?" deliberation ought to be conditioned by the themes of democracy, dignity, and diversity.

In making this claim I am not unaware of some of the objections that might be raised to it. One is that it places the school in a nonneutral position insofar as there are political, social, and economic implications in those themes. Obviously this is so, but the notion of the schools as "neutral" institutions is unrealistic; they are among many institutions that are maintained in large part for social purposes. Moreover, careful analysis of the curriculum, both planned and hidden, indicates that the school has been an active participant in many of the political, social, and economic inequities that have a long-standing history in the larger society.

A second objection to my claim may be that it appears to separate the school from the larger society and other institutions within it. Certainly it is true that where groups or institutions act in ways that detract from democracy, dignity, and diversity, the school would be (and is) placed in a contradictory position. But it is not true that all groups and institutions, either inside or outside the school, act against these concepts. Instead of separating the school from society, this approach places the school in the midst of a dynamic society as part of the stuggle to extend personal and social efficacy through the enduring themes I have described. This is not to say that such a role could be carried out without tension, conflict, or objection. After all, these concepts are not exactly dominant themes across public and private institutions and agencies other than the school. But this does not diminish the school's responsibility in that regard. Rather it is possible that the public school, with its long history of rhetorical attachment to the development of democratic attitudes, self-esteem, and cultural awareness, might well be placed in the forefront of the struggle.

Having made that general statement, I turn to one institution outside the school that requires particular attention, namely, the family. Just as there is a continuing dialectic between personal interests and the common good, so there is one between the rights of parents and the rights of the state regarding child rearing (Gutmann, 1987). In recent years, the most visible form of this dialectic has emerged at local, state, and federal levels in the form of conflict over value and moral content in the schools between radical fundamentalist religious groups and representatives of public schools. Other less visible or obvious examples include demands for censorship of books, demands for separating students of varying abilities, and insistence on more restrictive disciplinary policies. One way of looking at this conflict is as a dialectic between private and public values.

The public school that is guided by the themes of democracy, dignity, and diversity represents enduring themes in our society related to personal efficacy and the common good. Thus the curriculum of such a school could be objectionable to private interest groups, including sectarian religious groups, only if it contradicted these themes or if the personal values of such groups rejected them. Objections in the first case would be warranted; in the second they would not, because any alternative themes would require the public school to act against democracy, dignity, and diversity. My argument here is that the public school has not only a right but a responsibility to stand for these themes and to resist attempts by private interest groups, including parents, to act against them. Moreover, that right and responsibility extend to the development of educational experiences that promote those themes in the interest of the common good, even over the objection of parents. For those parents who strongly object to this concept, the legal right remains to form private schools, although we might seriously question the right of even those schools to reject our themes, because they too, and the young people who attend them, are part of our society.

Those who think that this way of positioning the rights of public schools is too harsh or unjust need only imagine the reaction of educators if a group of parents insisted that reading or arithmetic not be taught. At the present time, though, public school educators must not be glib in applying these rights. Not only do democracy, dignity, and diversity demand that voices of dissent at least be heard, but, as we have seen, there is much work to do in authentically placing these themes in the schools.

A third objection might involve the perception that my claim would result in a standard form of curriculum and thus contradict the concepts of diversity and local decision making. This objection would be a rather serious misinterpretation of the main grounds for the claim; that is, the concepts of democracy, dignity, and diversity are intended to guide rather than dictate curriculum forms. There are many ways in which these might be brought to life in the school. Given broad participation in creative and thoughtful decision making, it is likely that a diversity of ideas will emerge. In fact, if we recall the conditions for authentic democratic action, the search for such diversity is a critical imperative.

The objections noted above notwithstanding, this third approach to how the school might relate to the larger society serves several important purposes. It places democracy, dignity, and diversity in the forefront of curriculum deliberations and in so doing offers a set of enduring and defensible themes that may be consistently applied in response to affective issues. Such consistency, in turn, offers a way out of the contradictions and confusion that have plagued affect in the curriculum. Moreover, these themes provide grounds for reducing the school's vulnerability as well as for analyzing objections to the curriculum and rejecting those that are inappropriate for the purposes of public schools. Finally, those themes provide for the possibility that a diversity of practical forms may be identified through creative and thoughtful participation at the local level.

Again, though, we must not make the mistake of thinking that the public schools are presently in a position to fully exercise the rights attached to this approach; there is much about them that seriously contradicts the themes of democracy, dignity, and diversity. First, the task of engaging in discourse about those themes and how they might be brought to life in the school must be accomplished. So too must the effort be made to eliminate policies and procedures that detract from those themes, a process that is sure to be full of conflict and controversy, because they are found in the deep and powerful curriculum and institutional structures of the school to which so many people are attached.

CURRICULUM PLANS AND INSTITUTIONAL FEATURES

In this section we move to the very practical level in considering how affect might be brought to life in the school. Here, our focus will be on the pedagogical aspects of our efforts. Specifically, how might curriculum plans and institutional features be deliberately organized and developed to reflect and promote the foundational themes?

Direct and Indirect Instruction

One of the persistent issues in talk about affect in the curriculum is whether it should be carried out through direct or indirect instruction. By *direct instruction* I mean the explicit teaching of particular concepts in such a way that distinct time is allotted during which personal and social concerns are given primary attention through curriculum plans specifically designed for that purpose. Examples of the direct approach include the religious lessons found in nineteenth-century schools, the character education lessons that emerged in the earlier part of this century, and the more recent set-aside activities used with values clarification, sensitivity training, human relations, and packaged self-esteem programs. By *indirect instruction* I mean the implicit promotion of personal and social development themes through experiences that have some other explicit purpose or in which the affective themes are only one of several purposes. Examples of indirect approach include adding on affective questions to explicit studies of literature, history, and other subjects, and promoting particular attitudes or values through the hidden curriculum found in the institutional features of the school.

The question of whether direct or indirect instruction is best for placing affect in the curriculum has often been set up as an "either/or" proposition. Advocates of the direct approach argue that only by making affective themes explicit will they gain a recognized place in the school program and capture the serious attention of young people. They would submit that if we want young people to learn affective concepts, then we ought to teach them directly, just as we do in teaching reading, mathematics, writing, and so on. Advocates of the indirect approach argue their case in two ways. One is that the primary purpose of schooling has to do with academic knowledge and skills, and affective learnings follow from or after these. The other kind of argument is that people learn by doing, and thus the affect lived rather than the affect spoken presents the greatest potential for learning.

My position is that such arguments result in a false and unproductive dualism. The way out of this dilemma is to pose a third alternative in which both methods are repositioned as complementary and simultaneous ways of approaching affect in the curriculum. While it is true that real learning is best promoted through lived experience, its completion also requires explicit reflection about that experience. Thus personal and social meanings are most likely to be found through combining direct and indirect instruction in such a way that important affective themes are addressed in curriculum plans organized primarily around them, are integrated into other teaching-learning situations, and are deliberately used to form the institutional features of the school.

In defining the need for integration of direct and indirect instruction, we might also understand some of the empirical evidence on various programs or packages that suggests they have limited, if any, effects (Leming, 1981a; Lockwood, 1978; Schaefli, Rest, & Thoma, 1985). What is really learned about affective themes in school is not learned in any one place, but rather through an interpretation of the entire collection of experiences. It is hardly surprising when a controlled attempt to promote certain character traits or improved self-esteem in a particular course or class shows little in the way of lasting effects. All too often what is taught in those settings is contradicted in other places in the school, whether by lack of interest or sensitivity on the part of other teachers or by plain inconsistency across various settings. Moreover, what is included in many of those programs is limited to "contrived" activities that have relatively little to do with the ambiguous realities of life.

If we want to have more influence in affective matters, then we need to consider how those themes we wish to promote might permeate the entire school through both direct and indirect instruction. In other words, they must emerge in explicit curriculum plans, in the implicit meanings of institutional features, in nonformal interactions with young people, in teaching methods, and so on. Furthermore, if we are really interested in these themes, then they must also appear in talk and action that addresses their meanings outside the school. In the end, promoting affective themes is a matter of how those themes come to life in consistent and thoughtful ways across the whole school, not only in what we say but in what we do and what we stand for.

Critical Ethics

In Chapter 1, I referred to Phenix's (1977) analysis of "affective education" from the perspective of an ethicist. That viewpoint included two dimensions that are crucial to a complete consideration of how affect might be placed in the curriculum: judgments about personal and social conditions, and idealizations about progress toward more desirable conditions. These two dimensions clearly extend beyond typical "affective" talk about the insensitivity of adults and the need for self-esteem, toward the possibility of genuine personal and social efficacy. This does not mean that those other concerns are trivial; indeed, they are very important. Rather, it is to say that they are simply not sufficient to accomplish the fullest meaning of affect in the curriculum.

The problem that is set by the challenge to include judgments and idealizations is this: How might democracy, dignity, and diversity enter into young people's examination of affective issues and their sources? The appropriate response to this problem is perhaps best found in the exercise of *critical ethics*. Critical ethics combines two key concepts. One is the idea that affective issues are not simply abstract situations that present statistical pictures; for example, how many workers are displaced by technology, or how many people are living in shelters for the homeless? There are reasons why such phenomena occur, and those reasons often involve policies or actions that contradict democratic principles, diminish human dignity, and devalue diversity. The second concept is that democracy, dignity, and diversity are the ethical principles on which the possibilities for personal and social efficacy rest. As such they present an appropriate moral basis for judging whether policies, practices, and their outcomes in particular situations are right or wrong (Beyer & Wood, 1985). In short, critical analysis involves the search for full disclosure of what lies behind affective issues and judgments about the morality of what is found using the themes of democracy, dignity, and diversity.

Two curriculum examples might help clarify what I mean by critical ethics. It is not uncommon for young people to be engaged in a study of commercial media, particularly advertising. In such a unit they may study the difference between commercial and noncommercial media, keep logs of personal television viewing, conduct surveys of favorite programs and commercials among peers, learn how commercials are made, and even make their own commercials for real or fictitious products. Sometimes the study will also include discussion of commercials as propaganda, and analysis of claims made for particular products. On the surface this would seem to make for a pretty thorough as well as interesting unit. However, several important issues in commercial advertising have been left out. For example, why are special commercial advertisements designed for the youth market? What assumptions does commercial advertising make about young people? What aspects of youth development enter into commercial advertising? Why are selected products cycled off the market and replaced by new ones?

Even this quick analysis, which hardly scratches the surface of commercial advertising, begins to reveal such ethical issues as the following:

- Is it right for one group to capitalize on the self-esteem needs of another group?
- Is meaningful self-esteem a commodity that can be bought and sold?
- What happens to those who cannot afford to buy products that commercial interests suggest are desirable for status in the peer group?
- Are material possessions a desirable (as opposed to desired) basis for establishing conditions of status among peers?
- Does the peer group really decide the alternatives it will consider for establishing status within it, or are they partly (or largely) decided by the commercial media?
- Is the ideal self portrayed by the media really a desirable self?
- Is that self related to personal efficacy or is it dependent on someone else's definition?

Here again, these questions only begin to open up possible ethical issues, of which there may be many others; for example, how are the profits from the youth market spent, and do they make sense to the young people who create them? And, of course, in addition to all these questions there remains the one having to do with what action might be taken if young people do not like the answers to any or all of them.

Another example involves the complex and serious topic of education about drug use and abuse. Typically such programs include information about particular drugs, the consequences of their use, and admonitions not to use them. Unlike most other areas of the school program, this one often uses community resources, supplemented further by media pronouncements by well-known personalities, to more dramatically make its point. The emphasis here is on encouraging young people to assume personal responsibility for resisting drug use. However, the picture of drugs is more complicated than this; that is, it is only partly a matter of individual consumer action. Beyond that it involves a complex network of economic, political, and legal factors filled with ethical issues. For example, it is widely known that the production and distribution of drugs involve violent "cartels," corrupt governments, and morally bankrupt dealers who seduce young people into personal use of drugs and their distribution among peers. In the last case, the profits made among friends are surely attractive, but they are "small pickings" compared with those made by people who distribute to small-time "peer dealers," not unlike the relatively small profits of "farmers" who initially produce drug crops.

While these things are widely known, they are not necessarily brought to light in drug prevention programs. Obviously the information and admonition approach has an important place in the curriculum, but it stops short of raising crucial issues that might enter into how young people see themselves and others in relation to drugs. Engaging young people in critical ethics about this issue might well lead to helping them understand how drugs and the culture of which they are a part allow some people to prey upon others for profit, while simultaneously detracting from the dignity and integrity of the victims. Although it would be foolish to suggest that such an approach would guarantee resistance to drugs, it is just possible that for some it would encourage a kind of moral outrage at the way in which they are victimized for profit

From time to time we read of one or more young people taking action of some sort, as a result of a school project, to resolve some social, political, or economic problem. When this kind of news appears, which usually tells only about the action itself, we are seeing the results of critical ethics in the curriculum. If we listen or read carefully, we can usually see a double benefit for the young people involved. At the same time that they are seeking to resolve some issue that involves unsatisfactory conditions in the larger society, they are likely also building a sense of personal and social efficacy. This is, of course, in addition to the benefits others may enjoy as a result of their actions.

Critical ethics, then, is a crucial part of a complete view of affect in the curriculum. Without it the possibilities for finding authentic personal and social meanings in the curriculum are seriously limited. There are those who would clearly prefer that this aspect of authentic affective activity not be included in the curriculum. They may object on grounds that this activity makes the school and the curriculum political, as if it were not already political by virtue of the selective version of the world it portrays; that is, by what is chosen to be included in and what is thereby left out of the curriculum. Or they may say that young people should not be exposed to these harsh realities because they are too young or because the realities may be depressing, as if living under these conditions were not already part of their real life and in many ways already depressing to them. The real agenda behind such resistance is not hard to imagine: There is much about the world of school and the larger society that is ripe for critical analysis, and the results can obviously make some adults uncomfortable.

For this reason schools and particular teachers within them who engage young people in critical ethics often find themselves under attack from interest groups on the outside and some colleagues on the inside. I would thus be less than honest if I suggested that critical ethics is an easy road to travel in the curriculum. Yet if we accept the themes of democracy, dignity, and diversity, it is a road that must be traveled. Otherwise we are left with a selective and superficial curriculum that deprives young people of the opportunity to learn the ways of applying moral judgments to real-life situations.

The Problems Approach to Curriculum

There is perhaps no more obvious contradiction between the theory of affect and present curriculum practice than the almost universal overemphasis that schools place on academic matters. While goal statements may include concern for such concepts as democratic skills, self-esteem, social relations, and cultural awareness, the fact remains that curriculum plans are nearly always based on the learning of skills and content within various disciplines of knowledge. So strong is this tradition that the popular talk about restructuring schools, no matter how "radical" it may otherwise seem, almost never touches the pervasive subject-area approach.

The primary purpose of the subject-area approach is the mastery of facts, concepts, and skills within a particular discipline of knowledge. For example, in studying mathematics as a subject area, learners are to acquire relevant facts and skills as a distinct and differentiated body of knowledge. The same may be said for the chronological history approach to social studies, the subtopic approach to science (earth science, biology, chemistry), the reading and writing mechanics approach to language arts, and so on. The subject-area approach usually reduces the planned curriculum to a trivial level in which young people are asked to just "get the facts or skills" without regard for their meaning or their relation to other subjects (Freire, 1970). Described as a "patchwork" curriculum, this approach is most often thought of only in terms of middle level and high school, but it also characterizes many elementary school self-contained classrooms in which the day is simply divided into segments allotted to various subject or skill areas.

Detached as it is from personal and social meanings, the subject-area approach marginalizes affect in the planned curriculum and forces it into the hidden curriculum. This should not be taken as a simple oversight on the part of teachers and other school officials. Indeed, young people are often asked directly to concentrate exclusively on the subject or skill area at hand and to ignore distractions or irrelevant ideas. The latter may range from personal problems that are preoccupying their thinking to questions of why some concept is taken as a fact or where it came from. Such "distractions" are examples of affective dimensions, and it is their peripheral place in the subject-area approach that partly makes this way of organizing the curriculum so questionable.

If we mean to seriously restructure schools and if that restructuring is to include a genuine attempt to place the foundations of affect, as I have described them, in the curriculum, then we must consider alternative ways of organizing the curriculum. As is often true in situations like this, there is historical precedent in the curriculum field and in school practice for other curriculum approaches. In this particular case, a promising alternative is offered by what is known as the *social problems approach* (e.g., Smith, Stanley, & Shores, 1957).

Unlike the subject-area approach, the social problems, or problems, approach derives curriculum organizing centers from those themes and issues that emerge from the context of personal and social living. This approach involves young people in serious study of such problems as racism, cultural diversity, the distribution of wealth, environmental pollution, global interdependence, homelessness, effects of technology, politics and power, human relations, and commercial advertising, as well as more immediate and personal issues like peer group relations, personal decision making, living in the school, and so on. It is true that any of these may be "covered" in some way in one or another typical subject area. However, even when such coverage is provided, the subject area is still the dominant theme, and the problem is usually considered only within the boundaries of the subject and is given less than thorough treatment.

When the problems approach is properly used, the problem at hand becomes the primary focus. Facts, principles, concepts, and skills from various subject areas are not ignored; rather they are used where appropriate to explore and analyze the problem. For example, when investigating environmental pollution, concepts such as energy resource availability, population distribution, technology, social attitudes, and many more come into play. Similarly, to seriously work through the problem, skills like reading, writing, listening, observing, computing, and others are necessarily used. If we look at those concepts and skills, we can readily recognize themes often taught for their own sake and in isolation from one another in various subject areas. In the problems approach they are brought together in the context of some issue that has meaning in real life and to which they are related.

The problems approach offers opportunities to bring affective issues to a prominent place in the planned curriculum. It suggests that personal and social issues are not only important, but the central themes of living and learning both inside and outside the school. It correctly situates information and skills as means to larger ends rather than ends in themselves. It offers opportunities for critical thought and action. It offers the possibility to dissolve the barriers between the planned curriculum inside the school and the lived experiences of people outside the school. In short, the problems approach is one way to bring a larger and more complete view of affect to life in the school.

A major issue with the problems approach, however, has to do with where it will be placed in the school program. If the subject-area approach remains the unquestioned curriculum organizing pattern in the school, then the problems approach is likely to show up around the edges of one or another subject or perhaps somewhat more prominently where particular teachers have an interest in it. Or it may, as it often does, appear in some elective portion of the program available to those who have completed subject-area requirements.

I would argue instead that the problems approach ought to become the curricular pattern for general education, or that portion of the program that is experienced by all learners. Such an arrangement is relatively easy to imagine in self-contained classrooms at the elementary level. At the middle and high school levels, however, we will need to recall the concept of block-time core programs that enjoyed some popularity in theory and practice during the 1950s and early 1960s (Alberty & Alberty, 1962; Hock & Hill, 1962; Van Til, Vars, & Lounsbury, 1967). When an authentic problems approach was used in these arrangements, all learners were involved in a common experience involving topics related to personal and social issues (advanced or specialized work in particular subject areas was then offered on an elective basis). Careful readers of accounts of those programs recognize that they were often cast in the language of adaptation to social conventions related to the larger theme of social efficiency. Of interest here, though, is the structure of such programs and the possibility a renewed version of that structure would offer to the idea of placing affect at the very core of the curriculum.

Placing the problems approach at the center of the planned curriculum in this way would certainly not be an easy task to accomplish.

It would require widespread agreement on the importance of affect, the view of young people, and the relation of school and society I have described. Furthermore it would require deliberate resistance to domination of college and university subject-area requirements over the public school curriculum and considerable reorganization of state curriculum mandates. Faced with these obstacles, we might well ask whether there are any alternatives that might be considered. The answer is that there are, but none is as satisfactory as placing the problems approach at the core of the curriculum.

For example, in one alternative, the problems approach could become the way of organizing the social studies curriculum, and other subjects could be left intact. The difficulty here is that although this and related recommendations (e.g., Lockwood & Harris, 1985) already have a long tradition among the many ways in which social studies has been interpreted, other forms prevail, particularly the selective chronology of history. Also, this alternative suggests that personal and social problems enter only into social studies and are unrelated to science, mathematics, and other subject areas. In the end, this arrangement is not unlike the use of self-esteem "packages" in isolated courses, the shortcomings of which have already been noted.

Another alternative would be to plan subject areas so that they would systematically include affective issues. This approach has also been suggested in the past and is still popular (Ryan, 1986). The idea here is to recognize that any subject may be taught at three levels: facts, concepts, and values (Harmin, Kirschenbaum, & Simon, 1973). For example, a lesson on arithmetic could lead to one on comparative costing of products, which in turn could proceed to questions about the environmental effects of purchasing cheaper no-deposit cans rather than more expensive returnable bottles. A unit on the American Revolution could begin with the facts of the event, proceed to the concepts behind it, and then lead to a discussion of choices students think they would have made if they had been alive at the time. The difficulty with this alternative is that there is little guarantee that the value level would ever really be reached; teachers already claim that they are overburdened with the fact level. Moreover, this arrangement turns real life upside down in suggesting that one accumulates knowledge first and then secondarily looks for problems to solve.

Either one or both of these alternatives would indeed make a contribution to affect in the curriculum. But if we mean to think seriously about how to place affect in the curriculum, we should not turn to them easily, even on a temporary basis. In the reality of curriculum change, those things that are done temporarily often have a way of either becoming permanent or gradually fading out of the curriculum. In the long run, it would be better if we laid the careful groundwork that would give the problems approach a permanent and central place in the curriculum.

The Subject Matter of Affect

In arguing the case for using the problems approach as a major organizing pattern in placing affect in the curriculum, I have suggested that what is normally thought of as important content—what is found within various subject areas—ought to be used as a means of investigating powerful personal and social issues rather than as an end in itself. Moreover, it should be clear that when a broadly defined concept of affect occupies a prominent place in the curriculum, a new kind of content emerges, one that has previously been found only around the edges of the typical planned curriculum. That content is the facts, principles, concepts, and understandings that are related to the themes of democracy, dignity, and diversity as they emerge in the problems and issues of personal and social life.

Simply making such information available presents a continuing problem in schools, because it is often seen as controversial. On the one hand, the school is supposed to improve society by, for example, raising levels of awareness, promoting higher aspirations, and developing critical thinking. On the other hand, as young people engage in experiences intended for these purposes they are likely to discover information that would lead them to question conventional political, social, and economic arrangements and to seek alternatives to them. Following this line of reasoning, it is easy to see why the language of school purposes makes for powerful political rhetoric, while the subject-area approach offers contradictory but safe boundaries for subject matter to be learned.

When we place affect in the curriculum, it is inevitable that so-called controversial subject matter will come to the surface and will require thoughtful consideration. To attempt to critically analyze affective issues without admitting such "evidence" amounts to both undemocratic repression of information and professional failure of nerve. Yet, not all affective subject matter is of the same kind, and, depending on its content, it may be subject to different kinds of treatment by teachers and other adults in public schools. In this regard, I would suggest that there are at least three general kinds of affective content:

1. *Ideas that may be described, but not promoted.* Here I would place those topics and ideas that are value-loaded but are subject to conditional treatment insofar as they appear in the public school curriculum. The most obvious example of this type is the topic of religion. We may engage young people in studies of various religious views (indeed it is hard to imagine how we cannot if historical descriptions of value and moral sources are to be thorough), but we cannot promote religious viewpoints if we are to honor the constitutional proscriptions regarding the separation of church and state and the diversity of our society.

2. *Ideas that may be promoted, but not insisted upon.* Here I would place topics that may be preferable with regard to personal development and social relations, but that when actually applied to real situations are clearly the prerogative of the individual. For example, we may promote the idea of friendship between individuals, but we cannot insist that particular individuals actually be friends. Similarly we may strongly recommend participation in clubs and other social activities, but we cannot insist that an individual join such a group. And we may ask that students express their personal feelings on some social issue, but we cannot insist that they do so. In cases like these, our position is determined by individual rights to choice, participation, and privacy.

3. *Ideas that may be promoted and also insisted upon.* Here I would place those themes that I have previously described as the foundations of affect in the curriculum. For example, teachers not only may explicitly call for young people to respect the dignity of others, but may insist that they refrain from acting otherwise, such as using racial or ethnic slurs. In arguing for this placement, it is important to remember that ideas such as democracy, human dignity, equality, caring, justice, freedom, and peace, as well as constitutional citizens' rights and cultural diversity, are not simply abstract concepts made up in the office armchair. Rather they represent the very conditions under which personal and social efficacy are most possible as well as the ostensible political, social, and legal heritage to which young people in this society are entitled.

Recognizing that there are different types of affective subject matter, each requiring a particular kind of treatment, serves several important purposes. First, it begins to reduce the confusion that has surrounded how controversial topics ought to be regarded in the curriculum. The seemingly endless debates over one or another specific theme have frequently polarized and paralyzed affective discourse to a point where such themes are avoided altogether and the planned curriculum appears as a whitewashed version of real life. Second, it distinguishes between everyday social conventions and overarching themes, and between concepts that are legally or socially relegated to individual choice and those that are necessary conditions for personal and social efficacy. Third, and very important, it counters the argument that any version that does not honor absolute values external to human experience, middle-class social conventions, or classical moral virtues as the source of affective content is simply a system of relative values subject to individual preference.

Here, as in the problems approach, we must also be concerned with the access of all young people to the kind of affective content that I am describing. Too often such content is marginalized in the planned curriculum, held in the wings until academic content and skills have been covered, and, in that case, available only to those who achieve at higher academic levels or who are in higher tracks in homogeneous grouping structures. Such an arrangement has the hidden, though thinly veiled, result of denying such access to those who are in lower tracks or who experience difficulty with academic matters. As it turns out, these young people typically happen to be non-white and from lower socioeconomic groups. Thus, the content that involves personal and social efficacy becomes the reserve of already privileged and elite groups, a situation that was characteristic of the academy schools prior to the twentieth century, and of the curriculum differentiation of the social efficiency movement applied to immigrant working-class young people earlier in this century. That this condition still exists suggests that we must seriously rethink how access to particular content in the curriculum is related to the concepts of democracy, equality, and justice.

Access to particular kinds of content is limited not only by curriculum organization, teaching methods, and institutional features, but also by the selection of content, a powerful aspect of curriculum decision making. For many years the history and activity of white males have been almost exclusively privileged in the curriculum. While some progress has been made toward inclusion of content that presents the contributions and roles of women, people of color, and working-class people, this issue has been more prominent in curriculum theory than in school practice. Yet here is a case where we may easily see the integrated concepts of democracy, dignity (including self-esteem), and cultural diversity come together to suggest the need for deliberate action.

The theme of democracy requires that all pertinent information be disclosed, without privileging any particular source; that of dignity and self-esteem requires opportunities to make ancestral and contemporary connections to people of similar characteristics; and that of cultural diversity requires a full presentation of the rich contributions of the many groups that make up our society. Thus curriculum planning must *deliberately* include content that places more than only white males in the historical and contemporary episodes, struggles, issues, and achievements of our society. Of course it does not help if our treatment of history ends before the civil rights movement, or if we only set aside one month for "Black History." Nor is it sufficient to throw in a few poems by women or people of color among a long list of novels by white European males. Similarly, the concept of peace is not enhanced if history is revealed as a succession of wars, and the heroes of history as military leaders.

It is often said that if we want to know what learning schools value, we ought to look at what learning they measure. Here I am suggesting that if we want to look at what *affect themes* the schools value, we might look at the content they present. The claim that the selection process is determined by text publishers is true only to the extent that we use exclusively the materials they publish; given the current availability of other resources, that is not enough to justify a narrow selection process. People in schools, not publishers, control the resources actually used by young people, as well as the curricular emphasis and breadth. In situations where state adoption boards determine which textbooks are acceptable, the extent of their power is more than a little dependent on the degree to which local educators limit their choice of material resources to textbooks. Even so, among the possibilities for critical action beyond the school, educators must not overlook the need to insist on texts that portray a more complete and equitable treatment of all people (Apple, 1986).

Work in this direction is not simply a respectful nod toward women, people of color, and working-class people who have for so many years been deprived in school of their own story. This work is also important for white middle-class young men. As we understand more and more the interdependence among people, it becomes clear that the lives of this latter group are inextricably intertwined with the former in creating greater possibilities for both personal efficacy and the common good.

Finally, with regard to affective content in the curriculum, we must remember the need for critical analysis, previously described. Like any other subject matter, this can be presented in ways that make it sterile and selective. Affective content is value-loaded, and its presence in the curriculum is intended to provoke reflective thought and considered action. For this reason, full disclosure of alternative views and their meaning in relation to the foundations of affect is required. Attempts to suppress possible interpretations and their implications for considering present personal and social conditions will only leave us exactly where we are now—with an abstract set of difficult issues vulnerable to interpretation by slogan systems that have the appearance of solutions, but are really only disguised evasions of serious affective problems.

Cooperative Learning

In the past few years increasing attention has been given to the use of cooperative learning in schools. A good deal of this attention has been focused on the academic achievement gains demonstrated by this method in comparison with either competitive or individual learning. However, aside from these, cooperative learning is full of important affective meanings and possibilities (Johnson et al., 1984; Slavin, 1981).

One clue that may explain the power of cooperative learning has emerged from interviews conducted with young people regarding their self-perceptions in school (Beane & Lipka, 1986). When they talk about themselves in positive terms within the school context, they frequently explain that contributing experiences involve opportunities to work with peers, particularly friends. Such statements may be understood when we remember that self-esteem is based largely on interactions with significant others, a role that is increasingly assumed by peers. While peer interactions may take many less sophisticated forms than the carefully planned structures that have come to be associated with cooperative learning, the latter is obviously an important possibility for building upon the desire to be with peers.

Beyond this, however, the case for cooperative learning may also be based on its representation of the democratic way of life. The democratic process depends largely on the capacity of people to work together, rather than alone or against each other, in seeking the common good. At the same time, it operates under the assumption that groups of people represent diverse knowledge and skills whose integration is most likely to produce the most promising ideas and solutions (Kohn, 1986). Considered in this light, cooperative learning may be thought of as one of the ways in which democracy might be brought to life in the school in a variety of settings.

The process of cooperative learning also has implications relating to the concept of human dignity and the principles associated with it. When groups of young people are faced with problems that require knowledge and skill possessed by various members, each person has an important place in the group. As such, each has an opportunity to develop more positive self-esteem and sense of personal efficacy. As group work unfolds, participants may come to see the ways in which diverse ideas combine to create more complete and thorough projects. Moreover, as group members help one another, the concept of caring comes to life in whatever activity is undertaken.

Very often, teachers who hear about cooperative learning for the first time express a practical concern over what happens when one or another member of a group does not do a fair share of the work. They wonder about the justice of some members carrying the others along or dominating the group, and the related possibilities for dissension within the group. The correct answer to these questions is that they present social problems to be resolved and thus are important moments for social learning. Problems in group dynamics are, after all, characteristic of democratic processes. Here is an opportunity to learn some of the ways in which such dilemmas might be approached through group deliberation and action concerning topics like caring and justice. These real dilemmas are very different from the contrived situations that so often make up the problems to be solved in "affective education" classes.

From this brief discussion of cooperative learning, it is obvious that this method closely approximates the affective themes I have described. The extent to which its present growth across the schools continues should be a matter of much interest. Many adults both inside and outside the school seem so convinced that competition is the American way to get ahead. Moreover, parents of high-achieving students are sometimes concerned that cooperative learning relegates their children to the role of tutors of the less able rather than allowing them to press ahead to their own advantage. It is sad that we have come so far from an understanding of the democratic way of life and the concern for others that is associated with it. Such views are, of course, a reflection of how individualistic some segments of our population have become and how anxious they are to have more than others. Granted, cooperative learning has sustained much of its momentum on the basis of academic achievement gains, but there is clearly a need for educators to articulate its value in relation to promoting democracy, dignity, and diversity. To couch our language only in the safe ground of academics is, in the end, one of those failures of nerve that detract from the genuine affective purposes of the public schools.

Decision Making in the School

The theme of democracy is partly defined by the right of people to fully participate in decisions that affect them, a meaning that is enhanced by constitutional guarantees for citizens' rights. At the same time, the development of self-esteem depends on a sense of power or efficacy that partly comes from experiences that demonstrate that what one has to say counts for something. Thus it is sensible to conclude from these themes that schools would provide opportunities for meaningful participation of young people in important decision making in order to promote the themes and related skills.

A close look at life in schools, however, reveals that young people have little, if anything, to say about the planned structure of their time. This characteristic, along with compulsory attendance laws, has led a few observers to make an odious but not completely inaccurate comparison between students' lives in school and those of inmates in prisons and patients in mental facilities (Carlson, 1964; Haney & Zimbardo, 1975). Moreover, it is interesting to observe that in an oddly truncated way, young children often have more say in what they do in school than do adolescents, even though nearly every goal statement includes a recommendation that young people learn to be increasingly independent and self-directed in school.

Among the many ideas that are part of the history of attempts to create more democratic schools, two of the most prominent are *teacher-student planning* and *participatory governance*. Much recent attention has been given to the idea of empowering people to make curriculum decisions closer to the point of their implementation. Largely in reaction to centralized decision making, discussion of this possibility has focused mostly on empowering local teachers and local administrators and to a lesser extent on parents. Conspicuously absent from these discussions has been talk of the possibilities for empowering young people in their role as students in school. It is exactly to this issue that the idea of teacher-student planning has been addressed (Beane, Toepfer, & Alessi, 1986; Waskin & Parrish, 1967).

In planning teaching-learning situations, there is some combination of topics or problems to be considered, purposes to be accomplished, activities to be undertaken, resources to be consulted, and determinations to be made about what has been learned. The concept of teacher-student planning raises questions about who will make decisions about these various areas. In each case, there are possibilities for teachers or students to make decisions alone or for both to decide cooperatively. Moreover, teacher-student planning may be used with virtually any topic or subject and with any group of young people.

If we again think about the foundation themes of affect, the idea of teacher-student planning clearly has very important implications for bringing them to life in the curriculum. When students plan with teachers or alone, possibilities for democracy and personal efficacy are opened up. As students are recognized as having valuable ideas, their dignity is enhanced, and when those ideas enter into planning, the distribution of power shifts toward greater equality in teacher-student relationships. As in cooperative learning, the sharing of different views and ideas among the group members brings to light both the reality and the advantages of diversity.

A second possibility for promoting the themes of democracy and personal efficacy is participation in governance of the school as a whole or of particular parts within it, such as classrooms or interdisciplinary teams. Historically, many teachers, particularly at the elementary level, have begun the year by working cooperatively with students to determine ideas about how life in the classroom should be organized and carried out, and then provided time each week to talk about how things are going and to consider upcoming projects or special programs. Again, while one would expect such opportunities to continue and even increase across the school years, they tend to diminish or disappear into such generally ineffectual operations as "representative" student councils.

One common, but controversial, way of extending participatory governance is through the use of town meetings in which all young people and adults in a school come together to consider problems in the school as well as ways of improving school life. This organization gained some popularity in the 1960s and 1970s, partially as it became associated with the cognitive-developmental approach to moral reasoning (Reimer, 1981). More recently it has been named as one of the school arrangements that eroded the moral authority of teachers (Grant, 1988). Yet it is hard to believe that authority would be eroded unless it was defined as power held exclusively by adults and thus denied to young people. My own observation of school-wide town meetings, including at the elementary level, suggests that young people as well as adults are concerned about the quality of life in the school and, as a group, are very responsible in thinking through solutions to problems.

Participatory governance, whether in the classroom, team, or school, is, of course, not the entirely open situation that its critics maintain it is. For example, schools are governed partly by legal regulations such as those that forbid the presence of firearms and drugs. Obviously these regulations make sense and are not open to question. At the same time, however, other regulations governing everyday behavior, freedom of movement, organization of time, and so on, are left up to local schools to decide. It is these latter arrangements as well as projects and other activities that are the objects of discussion and consensus in many schools where successful and continuing efforts have been made to more justly distribute power through authentic participation by young people.

Sometimes school adults claim to involve students in planning and decision making when what they really do is lead student discussion toward decisions that they have already made. This kind of "cooperative" activity is what Graebner (1988), as we saw in Chapter 2, called the "engineering of consent," a popular form of protective democracy that involves subtle coercion. Teacher-student planning and participatory governance, as I am describing them here, are attempts to develop genuine cooperation through authentic participation in decision making. As Krug (1957) observed, this is not just a technique, but a "way of life" inasmuch as it grows from a sincere belief that what young people have to say counts for something in promoting democracy, dignity, and diversity in school life.

Community Service Projects

In discussing various programs designed to promote value and moral development, I have several times suggested that a consistent shortcoming among them is their use of contrived situations. This concern grows out of a belief that these kinds of activities have few, if any, more lasting effects than proselytizing about moral virtues. One of the ways in which opportunities may open for participation in genuinely value-loaded experiences is through community service project programs.

Community service projects are intended to engage young people in activities that make contributions to resolving real problems in their communities. Such experiences typically involve helping elders, assisting in hospitals and day-care centers, providing support networks for peers, working to improve community facilities, conducting community surveys, and the like. Particular projects may be sponsored by school clubs or done within regular classes, may be done either during or outside of school time, and may or may not involve school credit. Such programs have a long history in many communities and a serious body of empirical evidence to support their contribution to personal and social development, including self-worth, social awareness, and participation in community service in adulthood (Lipka, Beane, & O'Connell, 1985; Newmann & Rutter, 1983).

Some of the present interest in community service projects can easily be interpreted within a framework of virtues that recollects a nostalgic version of individual altruism. However, we must remember that the motivation for helping the "less fortunate" in the past was just as likely to have come from protective benevolence, nationalistic interests, and fear of collective action toward the redistribution of wealth and power on the part of those in lower socioeconomic positions. While the idea of altruism is crucial in considering affect in the curriculum, our concern here is not how it might be a discretionary sidelight on the relationship between privileged and nonprivileged classes, but rather its association with the moral concept of caring about others that derives from the larger theme of human dignity.

This is not to imply that the long history of community service programs has been thoroughly defined by the narrow version I have described. Indeed, many projects have involved such serious activities as voter registration, investigations of environmental pollution, and participation in adult literacy campaigns (Lipka, Beane, & O'Connell, 1985). Nevertheless, as we consider new possibilities for community service projects as part of affect in the curriculum, we must be careful to understand the difference between what Robert Starrat (undated) has called "works of mercy" and "works of justice," and the place of both within the curriculum.

The purpose of community service projects ought to involve not only resolving problems but recognizing their causes and implications. To simply help someone is important for this purpose, but not sufficient. If we want to bring the themes of affect to life, young people must also be encouraged to explore why that particular person or group is in need of help and what conditions gave rise to the situation. In other words, to the direct activity of helping is added the dimension of analysis and reflection. Here we again enter what I have called the area of critical ethics in which young people not only gain a sense of the problems that exist, but of the moral dimensions of those problems. For example, why are elders unable to pay for certain services? What conditions have led peers to need assistance, and what contributed to these conditions?

When these kinds of questions are raised, community service projects take on a new dimension. Certainly the promotion of altruism continues as young people think about how to care about other people, but they also have opportunities to become more than helpers; that is, they may learn to become critical members of the community who try to understand how problems arise and what they mean for the people involved. No doubt some adults would balk at this kind of rationale for fear that young people will begin to see some of the sociopolitical reasons why various problems arise and, in turn, become critical of powerful interests in the larger society. Yet to back away from such a possibility is to engage in a kind of information repression that is itself undemocratic.

If community service projects are to have a genuine place in affect in the curriculum, the service activity aspect must be broadened and the doors opened to larger understanding. The community problems and needs taken on must be genuine and carefully studied. And the participation must involve meaningful activity and thoughtful reflection rather than the engagement of young people in simple, unpaid labor to fill gaps in formal community service agency programs.

School Climate

So far the ideas I have described have addressed fairly specific aspects of the school program. However, these do not function in a random environment or as a simple collection of arrangements. Rather they are situated within an overall climate that presents the major affective themes as unifying concepts that permeate everyday life in the school.

Among the many theories of school climate, one of the most useful distinguishes two general types: custodial and humanistic (Willower, Eidell, & Hoy, 1967). Custodial climates emphasize maintenance of order, autocratic procedures, student stereotyping or labeling, punitive sanctions, moralizing by authorities, impersonalness, and obedience. Humanistic climates, on the other hand, are characterized by democratic procedures, high degrees of interaction, personalness, respect for individual dignity, self-discipline, flexibility, and participatory decision making. Placing these two types at opposite ends of a spectrum obviously implies the possibility for many shades of variation between them. However, aside from the very clear relationships between the language of these and our major themes, the two types offer an excellent way of thinking about the direction in which the general tone of the school tends.

My point is this: The public schools in the United States are presently leaning toward a custodial climate, but they ought to be moving in the direction of a humanistic climate. In language about schooling, the word *humanistic* presents something of a problem. For those on the right, it has become a code word for what is considered wrong with the schools and is used interchangeably with secular humanism, ethical relativism, and permissiveness. Yet if we look inside its meaning, we find the very themes that ostensibly define the society we live in; that is, concern for people as human beings and support for democracy, human dignity, and caring within the environment of the school. How is it, then, that so many schools have come to be characterized by custodial climates? The answer lies partly in the belief systems of adults in the school and partly in conditions outside the school that heavily influence what happens within it.

Since adults hold prior power over young people in the world of schools, they are largely responsible for creating the school climate. If, for example, they distrust young people or believe that students are in need of elaborate controls, such controls will undoubtedly be constructed. If adults believe that the school's major or sole purpose is academic achievement, they are likely to contrive mechanisms that will marginalize the personal and social dimensions of young people. If adults believe that young people are inherently ignorant or evil, they will expect failure and misbehavior and thus seek to immediately gain the upper hand over students by regulating their lives toward what is considered to be "right and good." In other words, the belief systems of adults in the school play a major role in creating the school's climate. Ironically, adults tend to get what they expect from young people, and so a custodial climate sets up a struggle between the adults' desire to control young people and the young people's resistance to that control. As a result both groups are subjects of continuing conflict that creates tension in their lives and limits the possibilities for expanding the efficacy of young people. Given the previously described evidence on stereotyped beliefs about nonwhite, non-middle-class young people, custodial climates in schools weigh most heavily on those who are least advantaged in the larger society as well.

Meanwhile, the beliefs and expectations of adults in a particular school are not entirely of their own doing. External expectations created by state curriculum mandates and special interest groups often have a strong impact on the climate of the school. As curriculum requirements, graduation standards, and standardized testing have increased, the academic aspects of the school have been emphasized and the human dimensions marginalized. For many teachers the test of their competence has become the test scores of their students and their capacity to keep order in the classroom, whatever that means. That they care about the real lives of young people or try to involve them in participatory decision making matters little. And so the teachers (and other school adults) are themselves set up for a kind of power that eventually turns back on them as the inevitabilities of affect enter into their relationships with young people. Clearly these adults will need to take action regarding their personal roles to find ways out of this dilemma, but it is important that we understand that the pervasive custodial climate of schools is not entirely self-chosen.

Recognizing the relationship between adult perceptions and school climate allows us to see one initial action that must be undertaken. If we want to work on school climate insofar as it affects young people, we must begin to think about how that climate affects adults in the school. Teachers, administrators, and other school adults do not shed their humanness when they assume the role of educator. In that role they still have needs for a sense of achievement, belonging, economic security, self-respect, affection, and so on. Yet so many work in the isolation of their classrooms, are rarely recognized for their competence, are left out of policy making, and are fearful of reprisal for any mistakes they might make in experimenting with new ideas. Moreover, they are subjected to ridicule in the media and deprofessionalized by top-down, "teacher-proof" curriculum packages from state departments and central offices. Nevertheless they are admonished by those same sources to enhance the self-esteem of young people and to promote better social development, especially among "at-risk" learners. We might well ask, who is really at risk here?

Though evidence on the relationship between teacher self-esteem and learner self-esteem is somewhat limited, what does exist suggests that there is a such correlation (Gilman, 1984). Thus it makes sense that part of the discourse around our affective themes would focus on the school climate insofar as it affects adults who work there. If we mean to move toward more humanistic climates, then we must explore ways of arranging for more professional interaction, broader involvement in policy decision making, more support for experimentation, less bureaucratic authority, more recognition for accomplishments, and more positive personal interactions among adults in the school. While some of these will involve new ways of thinking on the part of those outside the school, the primary workplace is the most powerful environment in professional self-esteem and much of the work must be done by adults in individual schools. Furthermore, specific arrangements cannot be made by administrators or other authorities and simply parceled out in a benevolent version of empowerment. Humanistic climates are meant to support and promote personal and social efficacy, and thus they will emerge in authentic forms only when people collectively work out the ways in which they will be created and sustained.

Many teachers and other adults in schools have grown weary of admonitions to enhance the personal and social development of young people, while they continue to work in settings that detract from their own efficacy. Their logic is hard to resist. Having a humanistic climate requires that its meaning be extended to all people in the school, both younger and older. We can surely understand how much more likely such a climate is to enter the lives of young people if it also enters the lives of the adults who work with them. Because the kinds of arrangements that would enhance the efficacy of adults turn out to be the same as those that would similarly affect young people, initial projects with adults would clearly demonstrate how they, in turn, might work with the young.

SUMMARY

In this chapter I have tried to describe examples of how affect might be placed in the curriculum if we think in terms of the broad themes of democracy, dignity, and diversity. However, if those themes are to have legitimacy in the school, the ways in which they might be brought to life cannot be defined simply by some voice on the outside. Rather, the meaning of the themes themselves must be explored and their practical life worked out by people at the local school level through cooperative, participatory, and reasoned discourse. So dominant is the tradition of top-down proposals that I was originally reluctant to offer even the examples I have. Yet I also realize that avoiding practical examples might leave this work in the position of others that have concentrated on theory alone. Furthermore, the examples I have chosen are meant to clearly suggest the scope of the work implied by the major themes.

Obviously, placing those themes in the curriculum cannot be reduced to a few packaged programs or neatly trimmed slogan systems. Instead it involves a comprehensive look at the deep and powerful curriculum and institutional structures of the school and a willingness to call into question even the most time-honored traditions of school life as well as the recent trend toward technical efficiency and accountability. In doing so, there is really no way to elude the important question of how we view young people in the school and how the relationship between the school and the larger society is constructed. Nor is it possible to ignore the long history of arrangements like participatory decision making, the problems approach, cooperative learning, and community service projects, or the need for critical ethics across the curriculum.

There are, of course, many practical examples beyond those I have used here. On the negative side, for example, I have not thoroughly treated the topic of corporal punishment, a senseless but continuing practice that obviously detracts from human dignity and is, not surprisingly, applied most frequently to the least advantaged young people. I hope that the present abolition movement will send it to the graveyard of irrational school practices. On the positive side, other examples, like heterogeneous grouping, have been placed in the context of larger issues, even though they might have stood alone. It is hard to imagine that these and other practical possibilities will not emerge early in local discourse about the major themes and their life in the school.

As we now turn to the topic of creating and sustaining a local discourse, we should not forget that the themes of democracy, dignity, and diversity are important for all people. Hence our work is concerned not only about what we do with young people, but with the personal and social efficacy of adults as well. As we shall see, discourse about affect in the curriculum raises this possibility and, in fact, is based on it.

6

Developing a Discourse
About Affect in the Curriculum

In the preceding chapters we have seen that the concept of affect in the curriculum is more than a little complex. Its history is one of confusion and contradiction over definitions of affect, conflicting interpretations of affective issues, and competing claims about the form of personal and social development in the curriculum. I have argued that we ought to rethink this area using the themes of democracy, human dignity, citizens' rights, developmental psychology (and its implications for social philosophy), and cultural diversity. In addition I have described some of the ways in which we might think through major questions about affect in the curriculum, as well as examples of how the basic themes could come to life in the school.

In this chapter, we will explore the question of how we might go about initiating and sustaining efforts to place affect, as I have described it, in the curriculum. In the past this process has usually involved the definition of some version of self-esteem, values, morals, character, and so on, by one or a few people outside the school or by a committee of representatives within it, followed by a proposal or mandate that the version be carried out with young people. Such proposals have typically been accompanied by suggestions implementing them, sometimes attractively packaged as collections of activities and materials. In this way, placing affect in the curriculum has not differed much from other curriculum topics, including subject-area units.

Here I want to suggest a quite different approach. At issue is not how we get people to use cooperative learning or how to implement heterogeneous grouping, though those are very important. Rather the question is how we open up the possibility that things like this could happen in schools. This way of wording the issue should not be taken to mean that I am avoiding the question of whether the schools are in need of change. Indeed, my arguments in previous chapters suggest that if the major themes (or any one of them) were taken seriously, a good deal of restructuring would follow. However, what the wording is intended to do is to open up a discourse about the affective themes and how they might be brought to life in the school and, it is hoped, the larger community. How do we begin such a discourse?

This effort does not begin at some "zero point." Instead the effort begins by clearly articulating the legitimate case for these themes in the curriculum. By this I mean that educators themselves need to say, "We believe that the public schools should promote democracy, human dignity (and related value and moral principles), citizens' rights, developmental psychology (including as a social philosophy), and cultural diversity; moreover, we believe the schools ought to present such themes in their ongoing life, including curriculum plans and institutional features." In other words, "not only should the schools promote those themes, but they ought to be a place where those themes may be found in practice."

On the surface these themes may (and probably will) seem like distant abstractions to some people and will undoubtedly be defined in many ways. I have argued that the theme of democracy includes such ideas as full participation and consideration of diverse viewpoints, that the theme of human dignity includes the need for personal efficacy and requires equality and caring, and that the theme of cultural diversity includes the prizing of cultural differences and the recognition of diversity in our own society. Moreover, I take these themes to be central in defining conditions for the kind of personal and social efficacy on which the idealization of our society depends. Alternatives to these themes, such as authoritarianism, elitism, cultural homogeneity, and so on, are based on a limited and differentiated distribution of personal and social efficacy, and detract from human dignity. Moreover, the themes are broad enough that their initial articulation does not prevent the possibility of many variations in which they may be brought to life in particular situations such as schools.

A critical aspect of the discourse I am proposing is the *continuing* examination of how these themes ought to be defined. The discourse I am proposing is long and involved; in fact, it is one that never ends. It is the continuing search for meaning and practice regarding the school's role in promoting personal and social efficacy, self-esteem and the common good, human dignity and equity. None of these is ever completed. The dynamics of social living continuously create new situations in which they must be reconsidered and reconstructed.

At this point we can only identify some of the questions that might emerge in the discourse either before curriculum plans and institutional features are created or in examining those that exist.

- How should power be distributed among individuals and groups within the school?
- What experiences are most likely to encourage caring and compassion among people in the school?
- What might lie behind unequal outcomes across various groups within the school?
- What does labeling mean for the self-esteem of young people?
- What rights do teachers or young people have regarding decisions about school policies?
- What conditions outside the school are detracting from the dignity of young people and what can be done about them?
- Do curriculum plans present the contributions of many cultures and both sexes to important historical episodes?

Such a list of possible questions could, of course, fill an entire book. Yet, obviously, even these few would be enough to support the discourse for a long time. The implications for restructuring affect in the curriculum are just as obvious.

Answering questions like these opens up possibilities for reflecting on how the school relates to the themes I have proposed. It also leads to the possibility for experimenting with forms that may bring these themes to life in the school. Just as the discourse itself is continuing, so is the effort to create practical ways of seeing it through to reality. This is a critical point. The discourse is not simply a process by which claims and counterclaims are made about abstract concepts. It is also one by which ideas lead to creative practices that are, in turn, examined and reflected upon, leading to new or revised ideas and practices. In other words, this is a discourse about theory and between theory and practice. If we think about the history of affect in the curriculum, it is clear that this is exactly the way in which the many theoretical proposals or versions of affect emerged throughout this century. Here, however, the grounds for the discourse are clearly articulated in and by the schools themselves and thus are immediately placed in the practical arena for consideration. Furthermore, the purpose is not confined to proposing specific practices, but extends to the possibility of searching for better meaning and practice through creative and thoughtful experimentation.

CONDITIONS OF THE DISCOURSE

The themes that serve as grounds for the discourse also place certain conditions on it. First among these is the idea that the discourse must be democratic. This means that all interested parties, including young people, professional educators, and citizens-at-large, must have access to full participation in it regardless of their present social, political, economic, or cultural positions. In using the term *parties*, I do not mean to allow an easy swing toward representative participation (which threatens to become "protective" democracy). Rather I mean to suggest the possibility that all individuals would have equal access to the discourse. While this may immediately conjure up images of unwieldy groups, it may also suggest the need to reposition the site at which the discourse takes place, a topic we will take up shortly.

In addition to the condition of full participation, in the democratic discourse all points of view are necessarily heard and considered seriously through what Habermas (1971) calls "undistorted communication"—the right of people to proceed from their own personal knowledge and belief as they pursue meanings and consensus with others. This does not mean that all ideas will be accepted or acted on, but that all have a right to be heard. At the same time, no point of view is permanently rejected, because new conditions or evidence may later arise that call for refinement of or even legitimate a previously unsatisfactory idea. Moreover, decisions that arise from the democratic discourse should be made by consensus. All participants need not agree heartily with a decision—an unlikely event to begin with—but all should be willing to go along with it, given the guarantee that it will be open to further examination.

Another condition that democracy places on the discourse about affect in the curriculum is that it be reasoned. This means that simply expressing an idea or defining a term does not necessarily legitimate it. Instead there is a need to argue a claim in sensible and defensible ways based on the facts as far as they can be known. This condition does not limit the grounds for making claims to "scientific" evidence alone, nor does it eliminate arguments based largely on feeling or intuition; rather it suggests that they be unbiased in their treatment of the facts and based on careful reflection. This condition leads back to the idea of critical analysis raised in Chapter 5. Just as affect in the curriculum requires a complete search for root conditions and reasons, so does a careful and reasoned discourse about affect in the curriculum.

As I write this description of democratic discourse, I am aware that we are living in a time when its practicality is open to serious question. As noted in the last section of Chapter 3, recent years have seen a steady erosion of gains made in the 1960s and 1970s in the efficacy of the views of particular groups in our society, especially poor and nonwhite people, women, and youth. At the same time we have seen the emergence of elite groups of professional technocrats representing private interests, who have gained increasing control over the definition of what constitutes "desirable" values, morals, ethics, and self-respect (Apple, 1988). Because of this, a particular issue arises in organizing ourselves for the discourse I am proposing. That is, some persons or groups may have an interest in affect in the curriculum, but may fail to honor the need for discourse conditioned by full participation of diverse people and groups.

The exclusion of certain people and groups is, of course, not only the result of efforts by others. In some cases lack of participation is chosen. In other words, those who have been disenfranchised may not want to participate. There are a number of possible reasons for this. One is that they may have had negative experiences in school and simply desire to avoid any further contact with it. A second reason is that they may distrust the school, either because of what it has done to them personally or because it is a social institution whose past and present policies have been constructed out of the interests of a particular class. Another reason may be that their personal obligations in terms of work, child care, and other concerns do not allow them time to participate. Or it may be that all of these reasons combined simply make some people feel unwelcome in school.

If the discourse about affect in the curriculum is to be genuine, there is a need for action that not only encourages widespread participation, but ensures it to the greatest extent possible. To begin with, those who initiate the discourse, and who therefore have an initial type of power, must insist that all persons be invited to join in it. Personal contacts (telephone calls, home visits, and so on) must supplement the usual mailed notices or newspaper bulletins. Second, the specific site for formal discussion might (and probably ought to) be moved outside the school to homes, community centers, public libraries, and the like, so as to reduce the implication of control by the school. Third, every possibility should be explored for arranging convenient meeting times, including work-release agreements, child-care provisions, and evening sessions. These kinds of practical arrangements are intended to press beyond the important concept of equal access, to the practical opportunity for those who are entitled to participate to actually do so. Moreover, they are intended to equalize the place and power of participants in the discourse.

The possibilities for realizing full participation are admittedly not as optimistic as they might be, especially at the present time when there is so little precedence for it or experience with it. Even when all are invited and arrangements such as those discussed above are made, there is still the strong likelihood that some people will choose not to participate, including some from within the school itself. Does this mean that the practical discourse cannot proceed? The answer here is "no," so long as all continue to be invited, arrangements are made to expedite their participation, and issues and concerns that nonparticipants might express are deliberately raised. The point is that work on affect in the curriculum cannot wait for those who do not see its necessity, nor can it be hindered by their reluctance. In time, perhaps, they will change their minds, but meanwhile those who choose to participate must proceed and do so empowered by the critical need to pursue the major themes I have proposed.

However, access and attendance are not sufficient to fulfill the condition of real participation. Many of us have at one time or another attended institutionally sponsored discussions only to find that we were actually participants in what Graebner (1988), as we saw in Chapter 2, described as episodes of the "engineering of consent." An example that comes to mind is the case where a group of citizens is invited to discuss the possible closing of a school. Upon arriving, they find that a decision has already been made to close the school and they are merely being asked to talk about how to procedurally carry the decision out. This is quite different from asking whether the school ought to be closed in the first place; yet participation in the discussion is taken to mean consent to the prior decision. Aside from the question of engineering consent in this way, this type of "participation" is what often leads to or confirms mistrust of school officials.

Beyond equal access and attendance, I interpret the concept of full participation to mean that possibilities for school policies and procedures really are open to consideration and that what participants in the discourse have to say really counts. Returning to our affective themes, suppose that a group meets to discuss how power in the school may be justly distributed. Assume for the moment that at present the genuine power is held by administrators and the school board, with teachers and students having little say in decisions. It may be in the end that such power relations will still be relatively imbalanced in this way (although it is hoped that they will be more equalized), but is the question at hand really open if the discussion is planned and led by administrators and board members? The answer most likely is "no" because regardless of the intentions of those people, the group is liable to sense from the tenor of the discussion that the original question is not really open.

To overcome this very real possibility, arrangements should be made to demonstrate in practical ways that the discourse process is really open to participants. This means that those who hold the least prior power should be placed in positions ordinarily held by those who would usually have the most prior power; that is, the discourse should deliberately advantage the least advantaged. Returning to our previous example, teachers and students ought to hold "leadership" positions in group work to plan the meeting about distribution of power and in the actual discussion. Similarly, when sessions are convened to discuss such matters as how cultural diversity might be better portrayed in the curriculum, people from the community, particularly those from nonprivileged "minority" groups, should assume leadership in discussions.

Arrangements such as the ones described above are suggested for two reasons. First, the very themes of the discourse require that it be carried out under conditions that bring to life the meaning of the themes. If a particular discussion is about distribution of power in the school, then the organization of the discussion must begin as if such power were equally distributed. From that point, participants may express views about the question at hand without being restricted by feelings that they are caught in the engineering of their consent under current definitions and stratification of roles. These arrangements attempt to recreate what Rawls (1971) calls the "original position" or the initial condition of "equality" prior to deliberation or interaction. By this I mean that at the moment of initial discussion the participant roles are arranged so that power is equalized among them. Certainly this does not suggest that, for example, young people will forget that they are also students, but that the usual positioning of such roles will not determine status within the group.

Second, given the fact that the formal discourse about affect in the curriculum will probably be initiated by the school, such arrangements are meant to demonstrate good faith on the part of those school administrators, board members, and others who would ordinarily assume leadership and power. Only in this way can we expect that over time those who have been left on the margins of participation in the past will continue to work with us in this area.

There is one special, but not unusual, case that also needs attention in this discussion. The fact is that this discourse is already under way in almost every community. Virtually everyone at one time or another has probably had something to say about the matter of affect in the curriculum or, at least, some aspect of it. So far I have described some ways in which this informal conversation might be formalized with leadership from the school. However, often one or more people approach school officials with suggestions or demands about some dimension of affect in the curriculum. Frequently these people are put off or "engineered" away as rude malcontents. Yet these episodes offer exactly the opportunity to begin a more formal discourse using real rather than created concerns.

I am suggesting here that when such complaints are made, the school should seize the opportunity to open up a larger, formal discussion about affect in the curriculum. Yet, again, we must not forget the democratic conditions of the discourse. Thus, the school must still seek broad participation, arrange for equalized distribution of power among participants, encourage the expression of all views, promote reasoned deliberation of them, and seek consensus among participants. It is under these conditions that the "democratic faith" enters in. That is, if these conditions are genuinely met, participants are not likely to consent to ideas that contradict the themes in which the discourse is grounded. In this case, they are the very themes that provide for open inquiry.

Before leaving this topic, there is one other piece of our memories that ought to be brought forth. Many of us, including myself, who have been involved in organizing school and community discussions about affect in the curriculum have at one time or another engaged in engineering consent. I am not speaking here about those who refuse outright to invite participation or who overtly manipulate others through political maneuvering. Rather I refer to those of us with "good" and perhaps defensible intentions who have organized participatory activities but have, for example, subtly veiled our own desired ends or strategically placed discussion leaders to guide conversations in desired directions. Perhaps it is that we forgot the deeper meaning of the democratic action we claimed to be promoting. Or perhaps we honestly and passionately believed that what we sought was good for others and they only needed to be guided to that realization. Whatever the case, we need to recognize now that with few exceptions those activities usually did not have lasting effects. "Participatory" groups and the decisions they made had no real staying power in the face of growing policy appropriation by professional elites, nor did they really shift the balance of power toward more equal distribution. The equilibrium that was created was only momentary.

Now we face a new possibility. Either we join the professional elites and do things for the "good" of others, or we turn back to our interest in participation and re-create those activities in light of the themes I have described. Much has been said recently about the concept of "empowerment," and it would appear that the time for talk about participatory discourse is upon us again. Perhaps we might do well to begin by realizing that there is still a dangerous thread in that talk. It still sounds as though people are empowered by institutions or by officials who are willing to let others have a say in things. But from a moral point of view, people are not "empowered" by officials or institutions. Instead, they are authentically empowered by the fact that they are people who live in a society where democracy, dignity, and diversity are ostensibly central themes. For that reason, a renewed effort at formal participatory discourse will require more thorough attention to the conditions those themes place on it.

THE SCHOOL AS THE LEVEL OF DISCOURSE

I have been describing a discourse about affect in the curriculum that requires meeting two conditions: (1) everyone who wishes to participate must have the opportunity to do so, and (2) those who do participate must be able to act personally and expeditiously on the ideas they develop.

A look at the existing structure for determining school policy suggests that in the present circumstances these two conditions are difficult to meet. In recent years there has been increasing centralization of policy making supported by a large and cumbersome bureaucracy. Power in curriculum planning has been largely appropriated by state legislatures and departments of education. State officials have created curriculum mandates based on popular political slogans, not the least of which has been the constant theme of the schools' relation to international economic competition. In some cases, state departments of education have even gone so far as to issue detailed curriculum guides tied to their own or national standardized tests. And power that is not assumed by the state is often controlled in local central offices that act as an intermediary between the state and the individual school.

The rhetoric (direct or implied) of this most recent centralization sounds much like a case description in opposition to the major themes we are considering here. For example, there is a basic assumption that people are unable to act intelligently in determining their own sense of what is educationally sound. Professional educators in local schools are characterized as inept and thus in need of further "monitoring," while citizens, including young people, are presumably either unaware of what they need or universally insistent on higher academic standards and more accountability. The human results over time are seen in the loss of power among local professionals, who increasingly become technicians merely carrying out the policies of state officials, as well as in the marginalizing of citizens, who simply have no place at all in educational policy discussions (Apple, 1986). Worse yet, these results become a way of life as local school officials clamor for recognition based on how well their schools perform on state or nationally determined measures of excellence.

What I am describing here is a pervasive loss of personal and social efficacy among people, compounded by loss of interest in participatory discourse, marginalization of the skills to carry it out, and disappearance of opportunities that involve those skills. I am not saying that everyone has had these dispositions and skills recently, but whatever supply there might have been is rapidly declining. Nor am I about to argue for completely dissolving the federal or state role in education; the memory of the need for federal intervention regarding, for example, school segregation is too recent. And obviously I do not mean to suggest that the debate among theorists over affect in the curriculum should cease. Voices like these ought to be heard in the discourse and must be heard if it is to consider a wide variety of viewpoints. What I am advocating is that the most important level of discourse—the one at which policy and practice based on the major themes are worked out—should be the individual school level.

Among the phrases often heard within the rhetoric of empowerment is one that refers to "site-based management." While the word *management* ought to make us immediately leery (remember "scientific management"), the concept behind this phrase offers some promise for the kind of discourse I am describing. Ostensibly the idea is that power in school policy making, including curriculum, would shift more heavily toward the local school building. If we return to the conditions placed on the discourse, this kind of shift makes a good deal of sense.

Placing the highest premium on discourse around the individual school has several advantages that cannot be matched at other levels. First, if everyone has access to the activities of formal discourse, the number of potential participants increases dramatically as one moves away from the individual building level, but so does the tendency toward "representation" rather than actual participation. However, at the school level the pool of potential participants is such that greater numbers of people have a chance to participate directly and with easy access. Second, at the individual building level, as participants think through affective themes they do not talk about abstract groups in other places. Instead, depending on who proposes what, they talk about "*my* life in school," "*my* children's education," and so on. Moreover, as consensus is reached or new curriculum arrangements are proposed, ideas may be acted on expeditiously, that is, without having to wait for official voices or other schools to agree.

This combination of the possibility for full participation, easier access, and expeditious action regarding issues in people's own lives describes heightened possibilities for personal and social efficacy. Ironically, it is possible that under these conditions the number of actual participants in the discourse might well increase beyond the number who would be concerned about it if it were carried on through representation at a level where the number of affected people would theoretically be greater. Just as important, however, is the possibility that experiences such as the local discourse may provide might not only promote predispositions related to efficacy, but help renew those that have diminished in the deskilling process of centralization.

In placing the site for critical discourse at the individual building level, we must again confront an issue raised in Chapter 4 in conjunction with the current democratic schools movement. In reviewing the *Equity and Excellence* report (Public Education Information Network, 1987), we noted that the authors took what might be perceived as a courageous, but dangerous, position. That is, they ignored the possibility that some local group might choose to act in ways that contradicted the principles of democracy. This stance is not naive; rather it is consistent with their overall belief that when people have a chance to work through ideas that affect them directly, they will not choose to detract from their own efficacy. Yet in describing the need for democratic schools, the problems of top-down mandates, and the culture and gender bias in standardized testing, the authors also suggest possible outcomes for the local decision making they recommend.

Here I am adding the notion that the themes of democracy, dignity, and diversity should be publicly articulated as defensible claims and should serve as the starting point for discourse about how to bring them to life in the curriculum. That the line between working toward personal and social efficacy and the "engineering of consent" can be thin has already been noted. However, the themes themselves are defensible in relation to that efficacy and thus are defensible starting points. That is, under the discourse conditions described here, their articulation is not a matter of showing less faith in people, but of expanding the meaning of the very concepts that support personal and social efficacy.

The discourse about affect in the curriculum I am recommending uses a parallel structure. The major themes of the discourse are articulated as *prior* conditions for both its content and process, and are defended in the ways I have described. However, primary emphasis in the discourse itself is placed at the local level, where there can be fuller participation in exploring the meaning of the themes and expediting action regarding their practical application. Again, to say that the prior definition of the themes is undemocratic or antithetical to human dignity is an empty argument of self-contradiction; to so enter these themes as an objection would, of course, require that they have somehow been previously defined and agreed upon.

DISCOURSE AS ACTION

So far we have looked at discourse with regard to engaging people in interaction about the meaning of the major themes and how to bring them to life in the school. However, discourse over affect in the curriculum ought not to involve talk alone. There must be a program of action as well. Almost all of us have been involved in episodes of school planning where long and involved discussions have come to nothing, and we have experienced the kind of frustration that inevitably results. In fact, one of the most difficult problems in opening up any current discussion of school restructuring is the reaction from many people that they have "been this route before" only to see their work blocked by inaction.

The action I want to portray here is not the type that is placed as a discrete stage in the usual technical-linear models associated with the management of change. Such models typically follow a series of steps from problem identification to planning of a program that solves the problem and subsequent implementation of the program (action), followed by an evaluation. This kind of model assumes that life stands still while each step is undertaken, that programs of action are implemented in the way they are planned, that particular parts of the school are independent, and that participants or practitioners do not plan and evaluate as they go along. Such assumptions are, of course, quite mistaken in the way they picture life inside and outside the school.

In contrast to this we need to see the themes of democracy, dignity, and diversity as permeating the everyday events of people's lives inside and outside the school. They are simultaneously grounds upon which to reflect about action and grounds that guide action in the continuing flow of experience. This is not a one-time attempt to

implement particular ideas, but rather a continuing struggle for
personal and social efficacy. It is by taking action that we demonstrate the meaning of the themes and the authenticity of our intentions. What kind of action might the discourse about affect involve?
One example is the kind of arrangements previously described in this
chapter, which now may be seen as more than merely ways of bringing people together for talk. Such organizing itself is a project that
presents the themes. A second example is the trying out of any curriculum or institutional arrangements like those described in previous
chapters.

A third example, and one we ought to particularly think about, is
projects that might involve action outside the school and in which
those inside and outside the school might work cooperatively. Just as
there are many examples of how the major themes are contradicted
within the school, so there are many that might be found in the local
community. As people become engaged in discourse about the school,
they are very likely to raise issues regarding the larger community.
Suppose, for example, that it is determined that young people in
school are exhibiting racial or ethnic bias or that practices in the
school reveal such bias. Obviously there are many possibilities for
action in the school to begin to counteract such bias, but the fact that it
exists within the school suggests that it is probably present in the
community as well. Moreover, action within the school alone is incomplete, because it may affect only a portion of certain people's lives,
namely, those people in the school and for the time they are there.

Thus the question arises as to what action might be undertaken to
counteract bias in the larger community. A project might be undertaken to engage young people and adults in the school and the community in cooperative action around the issue. This could involve investigating the sources and results of bias, sponsoring discussions and
seminars about it, media campaigns, and so on. The same might be
done with such issues as homelessness, poverty, commercialism, pollution, and others that continue to plague almost every community.
Such projects begin to idealize the relationship of the school to the
community and to show that discourse about affect is not merely a
school topic. At the same time they present a new problem in the sense
that they involve some risk for educators. When such issues are addressed, the themes and those who advocate them can run up against
some very powerful special interests. All too often, though, educators
who foresee such risks tend to see themselves standing alone in what
promise to be uncomfortable political situations. However, if the discourse I am describing is authentic, particularly in the sense of full

participation, educators would be joined in the search for personal and collective efficacy by many other people from the community, some of whom might otherwise have been silent on important issues.

The examples I have just been using obviously reflect serious social issues. However, the discourse action may involve projects of a less dramatic, but nevertheless important, sort. For example, educators and citizens might work together on curriculum plans focusing on a nonselective history of their community that includes all events and all people, or on raising money for famine relief in other countries. Similarly, they may form discussion groups about current events or sponsor voter registration drives. Each of these projects, and others like them, is obviously related to the major themes and may be seen as involving less risk and complexity than those described previously. In this sense, they may also be more attractive in the initial stages of the discourse and more likely to sustain the interest of participants who want to see less talk and more action. It is also possible that they may offer a kind of transition to the larger issues that we must inevitably consider if our discourse is truly legitimate.

Before leaving this discussion of discourse action, it is important to remind ourselves that such action and related projects require time for thoughtful consideration. As anxious as we may be for something concrete to happen, we must be careful to think ideas through completely. Too often we want to attach short deadlines to particular projects, which typically means that we short-cut critical aspects of deliberation. Arranging for as full participation as possible, hearing all points of view, and reaching consensus take time; furthermore, if participation is voluntary, there is the different matter of promoting ideas among those who have chosen not to participate. To say that we will have heterogeneous grouping by November or that the school climate will change by June may be theoretically desirable. But that does not mean that the practical conditions of the discourse can adequately be met in the same time frames. If projects related to the themes are worth doing, then they must also be worth taking the time to do well. If those undertaken first are done well, later efforts are more likely to be successful.

LANGUAGE AND MEANING IN THE DISCOURSE

The discourse described here is not new theoretically. Its possibility has been explored, for example, from the work of Dewey (1908) to that of Habermas (1971) and others like Maxine Greene (1985) who have more recently engaged in critical analysis of the school and society. Moreover, it is not a random tradition of disassociated thinkers. Rather the language of the discourse is part of the continuing progressive tradition that explores the possibilities for democracy, dignity, and diversity both inside and outside the school and that needs to be revived. Michael Apple (1986) makes this point in saying that "the languages of a genuine populism, of democratic faith, and, within education, of the progressive tradition, can be reappropriated, reconstructed, and made more politically astute" (p. 198).

The language of the discourse is also one of "shoulds" and "oughts" as well as "rights" and "wrongs." We cannot underestimate the degree to which such words elicit powerful feelings among people. After all, we are speaking of the ways in which people conduct their personal and social lives, a topic that brings us up against the enormous value that people in our society place on individual freedom. This certainly does not mean that individual freedom should be underestimated or deemphasized in the discourse about affect in the curriculum. Indeed, the way in which each of the major themes relates to personal efficacy requires that individual freedom be seriously and continuously emphasized. Rather it refers to the frequent tendency toward ultimately resolving value or moral differences on the grounds of personal choice and thus ultimately skirting the more complicated issue of the common good.

Oddly enough this individualistic tendency has come to be defined as the meaning of "progressive" by those on the conservative side of affective issues. This appropriation of meaning has, in turn, been used to argue for affect in the curriculum as a narrowly defined version of conventional social obligations (good manners, respect for authority) that marginalizes individual freedoms. Our work in pursuing a complete and defensible approach to affect in the curriculum must avoid exclusive emphasis on either personal or social interests. Instead it must be concerned with both and also with how they might be integrated to the advantage of personal and social efficacy.

Beyond this, however, the discourse about affect in the curriculum faces a formidable obstacle within the school itself. This obstacle is found in the social and cultural meanings of everyday language of the school, particularly as it evolved during the 1970s and 1980s. As interest in efficiency and technology has grown, the language of schools, including that of curriculum planning, has become overgrown with the language of "management systems." So, for example, we have become accustomed to identifying "target objectives" that are "monitored" so that we can maintain "quality control" over curriculum "products"; if properly "executed," these factors may come together to form an "accountable" curriculum "delivery system." Such terms are unmistakably those of management-efficiency systems found in the military and in professional as well as industrial businesses, too.

This point is not a simple semantic argument. Language has a good deal of power in shaping our relationships and limiting our thinking. For example, when we borrow terms like "chief executive officers" or "managers" to refer to superintendents or principals, and terms like "subordinates" or "front-line workers" to refer to teachers, we risk placing those two groups in a particular kind of relationship. In the world of business or the military, officers and managers make decisions while subordinates and workers do not. Similarly, when we cast curriculum planning within a framework of management-efficiency systems, we place limitations on what topics might be considered. In the forum where efficiency holds sway, "outcomes" that are thought to be quantifiable (like low-level academic skills or simple social behaviors) are acceptable, while qualitative possibilities like self-esteem and broad moral principles are not.

Hence it is not at all surprising that the kind of relationships and concepts that are part of larger and more complex affective themes have been marginalized in the curriculum, more narrowly redefined, or left out altogether. An excellent example is found in currently popular talk about self-esteem. In the context of democracy, dignity, and diversity, self-esteem has a broad and powerful meaning tied to personal efficacy, self-actualization, and the integration of individual and social interests. However, in schools it is often defined in relation to its widely publicized and quantifiable relationship with academic achievement.

Moreover, in an effort to systematically use this correlation, there is a constant search for tests that claim to measure levels of self-esteem, a search that often ends with one of the many "instruments" devised for this purpose. That these devices have little to do with the actual self-esteem of young people (Beane & Lipka, 1986) is apparently not important to those who use them. What is important is that they offer a numerical index that fits nicely into accountability schemes, often as an explanation of why various instructional practices, which remain unchallenged, do not work. In other words, by redefining the meaning of self-esteem, problems with academic achievement can be blamed on students, who, after all, "own" their self-esteem, while at the same time the larger meaning of self-esteem can be avoided. Meanwhile, the dominance of academics and other deep structures in the school escape scrutiny.

This line of thinking may seem to have taken us far afield from the matter of language. Yet, that is precisely the point in understanding how much our language in particular areas shapes our thought and action in a more general way. Thus the discourse I am recommending will have to pay particular attention to the language that is used. Just because particular terms are used in business or the military does not mean that they are appropriate for education—unless, of course, we see the purposes and relationships they imply as desirable. Just because the jargon of education allows for efficient communication among those who work in education does not mean that it is helpful in talking to those who do not—unless, of course, we mean to exclude them from our conversations.

The language and meaning of the discourse described in this chapter are intended to keep open and more broadly extend the themes of democracy, human dignity, and cultural diversity. They are also meant to recapture relationships that those themes suggest. Yet, this is not easy when we are accustomed to a different language or narrowly defined meanings. For example, even the designation of some people as educators and others as citizens is risky. For one thing, it could suggest that educators are not also citizens, when in fact they are, albeit a particular type of citizen. Also, and more important, it could suggest that educators are a privileged elite when it comes to talk about education, which they might be in having particular knowledge about aspects of schooling, but not when it comes to talk about affective issues that impinge upon the society as a whole. So it is that in our discourse we may need to use particular terms to define concepts or distinguish among groups, but we must also be careful to consider where those terms could lead us and to clarify how they are being used.

As a beginning point, for example, perhaps we might think carefully about the term *student* as it is commonly used in schools. As we have seen, student is only one of the many roles that a certain group of people plays in a life that extends beyond the school. Perhaps we might think differently about life in school if instead of *students*, we used a term like *young people*, which would suggest that we are concerned with a group of human beings who happen to be young. In this way, for example, our language might help us begin to view these people in a more complete and caring way. And while we are at it, we might also think about such phrases as *my* teachers or *my* students. In a discourse about affect in which democracy and dignity are prominent themes there is obviously no room for terms of "ownership" that conjure up images of life on the plantation.

A CASE IN POINT:
THE BALTIMORE COUNTY SCHOOLS PROJECT

One widely publicized attempt to create discourse about affect in the curriculum was undertaken by the Baltimore County public schools. As we shall see, its form differed somewhat from the one I have described, but it nonetheless demonstrated that such discourse is possible in public school settings. Initiated in 1981 by the superintendent and board of education, the project was intended to reclaim what was seen as a declining emphasis on values education in the county schools. To understand how the discourse unfolded, we will briefly look inside a document that emerged in its initial stages, *1984 and Beyond: A Reaffirmation of Values* (Task Force on Values Education and Ethical Behavior, 1983).

According to the report, a task force representing a diverse cross-section of the county was formed to investigate values education and ethical behavior. For most of the first year the group engaged in a study of the field, including general reading and discussion as well as specific investigation in such areas as conservative and progressive views; ethics in politics, business, and the media; and legal issues associated with values education. In addition, the group studied several versions of values education, including values "inculcation," values clarification, values analysis, and cognitive-moral development. While not specifically asked to do so, the task force eventually reached consensus on a "common core of values" that might be promoted in the schools. The list, in alphabetical order, included the following (p. 5):

Compassion	Loyalty
Courtesy	Objectivity
Critical Inquiry	Order
(e.g., Scientific Method)	Patriotism
Due Process	Rational Consent
Equality of Opportunity	Reasoned Argument
Freedom of Thought and Action	Respect for Others' Rights
Honesty	Responsibility
Human Worth and Dignity	Responsible Citizenship
Integrity	Rule of Law
Justice	Self-Respect
Knowledge	Tolerance
	Truth

The task force also outlined 10 premises it believed ought to underlie values education and ethical behavior. Among these were such ideas as

Values education needs to be defined . . . , there should be recognition
that a common core of values exists within our pluralistic society . . . ,
educators should be aware that values are taught implicitly and explicitly through the curriculum and by practices throughout the school
system . . . , [and] knowledge gained from research in the field of values
education and the developmental stages of children and youth should be
applied to our approach to the topic. (p. 2)

Each of the 10 was explained in the report, including a summary of
generalizations and critiques of approaches to values and moral education.

Having thus developed a framework for work in the area of
values education, the task force finally turned to a set of recommendations for continuing the discourse. It is here that we find perhaps the
most interesting twist in this story. Rather than suggesting development of a curriculum or mandating a program, the group instead
called for each individual school to convene its own task force to
consider ways of approaching the topic, including intensive study so
that more people could "experience the depth of understanding necessary to deal with issues of values and ethical behavior" (p. 30). However, in doing so, the task force made a number of recommendations
for ideas that ought to be considered. These included the need for
broad participation from inside and outside the school, standing com-
mittees to sustain work on values education, public articulation of
"core" values, a review of school policies and practices, development of
"human service projects," use of "critical commentary" activities to
enhance young people's capacity to examine and personally judge
value systems, and continued study of values education approaches
(pp. 30–33). The task force seemed particularly concerned about one
idea throughout the report and the recommendations: "Indoctrination
is not the purpose of values education; rather, that [values] education,
as the quest for truth, should foster tolerance, inquiry, and a healthy
respect for responsible dissent" (p. 33).

By 1988, representatives of the Baltimore County schools were
able to describe a wide array of attempts to continue work on both
theory and practice involving teachers, young people, parents, and
others (Dubel & Saterlie, 1988). In this sense, they had demonstrated
that it is possible to initiate and sustain discourse around affect in the
curriculum. If we examine the project using the discourse conditions
previously outlined in this chapter, there is obviously much similarity
between the two. Much of what is contained in the "core values"
statement reflects the major themes of democracy, dignity, and diver-

sity. The statement itself was arrived at through consensus after careful study by people from both inside and outside the school. The project presented a parallel structure in which themes were widely articulated and local schools asked to explore their meanings and how they might be brought to life through cooperative work. Finally, and of particular interest, is the fact that even though the content of "core values" was originally left open, the major themes I have suggested emerged from a diverse group of participants.

However, without in the least denigrating the project, several questions might be raised.

- Are we really to assume that all of the "core values" are of equal importance; for example, are patriotism and courtesy to be seen at the same level as human dignity?
- Are some of these values more likely "contained" within others and thus subject to greater ambiguity?
- Is it really necessary to develop such a long list of "core values," or is that length actually meant to more easily gain consent among diverse groups?
- Could the same effort initially have been undertaken in each individual school and thus involved fuller participation?
- Given the county level "core values," are groups in individual schools likely to engage in a really full examination of possibilities or to simply consent to the original statement?
- Why were young people not included in either county or individual school level task forces?

Again, these questions are not meant to denigrate the project. Rather they are meant to demonstrate the need for continued analysis of the discourse and to remind us of even greater possibilities. Despite the questions, we must still recognize that this project, and others like it, are bold and important efforts.

SUMMARY

Of the various chapters in this book, this one raises the most crucial question from a practical standpoint; that is, how might we initiate and sustain efforts to place affect in the curriculum in complete and appropriate ways? The answer is important because the means we use are themselves part of that affect. I have described a discourse of parallel structure in which our work is conditioned by prior themes, but carried out through grass-roots efforts at the individual school level. Theoretical as the sketch may seem, it is quite possible in practice if we choose to make it happen. The historical failure of top-down proposals and the risk of athematic bottom-up projects leave us with little choice but to create this kind of structural possibility.

To understand this, let us look once more at some of the problems found in more conventional efforts to work on affect in the curriculum. Historically, proposals about affect have typically considered only one or two of the various aspects of personal and social development, such as self-esteem or moral reasoning. Moreover, in doing so they have entered the discourse at a kind of intermediate level in the nomenclature of affect, where the original basis for their claim has not always been clear. For example, talk about self-esteem or caring, important as it is, does not necessarily in itself reveal the broader theme of human dignity from which they follow. Surely talk about character, the "conduct" aspect of affect in the curriculum, does not in itself begin to reveal the reasons why such expectations are justifiable. It is only by placing these aspects within a broader discourse around the larger themes that we can expect their real meaning to be fully explored and their implications made known.

Another problem with typical proposals about affect in the curriculum is that they have tended to follow a linear-technical change model; that is, the problem and solution are identified "at the top" and then handed down to schools where implementation is expected to follow. Like so many other curriculum reform proposals, these assume that teachers and parents will easily consent to the solution and also be committed to carrying it out. Such an assumption is tenuous at best, as the history of confusion and resistance described in Chapter 2 revealed. Worse yet, this legislated form of curriculum planning not only incorrectly supposes that those "at the bottom" are themselves unskilled, but works against their efficacy by isolating them from the point where decisions are actually made. The inevitable tension created between top-down proposals and bottom-up resistance has been one among many reasons for the confusion and contradiction that now characterize affect in the curriculum.

At the same time, there is an obvious danger in an unconditional discourse over affect from the bottom up. One need not look far to see that special interests have a way of dominating talk about affective issues even when the way seems clear for broad participation. The history of "engineered consent" and the appropriation of morality by intellectual and other elites is but one example. Another is the tendency by majorities to marginalize the place of minorities in political, economic, social, and institutional life, including within the school itself. For example, if not for top-down mandates from courts and legislatures, racial segregation would undoubtedly continue to be an overt practice in public schools. Furthermore, discourse over affect in the curriculum is not supposed to be unconditional in public schools in the United States. Instead it is ostensibly governed by the same deep themes of democracy, dignity, and diversity that are central to personal and social efficacy in the larger society of which the schools are a part.

The discourse I have proposed presents a possibility for resolving this typically "either/or" dilemma. Its parallel structure begins with defensible themes that place conditions on the critical practical discourse that follows. Among these are requirements that counter the possibility of domination by special interests, namely, full participation, equal distribution of power, and rational consent. Moreover, the local discourse is about theory and the relation between theory and practice—a discourse that leads to deliberate and thoughtful action and that insists on critical reflection about that action.

Such discourse is a linguistic act—it involves "talk"—yet in naming the themes and the actions they imply it is not simply a trivial semantic exercise. Rather it recognizes the hidden meanings and the consequences of language for everyday life in the school. On the other hand, it does have a semantic side in that it redeems the language of progressive theory and practice that has long been associated with the themes of democracy, dignity, and diversity.

The themes with which this discourse begins were meant to extend personal and social efficacy in our society. Thus the discourse is not without an obvious purpose that we can now unmistakably name. The purpose is this: to share the legacy of democracy, dignity, and diversity not only with the young people who experience affect in the curriculum, but with all of those, older and younger, who participate in the discourse itself. In doing so, it is more and more likely that those themes will enter not only into affect in the curriculum but into the larger society as well.

7

Legacy and Liberation

Many educators like to interpret historical accounts of their work in terms of the "swinging pendulum" metaphor. Ideas come and go, they say, and if any one "disappears" we need only wait awhile and it will show up again. As we have seen, this is not really an appropriate metaphor. While one or another idea may be in ascendance at a given moment, others, including competing ones, are almost sure to be close by—not forgotten, but less popular; and not completely out of sight, but coexisting in both theoretical discussion and everyday life in the school. And unlike the "swinging pendulum" in physics, educational ideas are moved not by unseen forces of nature, but by the struggles among people to promote particular ideas.

In this book I have presented a case for how we might think about affect in the curriculum. The major themes of democracy, dignity, and diversity that serve as grounds for the case have certainly been less popular during the 1980s than the competing claims associated with the emergence of the individualistic "excellence" movement in schools and society. Nevertheless, these themes have not disappeared, as the usual metaphor might suggest. Rather their meanings have been defined in relatively narrow ways and their broader interpretation has been marginalized by self-interest and the call for a return to a past that is perceived to have been more stable and secure than historical facts would suggest. The purpose of my case has been to reclaim the broader meanings from which democracy, dignity, and diversity may be seen as the bases of integrating self-interest and the common good and for extending the possibilities for personal and social efficacy in our society. In this chapter I want to summarize the major aspects of this case and to explore its implications for young people, their schools, and the society in which they, and we, live.

THE FRAMEWORK FOR AFFECT CLAIMS

In Chapter 1, I suggested ten guidelines for constructing a coherent and reasonably complete framework for proposals about affect in the curriculum. We will now recall these guidelines in order to summarize and examine the claims I have made in this book. The order in which they will be examined here follows approximately the order in which they were presented in the first six chapters. However, I want to be clear that this order must not suggest a linear (step-by-step) model for developing proposals regarding affect in the curriculum. Entry into the discourse around this topic should be (and is) made at any point where participants see the need for examining aspects of theory and/or practice. In fact, engagement in such discourse most often seems to begin in the latter components, as they are presented here; that is, the points at which particular practices are either suggested or called into question. Thus, the components should be viewed as areas of concern to which we can refer in constructing or examining proposals. With that in mind, we will now turn to the topic of how the claims I have made fit within the framework.

1. *Proposals regarding affect in the curriculum should define what is meant by "affect" and its relations with other dimensions of humanness.* I have defined "affect" as a dimension of humanness that involves preferences and choices. It is related to cognition inasmuch as those preferences and choices are informed by experiences that we reflect on in framing thought and action regarding self and others. The content of those reflections centers on what is "desired" and "desirable" in personal and social activity. Taken this way, curriculum interest in affect involves personal and social development, and their integration, including self-perceptions, values, morals, ethics, and the like. Furthermore, affect enters into the curriculum as an antecedent, as a feature of school transactions, and as an intended outcome of school experiences. Finally, I have argued that wherever claims are made about any of these aspects in education, those claims fall under the general framework of "affect in the curriculum."

2. *Proposals regarding affect in the curriculum should be attached to a particular culture or society.* Because the political, economic, legal, and social factors that drive education and schooling are bound to particular societal and cultural configurations, I have limited my claims to public schools in the United States. This does not mean that any of the claims, such as human dignity, would not be

worthwhile in other societies, but rather that their meanings would have to be worked out in light of configurations of factors in those societies. On the other hand, while I have stated my claims in terms of public schools, they certainly ought to be taken seriously in private schools; those institutions and the young people who attend them are a part of this society and ought to be concerned with the themes that ostensibly support personal and social efficacy within it. Furthermore, while my claims are attached to the national society, I have emphasized the themes of cultural diversity within it and the need to prize and build on the richness of that diversity in deliberate ways.

3. *Proposals regarding affect in the curriculum should articulate a philosophic basis that names the sources of its views and positions on affect, affective issues, and the curriculum.* I have called forth the themes of democracy, human dignity, and cultural diversity and defined them in terms of the progressive tradition that seeks to extend them broadly as grounds for personal and social efficacy. In so doing, the validity of related values and moral principles has also been claimed: freedom, equality, caring, justice, human life, peace, and citizens' rights. From that position I have examined several current trends and issues in society and the schools that inhibit people's access to those themes, values, and moral principles in their real lives. This analysis suggests the need for both personal and collective action toward restructuring certain aspects of both the school and the society, a view that is aligned with the historical thread of reconstructionism.

4. *Proposals regarding affect in the curriculum should articulate a psychological theory that explains how affect develops and is influenced.* I have suggested that among the themes that ought to guide affect in the curriculum is developmental psychology. My particular interest here is with the constructivist aspect of this view that suggests people develop a sense of the "desired" and "desirable" out of their own experiences and perceptions. In this case, I have given priority to self-perceptions as a central feature in the human personality that influences social interactions, but also emphasized the importance of the common good rather than individualistic self-interest. At the same time, strong adherence to rigid "stage" theories has been avoided in the belief that they tend too often to trivialize the perceived capacities of young people to make judgments about self and others; in other words, the themes suggested above should be introduced into the lives of young people as soon as possible and as much as possible.

The developmental view is claimed here because its prizing of human experiences, perceptions, and the constructivist capacity of people matches the themes of democracy, dignity, and diversity more closely than behavioristic theories that favor conditioning toward compliance with externally imposed behavior rules without reasoned consent and in defiance of dignity and choice. Taken this way, the developmental view suggests more than a psychological position. It also presents a possibility for a social philosophy of collective efficacy whereby groups work out conceptions of the common good.

5. *Proposals regarding affect in the curriculum should define what is meant by personal development, social development, and the relations between the two.* I have emphasized the concept of efficacy in personal and social development; that is, young people (and others) should not simply be happy or comfortable as a result of benevolent action by others, but should have a sense of personal and collective capacity to construct the conditions necessary for such development. That sense, of course, comes from experiences in which they are genuinely involved in making decisions that affect their lives. In this sense, development is seen as a concept of liberation by which they are free and freed to think and act for self-actualization and the common good. Those two are integrated through the themes of democracy, dignity, and diversity—not as simple recipes, but as grounds for continuing efforts to reflect on tensions and contradictions between self-interests and the common good (or individualism and the collective good). It is this integration, for example, that helps us to understand that even the most privileged in our society are affected by the restrictive conditions facing the less privileged, because their lives are inextricably tied to the fate of the common good.

6. *Proposals regarding affect in the curriculum should articulate the view of relations they imply between public and private values.* I have recognized that in the affective dimensions of lived experiences, people integrate public and private values. Yet, the word *public* in "public schools" is not only part of a compound noun, but an adjective. Because the public schools are for public use, they must honor the need to respect diverse views, but must promote no view that privileges particular parts of society. To resolve the tension between that responsibility and the democratic right of access to all points of view, I have suggested three levels at which we might view affective content in the curriculum. The first includes those ideas, such as religious concepts, that we may describe, but not promote. The second includes

ideas that we should promote, such as friendship between individuals, but cannot insist on. The third level includes ideas that we should promote and that we may insist on, such as democracy, human dignity, and cultural diversity. Ideas appropriate for the third level are so identified because they present the very themes on which personal and social efficacy in our society are ostensibly extended.

7. *Proposals regarding affect in the curriculum should review the history, if any, of their forms.* I have gone beyond the requirements of this component by reviewing the history of many versions of affect in the curriculum, because the field tends to be so ahistorical in general. In doing so, perhaps my claims may be better understood in relation to others that have been made over time. Specifically, though, my claims present an integration of concepts related to developmental theory, democratic schools, school and social reconstruction, humanistic restructuring of institutions, and interest in advanced multicultural diversity. Moreover, those claims have addressed not only cognitive work around the major themes, but behavior and action toward their realization in personal and social activity.

8. *Proposals regarding affect in the curriculum should clearly define their curriculum intentions.* I have made clear the need for restructuring of affect in the curriculum, but I have also recognized the historical threads that offer valuable ideas. To pursue personal and social efficacy based on the major themes, I have named a number of examples of curriculum arrangements that might emerge from discourse about those themes. These included integration of direct and indirect instruction, inclusion of critical ethics, use of the social problems and emerging-needs curriculum approaches, involvement of young people in curriculum planning and school governance, heterogeneous grouping, and development of humanistic climates. Moreover, I have described how the major themes might guide our view of young people in school and the relations between school and society, including the right of public schools to promote those themes in opposition to special interests that would detract from them. These examples are only suggestive, though, because the continuing question of how to bring the themes to life must be worked out at the individual school level.

9. *Proposals regarding affect in the curriculum should define their relations with other, existing aspects of the school program.* I have used the themes of democracy, dignity, and diversity to analyze

both the everyday affect in schools and the many versions of affect in the curriculum that are presently on the scene. Again, the major implication of this analysis is that affect in the curriculum is in need of serious restructuring. The present versions are either incomplete or inappropriate. For example, self-esteem "packages" isolate affect from the rest of the school, character education reduces morality principles to a simple list of conventional behavior rules, classical humanism detracts from cultural diversity, and all three ignore the powerful effects of the larger society on young people's lives. If the themes are indeed the common legacy of all people and the ostensible grounds for their efficacy, then general education—the common school experience of all young people—ought to be developed around those themes. At the same time, other curriculum plans, and institutional features as well, should be deliberately examined in light of those themes and restructured (where necessary) to bring them to life. In other words, my claims are intended to permeate the entire institution, not simply to be parceled out to some place or program in the schools.

The school imagined here is very different in very important ways from most that are presently in place. Obviously those who work in schools have loyalties to present arrangements. However, if schools are to finally present possibilities for personal and social efficacy and find their way out of the current confusion and contradictions of affect in the curriculum, those arrangements, and the loyalties to them, must be reconsidered.

10. *Proposals regarding affect in the curriculum should describe a process by which discourse about them may proceed.* I have proposed a continuing discourse about affect in the curriculum. Its focus is on the meaning of the major themes of democracy, dignity, and diversity and how to bring them to life in the school. It is a discourse about theory and practice, and the relations between the two. In this sense, I have tried to be clear that my claims are not to be viewed as rigid, final, or closed, but rather that they present one voice among the many that ought to be involved in the discourse. On the other hand, because the themes derive from the ostensible sources for personal and social efficacy in our society, they are placed at one level in a parallel structure that names the conditions upon which fuller discourse and appropriate arrangements for it are developed at the other level, namely, the local school. Attention has also been called to the language aspects of the proposed discourse, including the problems in using "ought" and "should" claims, the place of this discourse proposal

in the progressive language tradition, and the ways in which language casts a long shadow across our relationships. In the end, the discourse proposed here is one of possibility for personal and collective action regarding affect not only in the curriculum but in the larger society in which its participants live.

At the very least, my claims have touched all of the components and thus meet the condition of reasonable completeness. Again, however, I do not want to imply that they are taken to be thoroughly correct or final. As with any set of claims, these are in need of evaluation for coherence and consistency as well as validity in the lived experiences of people. Yet, they cannot be ignored—not because I have made them, but because they recall the very themes that are supposed to support personal and social efficacy in our society. Thus, while we may refine the definitions of democracy, dignity, and diversity or add other themes, it is hard to imagine that we could simply reject those three and the others that they imply.

THE ROAD AHEAD

A school administrator who read parts of a draft of this book suggested that I was calling on educators to "storm the Bastille." To a certain extent this may well be true. If we define "the Bastille" as those conditions that detract from democracy, human dignity, and the prizing of cultural diversity, *and* if we define "storming" as discourse about how we might remove those conditions, then this metaphor is appropriate. If we define "the Bastille" as features of the school that inhibit personal and social efficacy, *and* if we define "storming" as discourse that creates alternative features that support such efficacy, then the metaphor is particularly correct. On the other hand, that comment by a person working in the schools, conjuring up as it does a violent break from our traditions, might be taken as a sad commentary on how far we have come from the very themes that ostensibly set the grounds for personal development and the common good in our society and our schools.

We are living in troubled times. Those of us who are adults know that we are having a hard time finding anything to hang onto. Ours is an age of discontinuity and disbelief, of ambiguity and ambivalence. Imagine what all of this must look like through the eyes of the young who often lack our more matured insights and skills and yet must try to see themselves living out the greater part of their lives in this world. Surely the increased incidence of self-destructive behaviors among the young must tell us something of how they view their chances. Surely we must realize that many see little hope for themselves and society.

To say that these young people are simply engaging in individualistic hedonism is to sadly ignore the "yellow wall" on which are written the facts of the environment that surrounds them—facts that powerfully inform their self-perceptions, their values, their sense of morality and ethics, their aspirations, and the lived experiences in which these are formed and tested. To say that they simply need to exercise self-control and self-reliance, to "pull themselves up by their own bootstraps," is to misunderstand and underestimate the power of political, social, and economic forces with which they must contend. Can we possibly be so crass as to suggest, for example, that homeless children, living in abject poverty, should play out their self-images as if their living conditions did not affect virtually all their experiences? Can we be so blind as to say that these are only isolated examples, when the facts suggest that more and more young people find themselves in exactly these and comparable situations? Can we be so shortsighted that we do not see how the lives of "privileged" young people are inextricably intertwined with the fate of their nonprivileged peers? Have we forgotten that the common good is not just an ideal vision, but a condition that affects us all?

These young people are not like Beethoven, deaf to what was around him while creating beautiful music inside his own mind. They hear, and are forced to hear, the sounds of real life around them no matter how much we exhort them to ignore those sounds: sounds that have grown louder, playing out themes that are neither beautiful nor even nice. Those sounds have largely been created by adults, among whom are, of course, many in the education profession. So it is that we must now take action to create different sounds—a different environment—because while the ideas about affect in the curriculum may be written out on chalkboards like the one in the classroom where I taught, those chalkboards, like mine, are riveted to the "yellow wall" on which are written the facts of the larger society.

In taking such action we are faced, theoretically, with two major choices. In the first, we may try to turn the clock back to what are perceived to have been simpler and more stable times. In the second, we may face up to the realities of the world in which we live, which is filled with ambiguity and contradiction. However, our experiences and the facts at hand suggest that the choice is really only theoretical. The first alternative involves mostly selective and nostalgic recollection of a past that was as full of inequity, injustice, and lack of care as our present, whether we knew or wanted to know it. How else can we account for the histories of the poor, the nonwhite, immigrants, women, the aged, and others who were so often forced to live on the margins of society? How else can we account for the struggles of such people, so often unsuccessful, to gain full status in the political, economic, cultural, and social workings of our society? How else can we explain their resistance to many of the proposals for affect in the curriculum that presented "high culture" and other privileged views? Turning the clock back will not do the trick its proponents claim. It is a past that never really existed except for certain people.

We are left, finally, with the second alternative: to face the facts squarely and search for ways to do what has not been done well before; a search for a "lever long enough" to extend and broaden the powerful themes of democracy, dignity, and diversity in the lives of people and across our society, including in the institutions we maintain, like schools. This search begins with those themes, and its arrangements are conditioned by them—it demonstrates in action what they might begin to look like if we took them seriously. It brings us, as educators, into cooperative relations with others in our community to explore and act upon these themes both inside and outside the school. Unlike many other proposals regarding affect in the curriculum, this discourse is created and carried out through reasoned consent, fuller participation, and creative action.

In accepting this choice, we must not be fooled by the way in which popular rhetoric has attempted to redefine the themes that must guide the work ahead. Arguments have been co-opted and powerful language has been used to reposition them. For example, the defense of democracy has become the pursuit of global economic predominance; freedom is postulated as "free market competition"; morality is interpreted as compliance with conventional norms; survival of the most fit is conceived as the corollary of equality of opportunity; the rights of citizenship are expressed as the responsibility to conform to political opinion; statistics on economic gains (skewed as they are toward one group) are posited as evidence of universal prosperity; and the impoverished who receive economic assistance are construed as privileged (Apple, 1988). By these linguistic tricks, the fundamental themes of democracy, dignity, citizens' rights, and cultural diversity lose the meaning and power of their proper definitions.

No place is this issue more hotly contested than within the public schools. It is here, in creating and resisting particular programs intended to "affect" the lives of young people, that so many people from policy makers to parents to professional educators find the most urgent ground for thinking about the course of social affairs. And it is in the local schools that they also find perhaps the most accessible symbol of the institution upon which to exercise their preferred version of personal and social efficacy. So it is that we must recapture the authentic meanings of democracy, dignity, and diversity and invite others to join us in our work. The need in our own times is not unlike that called for by Dewey (1934) some 50 years ago.

> The things in civilization we most prize are not of ourselves. They exist by grace of the doings and sufferings of the continuous human community in which we are a link. Ours is the responsibility of conserving, transmitting, rectifying and expanding the heritage of values we have received that those who come after us may receive it more solid and secure, more widely accessible and more generously shared than we have received it. (p. 87)

FAILURE OF NERVE

The work that I have proposed is not something that can easily be done. It requires a continuing struggle to explore what democracy, dignity, and diversity mean; to imagine ways of bringing them to life in the curriculum; and to sharpen our understanding of the environment in which they are acted upon. How much easier it would be to define them in simple and narrow terms, to pretend that the school is a "limited" environment in which they need not be pursued, or to provide a few activities that supposedly will allow young people to "cope" with the realities of their lives. As illusory as such pretensions may be, they precisely describe much of what has passed for affect in the curriculum in our schools.

This is not only the case with those who want to deny that those themes ought to be alive in the school. It also involves many who would agree with the themes yet stop short of fully advocating them, particularly for fear of criticism by colleagues and special interests in the community. In the latter case, we often find a version of affect in the curriculum that explores possibilities for personal and social efficacy only up to the point where conflict may emerge. It is this version that largely defines a "failure of nerve" among some individuals and groups in our profession. That is, when we promote enhanced self-esteem in conjunction with ethical analysis of those conditions that detract from personal and social efficacy, we risk the very real possibility of coming up against powerful interests that benefit from those conditions; for example, commercial interests that profit from the desire for social acceptance among peers.

Such failure of nerve has not been without consequences. For one thing, it has meant that the school is full of contradictions, such as exhorting young people to act ethically while failing to allow them to name ethical lapses in the larger society for what they are. For another, it has meant that we have been open to accusations that we stand for nothing except relativistic individualism. And it has left us in a "sterile" position with regard to pressing issues in our society that work against our best efforts and often wash away whatever salutary effects we might have within the school.

The themes of democracy, dignity, and diversity present a powerful argument for overcoming this failure of nerve. They offer a compelling challenge for restructuring affect in the curriculum and a line of thinking to guide our efforts. Moreover, should conflict with special interests arise, those themes provide the solid grounds upon which we may stand in resisting them and inviting their proponents to join in our continuing discourse, to add their voices to the attempt to develop a reasoned consent about our work.

LEGACY AND LIBERATION: A FINAL WORD

Recall once more the suggestion that my case is a call for "storming the Bastille" and implies a violent break with our traditions. Nothing could be further from the truth. As I have pointed out many times, the themes of democracy, dignity, and diversity ostensibly support personal and social efficacy in our society—they are *supposed* to be in evidence in our own lives and those of others. In this sense, the case I have argued partly amounts to an act of tradition; that is, it shares with young people the *legacy* of our past in which those themes are proposed as the guiding principles for our society.

In defining those themes as grounds for personal and social efficacy, we also saw that they free people to search for ways to extend and broaden democracy, dignity, and diversity in their lives. So it is that the case I have argued involves not only legacy but *liberation*. It opens up possibilities for young people to go beyond the conditions that their elders have created, to examine conditions in their lives, and to act upon them as they detract from or enhance the possibilities for personal development and the common good. At the same time it also engages adults in this effort in terms of restructuring conditions that affect not only the lives of the young, but their own as well.

Some may say that the case I have argued is soft-headed or naive. That would ignore the very hard work that is ahead and the power of the themes I have proposed. Others might say that it involves too many forces outside the school and that we cannot go this route alone. This is, of course, quite correct. Yet the work must begin somewhere and with someone. As I look around at the possibilities for where and whom this might mean, the alternatives seem relatively few. Certainly there are many who would join us in this effort if only we would invite them to do so and say clearly what it is we want to pursue. Just as certainly some of these people are located in other institutions, and many are presently living on the margins of our society. Yet no institution has more clearly been called on to pursue the possibilities for personal and social development than the schools, and none is so assured of being part of the common experience of virtually all people. Thus, what better place to start this deliberate and conscious work than in the schools, and in the way we place affect in the curriculum?

Notes

CHAPTER 1

1. This statement refers to the normal course of events experienced by mentally stable persons and excludes arational behavior due to instability.

CHAPTER 2

1. I am indebted to Michael Olneck for our long discussion about this, though he may not share my interpretation.

2. I am indebted to James Ladwig for this important insight.

CHAPTER 3

1. In thinking this through, I am indebted to Robert S. Harnack for sharing an unpublished manuscript on curriculum planning in the affective domain.

2. At one level the white majority, nonwhite minority portrait is a curious and arrogant piece of ethnocentrism, because whites constitute a very small percentage of the world population.

CHAPTER 4

1. James Ladwig, personal correspondence, September 1988.

2. I served on the panel and am thus interpreting the document as text and as lived experience.

References

Abington School District v. *Schempp*. 1963. 374 U.S. 203.

Adler, Mortimer. 1981. *Six Great Ideas*. New York: Macmillan.

Adler, Mortimer. 1982. *The Paideia Proposal*. New York: Macmillan.

Aiken, Wilford. 1941. *The Story of the Eight Year Study*. New York: Harper & Row.

Alberty, Harold B. 1953. *Reorganizing the High School Curriculum*. New York: Macmillan.

Alberty, Harold B., & Elsie J. Alberty. 1962. *Reorganizing the High School Curriculum*, rev. ed. New York: Macmillan.

Alschuler, Albert S. 1969. Psychological Education. *Journal of Humanistic Education* 9, pp. 1–16.

Alschuler, Albert S. 1982. *Values Concepts and Techniques*, rev. ed. Washington, DC: National Education Association.

American Federation of Teachers. 1987. *Education for Democracy: A Statement of Principles*. Washington, DC: American Federation of Teachers.

Apple, Michael W. 1979. *Ideology and Curriculum*. London, Boston, and Henley: Routledge & Kegan Paul.

Apple, Michael W. 1982a. *Education and Power*. Boston and London: Routledge & Kegan Paul.

Apple, Michael W. (ed.). 1982b. *Cultural and Economic Reproduction in Education*. London, Boston, and Henley: Routledge & Kegan Paul.

Apple, Michael W. 1986. *Teachers and Texts: A Political Economy of Class and Gender Relations in Education*. New York and London: Routledge & Kegan Paul.

Apple, Michael W. 1988. Redefining Equality. *Teachers College Record* 90, pp. 167–84.

ASCD Panel on Religion in the Curriculum. 1987. *Religion in the Curriculum: A Report of the Panel on Religion in the Curriculum*. Alexandria, VA: Association for Supervision and Curriculum Development.

ASCD Panel on Moral Education. 1988. *Moral Education in the Life of the School*. Alexandria, VA: Association for Supervision and Curriculum Development.

Aspy, David N., & Flora N. Roebuck. 1977. *Kids Don't Learn From People They Don't Like*. Amherst, MA: Human Resource Development Press.

Baier, Annette C. 1987. Hume: The Women's Moral Theorist? In Eva Feder Kittay & Diana T. Meyers (eds.), *Women and Moral Theory* (pp. 37–55). Totowa, NJ: Rowman & Littlefield.

Ball, William B. 1967. Religion and Public Education: The Post-Schempp Years. In Theodore R. Sizer (ed.), *Religion and Public Education* (pp. 144–63). New York: Houghton Mifflin.

Banks, Olive. 1981. *Faces of Feminism: A Study of Feminism as a Social Movement.* New York: St. Martin's.

Banks, Olive. 1987. *Becoming a Feminist: The Social Origins of 'First Wave' Feminism.* Athens: University of Georgia Press.

Baran, Barbara. 1986. The Technological Transformation of the Insurance Industry. In Heidi Hartman, Robert Kraut, & Louise Tilly (eds.), *Computer Chips and Paper Clips* (pp. 25–62). Washington, DC: National Academy Press.

Bastian, Ann, Norm Fruchter, Marilyn Gittell, Colin Greer, & Kenneth Haskins et al. 1986. *Choosing Equality: The Case for Democratic Schooling.* Philadelphia, PA: Temple University Press.

Battistoni, Richard. 1985. *Public Schooling and the Education of Democratic Schooling.* Jackson: University of Mississippi Press.

Beane, James A. 1985/1986. The Continuing Controversy Over Affective Education. *Educational Leadership* 43, pp. 26–31.

Beane, James A., & Richard P. Lipka. 1986. *Self-Concept, Self-Esteem, and the Curriculum.* New York: Teachers College Press.

Beane, James A., & Richard P. Lipka. 1987. *When the Kids Come First: Enhancing Self-Esteem.* Columbus, OH: National Middle School Association.

Beane, James A., Conrad F. Toepfer, Jr., & Samuel J. Alessi, Jr. 1986. *Curriculum Planning and Development.* Boston: Allyn & Bacon.

Bell, Bernard I. 1949. *Crisis in Education: A Challenge to American Complacency.* New York: Whittlesey House.

Bellah, Robert N., Richard Madsen, William M. Sullivan, Ann Swidler, & Steven M. Tipton. 1986. *Habits of the Heart: Individualism and Commitment in American Life.* New York: Harper & Row.

Bennett, William J. 1986. Moral Literacy and the Formation of Character. Address given to the Manhattan Institute (available from the United States Department of Education).

Berscheid, Ellen. 1982. Attraction and Interpersonal Relations. In Margaret Sydnor Clark & Susan T. Fiske (eds.), *Affect and Cognition,* the Seventeenth Annual Carnegie Symposium on Cognition (pp. 37–54). Hillsdale, NJ: Lawrence Erlbaum.

Berscheid, Ellen. 1985. Interpersonal Modes of Knowing. In Elliot Eisner (ed.), *Learning and Teaching the Ways of Knowing,* 84th Yearbook of the National Society for the Study of Education, Part II (pp. 60–76). Chicago: University of Chicago Press.

Bestor, Arthur E. 1953. *Educational Wastelands: The Retreat from Learning in Our Public Schools.* Urbana, IL: University of Illinois Press.

Bestor, Arthur E. 1956. *The Restoration of Learning.* New York: Knopf.

Beyer, Landon E., & George H. Wood. 1985. Critical Inquiry and Moral Action in Education. *Educational Theory* 36, pp. 1–14.

Birnbaum, Max. 1969. Sense About Sensitivity Training. *Saturday Review,* November 16, pp. 82–83 ff.

Bloom, Allan. 1987. *The Closing of the American Mind.* New York: Simon & Schuster.

Bloom, Benjamin S. (ed.). 1956. *Taxonomy of Educational Objectives, Handbook I: Cognitive Domain.* New York: David McKay.

Bobbitt, Franklin. 1918. *The Curriculum.* Boston: Houghton Mifflin.

Bobbitt, Franklin. 1924. *How to Make a Curriculum.* Boston: Houghton Mifflin.

Bode, Boyd H. 1935. Education and Social Reconstruction. *The Social Frontier* 1, pp. 12–23.

Brown, George Isaac. 1969. *Human Teaching for Human Learning.* New York: Viking.

Bryan, Tannis, & James Bryan. 1986. Self-Concepts and Attributions of the Learning Disabled. *Transescence* 14, pp. 33–40.

Bureau of Labor Statistics. 1982. *Economic Projections to 1990,* Bulletin 2121. Washington, DC: Department of Labor.

Butts, R. Freeman, & Lawrence A. Cremin. 1953. *A History of Education in American Culture.* New York: Holt, Rinehart, & Winston.

Callahan, Raymond E. 1962. *Education and the Cult of Efficiency.* Chicago: University of Chicago Press.

Carlson, Richard O. 1964. Environmental Constraints and Organizational Consequences: The Public School and Its Clients. In D. E. Griffiths (ed.), *Behavioral Science and Administration,* Part II (pp. 262–78). Chicago: University of Chicago Press.

Carnoy, Martin, Derek Shearer, & Russell Rumberger. 1983. *A New Social Contract.* New York: Harper & Row.

Chapman, William E. 1969. *Roots of Character Education.* Schenectady, NY: Character Research Press.

Charters, W. W. 1926. Curriculum for Women. *Bulletin of the University of Illinois* 23, pp. 327–30.

Charters, W. W. 1927. *The Teaching of Ideals.* New York: Macmillan.

Chazan, Barry. 1985. *Contemporary Approaches to Moral Education.* New York and London: Teachers College Press.

Coe, George Albert. 1917. *A Social Theory of Religious Education.* New York: Scribner's.

Cohen, Joshua, & Joel Rogers. 1983. *On Democracy: Toward a Transformation of American Society.* New York: Penguin Books.

Combs, Arthur (ed.). 1962. *Perceiving, Behaving, Becoming.* Washington, DC: Association for Supervision and Curriculum Development.

Counts, George S. 1932. *Dare the School Build a New Social Order?* New York: John Day.

Cremin, Lawrence A. 1961. *The Transformation of the School.* New York: Random House.

Crisci, Pat Eva. 1986. The Quest National Center: A Focus on Prevention of Alienation. *Phi Delta Kappan* 67, pp. 440–42.

Curti, Merle. 1935. *The Social Ideas of American Educators.* New York: Scribner's.

Davis, O. L. 1985. *Looking at History: A Review of Major U.S. History Textbooks.* Washington, DC: People for the American Way.

DeGarmo, Charles. 1896. *Herbart and the Herbartians.* New York: Scribner's.

Dewey, John. 1902. *The Child and the Curriculum.* Chicago: University of Chicago Press.

Dewey, John. 1908. *Theory of the Moral Life.* New York: Holt, Rinehart, & Winston.

Dewey, John. 1909. *Moral Principles in Education.* Boston: Houghton Mifflin.

Dewey, John. 1910. *How We Think.* Boston: D. C. Heath.

Dewey, John. 1911. Character. In Paul Monroe (ed.), *Cyclopedia of Education* (pp. 569–72). New York: Macmillan.

Dewey, John. 1915. *The School and Society,* rev. ed. Chicago: University of Chicago Press.

Dewey, John. 1916. *Democracy and Education.* New York: Macmillan.

Dewey, John. 1929. *The Quest for Certainty.* New York: Minton, Balch.

Dewey, John. 1934. *A Common Faith.* New Haven, CT: Yale University Press.

Dewey, John. 1939. *Theory of Valuation.* Chicago: University of Chicago Press.

Dewey, John. 1944. The Democratic Faith and Education. *Antioch Review* 4, pp. 274–83.

Dewey, John. 1946. *Problems of Men.* New York: Philosophical Library.

Donovan, Josephine. 1985. *Feminist Theory: The Intellectual Traditions of American Feminism.* New York: F. Ungar.

Dubel, Robert Y., & Mary Ellen Saterlie. 1988. *The Baltimore County Values Project.* Paper presented to the ASCD Institute on Character Development in Public Schools, Williamsburg, VA.

Du Bois, W. E. B. 1902. *The Negro Artisan.* Atlanta, GA: Atlanta University Press.

Durkheim, Emile. 1961. *Moral Education: A Study in the Theory and Application of the Sociology of Education,* translated by Everett K. Wilson & Herman Schnurer. New York: The Free Press.

Education Week, February 27, 1985, pp. 1 & 28.

Education Week, September 9, 1987, p. 8.

Educational Policies Commission. 1944. *Education for ALL American Youth.* Washington, DC: National Education Association and American Association of School Administrators.

Edwards v. *Aguillard.* 1987. 55 L.W. 4860 (No. 85–1513), U.S.

Eisner, Elliot. 1979. *The Educational Imagination: On the Design and Evaluation of School Programs.* New York: Macmillan.

Euch, Forest S. 1987. Cultural Perspectives on Indian Education. *Equity and Excellence* 23, pp. 65–76.

Falwell, Jerry. 1979. *America Can Be Saved.* Murfreesboro, TN: Sword of the Lord Press.

Feldberg, Michael. 1975. *The Philadelphia Riots of 1844.* Westport, CT: Greenwood.

Finn, Chester E. 1987. The High School Dropout Puzzle. *The Public Interest* 87, pp. 3–22.

Foshay, Arthur W. 1980. Curriculum Talk. In A. W. Foshay (ed.), *Considered Action for Curriculum Improvement* (pp. 82–94). Washington, DC: Association for Supervision and Curriculum Development.

Fraenkel, Jack R. 1978. The Kohlberg Bandwagon: Some Reservations. In Peter Scharf (ed.), *Readings in Moral Education* (pp. 250–63). Minneapolis, MN: Winston.

Fraenkel, Jack R. 1980. *Helping Students Think and Value: Strategies for Teaching the Social Studies*, 2nd ed. Englewood Cliffs, NJ: Prentice-Hall.

Franklin, Barry. 1986. *Building the American Community: The School Curriculum and the Search for Social Control*. London and Philadelphia: Falmer.

Freire, Paulo. 1970. *Pedagogy of the Oppressed*. New York: Herder & Herder.

Gabler, Mel, & Norma Gabler (with James C. Hefley). 1985. *What Are They Teaching Our Children?* Wheaton, IL: Victor.

General Education Provisions Act. 1974. 20 USC 1232h, Sec. 439.

Gerler, Edwin R. 1986. Skills for Adolescence: A New Program for Young Teenagers. *Phi Delta Kappan* 67, pp. 436–39.

Germane, Charles E., & Edith Germane. 1929. *Character Education*. New York: Silver Burdett.

Gilligan, Carol. 1977. In a Different Voice: Women's Conception of the Self and Morality. *Harvard Educational Review* 47, pp. 481–517.

Gilligan, Carol. 1982. *In a Different Voice*. Cambridge, MA: Harvard University Press.

Gilman, Francis. 1984. Teacher Self-Perceptions and Their Perceptions of Student Characteristics. *Journal of Classroom Interaction* 19, pp. 9–11.

Giroux, Henry. 1981. *Ideology, Culture, and the Process of Schooling*. Philadelphia, PA: Temple University Press.

Giroux, Henry, & David Purpel (eds.). 1983. *The Hidden Curriculum and Moral Education*. Berkeley, CA: McCutchan.

Glasser, Ira. 1969. Schools for Scandal—The Bill of Rights and Public Education. *Phi Delta Kappan* 51, pp. 190–94.

Goble, Frank G., & B. David Brooks. 1983. *The Case for Character Education*. Ottawa, IL: Green Hill.

Graebner, William. 1988. *The Engineering of Consent*. Madison: University of Wisconsin Press.

Grant, Carl A., & Christine E. Sleeter. 1985. The Literature on Multicultural Education: Review and Analysis. *Educational Review* 37, pp. 97–118.

Grant, Gerald. 1988. *The World We Created at Hamilton High*. Cambridge, MA: Harvard University Press.

Greene, Bert I., & Marvin Pasch. 1985/1986. Observing the Birth of the Hatch Amendment Regulations: Lessons for the Education Profession. *Educational Leadership* 43, pp. 36–41.

Greene, Maxine. 1985. The Role of Education in Democracy. *Educational Horizons* 63, pp. 3–9.

Gumaer, Jim. 1975. Affective Education Through Role Playing. *Journal of Personnel and Guidance* 53, pp. 604–08.

Gumaer, Jim. 1976. Affective Education Through The Friendship Class. *School Counselor* 23, pp. 257–63.

Gutmann, Amy. 1987. *Democratic Education.* Princeton, NJ: Princeton University Press.

Habermas, Jurgen. 1971. *Knowledge and Human Interests.* Boston: Beacon.

Habermas, Jurgen. 1979. *Communication and the Evolution of Society.* Boston: Beacon.

Hadley, Arthur Twining. 1907. *Standards of Morality.* New York: Macmillan.

Hall, G. Stanley. 1901. How Far Is the Present High-School and Early College Training Adapted to the Nature and Needs of Adolescents? *The School Review* 9, pp. 649–65.

Hall, G. Stanley. 1909. Evolution and Psychology. In Charles E. Strickland & Charles E. Burgess (eds.), *G. Stanley Hall: Health, Growth, and Heredity.* New York: Teachers College Press, 1965.

Hamachek, Donald E. 1978. *Encounters With the Self,* 2nd ed. New York: Holt, Rinehart, & Winston.

Haney, Charles, & Philip Zimbardo. 1975. The Blackboard Penitentiary: Its Tough to Tell a High School from a Prison. *Psychology Today* 9, pp. 26 ff.

Harmin, Merrill E., Howard Kirschenbaum, & Sidney B. Simon. 1973. *Clarifying Values Through Subject Matter.* Minneapolis, MN: Winston.

Harmin, Merrill E., Howard Kirschenbaum, Leland Jacobs, & Sidney B. Simon. 1977. In Defense of Values Clarification. *Phi Delta Kappan* 58, pp. 743–46.

Harris, William Torrey. 1896. What Shall We Study? *Journal of Education* 2, pp. 1–3.

Hartshorne, Hugh, & Mark A. May. 1928, 1929, 1930, respectively. *Studies in the Nature of Character: Volume I: Studies in Deceit, Volume II: Studies in Service and Self-Control, Volume III* (with Frank K. Shuttleworth): *Studies in the Organization of Character.* New York: Macmillan.

Harvard University Committee on the Objectives of General Education in a Free Society. 1945. *General Education in a Free Society: Report of the Harvard Committee.* Cambridge, MA: Harvard University Press.

Haubrich, Vernon (ed.). 1971. *Freedom, Bureaucracy, and Schooling.* Washington, DC: Association for Supervision and Curriculum Development.

Henry, Jules. 1963. *Culture Against Man.* New York: Random House.

Higham, John. 1970. *Strangers in the Land.* New York: Atheneum.

Hirsch, E. D. 1987. *Cultural Literacy.* Boston: Houghton Mifflin.

Hock, Louise, & Thomas Hill. 1962. *The General Education Class in the Junior High School.* New York: Holt, Rinehart, & Winston.

Hodgkinson, Harold L. 1985. *All One System.* Washington, DC: Institute for Educational Leadership.

The Holmes Group. 1986. *Tomorrow's Teachers.*

Hopkins, L. Thomas. 1941. *Interaction: The Democratic Process.* New York: D. C. Heath.

Humanist Manifestos I and II. 1973. Buffalo, NY: Prometheus.

Inhelder, Bärbel, & Jean Piaget. 1958. *The Growth of Logical Thinking from Childhood to Adolescence.* New York: Basic.

Jenkinson, Edward B. 1979. *Censors in the Classroom: The Mindbenders.* Carbondale: Southern Illinois University Press.

Johnson, David W., Roger T. Johnson, Earl J. Holubec, & Patricia Roy. 1984. *Circles of Learning: Cooperation in the Classroom.* Alexandria, VA: Association for Supervision and Curriculum Development.

Junell, Joseph S. 1979. *Matters of Feeling: Values Education Reconsidered.* Bloomington, IN: Phi Delta Kappa Foundation.

Kaestle, Carl F. 1983. *Pillars of the Republic: Common Schools and American Society, 1790–1860.* New York: Hill & Wang.

Kaestle, Carl F. 1984. Moral Education and Common Schools in America: A Historian's View. *Journal of Moral Education* 13, pp. 101–11.

Kaiser-Carlso, Arlene Marie. 1986. *A Program Description and Analysis of Self-Esteem Programs for the Junior High School.* Santa Clara, CA: Educational Development Center.

Kelley, Earl. 1962. The Fully Functioning Self. In Arthur Combs (ed.), *Perceiving, Behaving, Becoming.* Washington, DC: Association for Supervision and Curriculum Development.

Kilpatrick, William H. 1918. The Project Method. *Teachers College Record* 19, pp. 319–35.

Kliebard, Herbert M. 1986. *The Struggle for the American Curriculum: 1893–1958.* Boston, London, and Henley: Routledge & Kegan Paul.

Kohlberg, Lawrence E. 1966. Moral Education in the Schools. *School Review* 74, pp. 1–29.

Kohlberg, Lawrence E. 1980. High School Democracy and Educating for a Just Community. In Ralph Mosher (ed.), *Moral Education* (pp. 20–57). New York: Praeger.

Kohlberg, Lawrence E., & Rochelle Mayer. 1972. Development as the Aim of Education. *Harvard Educational Review* 42, pp. 449–96.

Kohn, Alfie. 1986. *No Contest: The Case Against Competition.* Boston: Houghton Mifflin.

Kozol, Jonathan. 1987. *Rachel and Her Children: Homeless Families in America.* New York: Crown.

Krathwohl, David R., Benjamin S. Bloom, & Bertram B. Masia. 1964. *Taxonomy of Educational Objectives, Handbook II: Affective Domain.* New York: David McKay.

Krug, Edward A. 1950. *Curriculum Planning.* New York: Harper & Row.

Krug, Edward A. 1957. *Curriculum Planning,* rev. ed. New York: Harper & Brothers.

Krug, Edward A. 1960. *The Secondary School Curriculum.* New York and Evanston: Harper & Row.

Laird, Susan. 1988. Women and Gender in John Dewey's Philosophy of Education. *Educational Theory* 38, pp. 111–29.

Lazerson, Marvin, Judith Block McLaughlin, Bruce McPherson, & Stephen K. Bailey. 1985. *An Education of Value: The Purposes and Practices of Schools.* Cambridge: Cambridge University Press.

Leming, James S. 1981a. Curricular Effectiveness in Moral/Value Education. *Journal of Moral Education* 10, pp. 147-64.

Leming, James S. 1981b. On the Limits of Rational Moral Education. *Theory and Research in Social Education* 9, pp. 7-34.

Lickona, Thomas. 1988. Four Strategies for Fostering Character Development in Children. *Phi Delta Kappan* 69, pp. 419-23.

Lipka, Richard P., James A. Beane, & Brian E. O'Connell. 1985. *Community Service Projects: Citizenship in Action.* Bloomington, IL: Phi Delta Kappa Foundation.

Lockwood, Alan L. 1977. Values Education and the Right to Privacy. *Journal of Moral Education* 7, pp. 743-46.

Lockwood, Alan L. 1978. The Effects of Values Clarification and Moral Development Curricula on School-Age Subjects: A Critical Review of Research. *Review of Educational Research* 48, pp. 325-64.

Lockwood, Alan L. 1982. Bedding Down in Democratic High Schools. *Harvard Educational Review* 52, p. 216.

Lockwood, Alan L. 1985/1986. Keeping Them in the Courtyard: A Response to Wynne. *Educational Leadership* 43, pp. 9-10.

Lockwood, Alan L. October, 1989. Do Public Schools Teach Secular Humanism? Why We May Never Know. *Counseling and Values* 34, pp. 3-11.

Lockwood, Alan L., & David E. Harris. 1985. *Reasoning With Democratic Values.* New York: Teachers College Press.

Lufler, Henry S. 1986. Courts and School Policies. Paper presented at the Conference on Student Discipline Strategies, U.S. Department of Education, Washington, DC.

Macdonald, James B., & Esther Zaret (eds.). 1975. *Schools in Search of Meaning.* Washington, DC: Association for Supervision and Curriculum Development.

Mandler, George. 1984. *Mind and Body: Psychology of Emotion and Stress.* New York: Norton.

McKown, Harry C. 1935. *Character Education.* New York: McGraw-Hill.

McLeod, Douglas. (ed.). In press. *Affect and Mathematical Problem Solving.*

McNeil, Linda. 1986. *Contradictions of Control: School Structure and School Knowledge.* New York and London: Routledge & Kegan Paul.

Mosher, Ralph L., & Norman A. Sprinthall. 1970. Psychological Education in Secondary Schools: A Program to Promote Individual and Human Development. *American Psychologist* 25, pp. 911-24.

Moustakas, Clark (ed.). 1956. *The Self: Explorations in Personal Growth.* New York: Harper & Row.

National Association for Education of Young Children. 1988. Developmentally Appropriate Practice in Early Childhood Programs Serving Children From Birth Through Age 8. *Young Children*, pp. 64-84.

National Commission on Excellence in Education. 1983. *A Nation at Risk: The*

Imperative for Educational Reform. Washington, DC: U.S. Government Printing Office.

National Education Association. 1893. *Report of the Committee on Secondary School Studies*. Washington, DC: U.S. Government Printing Office.

National Education Association. 1895a. *Report of the Committee of Fifteen on Elementary Education, with Reports of the Subcommittees: On the Training of Teachers; On the Correlation of Studies in Elementary Education; On the Organization of City School Systems*. New York: American Book.

National Education Association. 1895b. Report of the Committee of Fifteen. *Educational Review* 9, pp. 264–85.

National Education Association. 1918. *Cardinal Principles of Secondary Education: A Report of the Commission on the Reorganization of Secondary Education*. Washington, DC: U.S. Government Printing Office.

National Education Association. 1919. *Fourth Report of the Committee on Economy of Time in Education*, 18th Yearbook of the National Society for the Study of Education, Part II. Bloomington, IL: Public School Publishing.

Newmann, Fred, & Robert Rutter. 1983. *The Effects of High School Community Service Programs on Students' Social Development*. Report to the National Institute of Education. Madison: Wisconsin Center for Educational Research.

Niebuhr, Herman. 1984. *Revitalizing American Learning: A New Approach That Just Might Work*. Belmont, CA: Wadsworth.

Nobles, Wade W. 1976. Extended Self: Rethinking the So-Called Negro Self-Concept. *Journal of Black Psychology* 2, pp. 15–24.

Noddings, Nel. 1984. *Caring: A Feminist Approach to Ethics and Moral Education*. Berkeley: University of California Press.

Nucci, Larry. 1987. Synthesis of Research on Moral Development. *Educational Leadership* 44, pp. 86–92.

Oakes, Jeannie. 1985. *Keeping Track: How Schools Structure Inequality*. New Haven, CT: Yale University Press.

Oliver, Donald W., & James P. Shaver. 1966. *Teaching Public Issues in the High School*. Boston: Houghton Mifflin.

Overly, Norman V. (ed.). 1970. *The Unstudied Curriculum: Its Impact on Children*. Washington, DC: Association for Supervision and Curriculum Development.

Oxford English Dictionary. 1961. Oxford: Clarendon Press.

Patterson, Cecil H. 1977. Insights About Persons: Psychological Foundations of Humanistic and Affective Education. In Louise M. Berman & Jessie A. Roderick (eds.), *Feeling, Valuing, and the Art of Growing: Insights Into the Affective* (pp. 145–160). Washington, DC: Association for Supervision and Curriculum Development.

Phenix, Philip J. 1961. *Education and the Common Good*. Westport, CT: Greenwood.

Phenix, Philip J. 1977. Perceptions of an Ethicist about the Affective. In Louise M. Berman & Jessie A. Roderick (eds.), *Feeling, Valuing, and the Art of Growing: Insights Into the Affective* (pp. 59–82). Washington, DC: Association for Supervision and Curriculum Development.

Piaget, Jean. 1932. *The Moral Judgment of the Child*. London: Routledge & Kegan Paul.

Public Education Information Network. 1987. *Equity and Excellence: Toward an Agenda for School Reform*. St. Louis, MO: Public Education Information Network.

Public Law 94–142. *The Right to Education for All Handicapped Children Act*. 1975. 20 U.S.C. 1412.

Purkey, William W. 1970. *Self-Concept and School Achievement*. Englewood Cliffs, NJ: Prentice-Hall.

Purkey, William W., & John Novak. 1978. *Inviting School Success: A Self-Concept Approach to Teaching and Learning*. Belmont, CA: Wadsworth.

Raths, Louis E. 1969. *Teaching for Learning*. Columbus, OH: Charles E. Merrill.

Raths, Louis E. 1972. *Meeting the Needs of Children: Creating Trust and Security*. Columbus, OH: Charles E. Merrill.

Raths, Louis E. 1975. Social Change and Values. *Impact on Instructional Improvement*, pp. 8–11.

Raths, Louis E., Merrill Harmin, & Sidney B. Simon. 1966. *Values and Teaching*. Columbus, OH: Charles E. Merrill.

Raths, Louis E., Selma Wasserman, Arthur Jonas, & Arnold Rothstein. 1967. *Teaching for Thinking: Theory and Application*. Columbus, OH: Charles E. Merrill.

Ravitch, Diane, & Chester Finn. 1987. *What Do Our 17 Year Olds Know?* New York: Harper & Row.

Rawls, John. 1971. *A Theory of Justice*. Cambridge, MA: Harvard University Press.

Reasoner, Robert W. 1982. *Building Self-Esteem*. Palo Alto, CA: Consulting Psychologists.

Reimer, John. 1981. Moral Education: The Just Community Approach. *Phi Delta Kappan* 62, pp. 485–87.

Rice, Joseph Mayer. 1893. *The Public School System of the United States*. New York: Century.

Rickover, Hyman G. 1959. *Education and Freedom*. New York: E. P. Dutton.

Roberts, Thomas B. 1972. Seven Major Foci of Affective Experiences: A Typology of Educational Design, Planning, Analysis, and Research. *ERIC Reports*, ED 063 215.

Rogers, Carl. 1969. *Freedom to Learn*. Columbus, OH: Charles E. Merrill.

Rorty, Amelie Oksenburg (ed.). 1980. *Explaining Emotions*.Berkeley: University of California Press.

Rugg, Harold O. (ed.). 1939. *Democracy and the Curriculum*, 3rd Yearbook of the John Dewey Society. New York: Century.

Rugg, Harold O. 1947. *Foundations for American Education*. Yonkers-on-Hudson, NY: World Book.

Rugg, Harold O., & Ann Shumaker. 1928. *The Child-Centered School*. Yonkers-on-Hudson, NY: World Book.

Russell, William. 1830. Quotation from *American Journal of Education* 5, p. 117, cited in Daniel Tanner & Laurel N. Tanner, *Curriculum Development: Theory into Practice*. New York: Macmillan, 1980.

Ryan, Kevin. 1986. The New Moral Education. *Phi Delta Kappan* 68, pp. 228–33.

Saylor, J. Galen, & William Alexander. 1954. *Curriculum Planning for Better Teaching and Learning*. New York: Holt, Rinehart, & Winston.

Schaefli, Andre, James Rest, & Steven Thoma. 1985. Does Moral Education Improve Moral Judgment? A Meta-Analysis of Intervention Studies Using the Defining Issues Test. *Review of Educational Research* 55, pp. 319–52.

Schneir, Miriam (ed.). 1972. *Feminism: The Essential Historical Writings*. New York: Random House.

Selden, Steven. 1985. Educational Policy and Biological Science: Genetics, Eugenics, and the College Textbook. *Teachers College Record* 87, pp. 35–51.

Silberman, Charles E. 1970. *Crisis in the Classroom*. New York: Random House.

Silver, Michael. 1976. *Values Education*. Washington, DC: National Education Association.

Skinner, B. F. 1968. *The Technology of Teaching*. New York: Appleton.

Slavin, Robert. 1981. Synthesis of Research on Cooperative Learning. *Educational Leadership* 38, pp. 655–60.

Sleeter, Christine E. 1987. Why Is There Learning Disabilities? A Critical Analysis of the Birth of the Field in Its Social Context. In Thomas S. Popkewitz (ed.), *The Formation of the School Subjects* (pp. 210–37). New York: Falmer.

Smith, B. Othanel, William O. Stanley, & J. Harlan Shores. 1957. *Fundamentals of Curriculum Development*, rev. ed. New York: Harcourt, Brace, & World.

Smith, Mortimer B. 1949. *And Madly Teach: A Layman Looks at Public School Education*. Chicago: Henry Regnery.

Sneath, E. Hershey, & George Hodges. 1914. *Moral Principles in the School and Home*. New York: Macmillan.

Snedden, David. 1921. *Sociological Determinants of Objectives in Education*. Philadelphia: Lippincott.

Snygg, Donald, & Arthur W. Combs. 1949. *Individual Behavior: A New Frame of Reference for Psychology*. New York: Harper & Row.

Spender, Dale (ed.). 1981. *Men's Studies Modified: The Impact of Feminism on the Academic Disciplines*. New York: Pergamon.

Starrat, Robert J. Undated. *Sewing Seeds of Faith and Justice*. Washington, DC: Jesuit Secondary Education Association.

Stedman, Lawrence C., & Marshall S. Smith. 1983. Recent Reform Proposals for American Education. *Contemporary Education Review* 2, pp. 85–104.

Stillwell, William E. 1976. A Systems Approach for Implementing Affective Education Programs. *Counselor Education and Supervision* 15, pp. 200–10.

Stocker, Michael. 1980. Intellectual Desire, Emotion, and Action. In Amelie Oksenburg Rorty (ed.), *Explaining Emotions* (pp. 323–38). Berkeley: University of California Press.

Stocker, Michael. 1987. Duty and Friendship: Toward a Synthesis of Gilligan's

Contrapositive Moral Concepts. In Eva Feder Kittay & Diana T. Meyers (eds.), *Women and Moral Theory* (pp. 56–68). Totowa, NJ: Rowman & Littlefield.

Strike, Kenneth A. 1982. *Educational Policy and the Just Society.* Urbana: University of Illinois Press.

Tanner, Daniel, & Laurel N. Tanner. 1980. *Curriculum Development: Theory into Practice.* New York: Macmillan.

Task Force on Education for Economic Growth. 1983. *Action for Excellence: A Comprehensive Plan to Improve Our Nation's Schools.* Denver, CO: Education Commission of the States.

Task Force on Values Education and Ethical Behavior. 1983. *1984 and Beyond: A Reaffirmation of Values.* Towson, MD: Baltimore County Public Schools

Taylor, Frederick. 1911. *The Principles of Scientific Management.* New York: Harper & Brothers.

Teitelbaum, Kenneth. 1987. Outside the Selective Tradition: Socialist Curriculum for Children in the United States, 1900–1920. In Thomas S. Popkewitz (ed.), *The Formation of the School Subjects* (pp. 190–209). New York, Philadelphia, and London: Falmer.

Torcaso v. Watkins. 1961. 367 U.S. 488.

Tronto, Joan. 1987. Beyond Gender Difference to a Theory of Care. *Signs: Journal of Women in Culture and Society* 4, pp. 644–63.

Tubbs, Mary, & James A. Beane. 1981. Curricular Trends and Practices in High Schools. *High School Journal* 65, pp. 103–08.

United States Department of Education. 1984. *Public Hearing on Proposed Rulemaking Implementing the Hatch Amendment.* Washington, DC.

Valett, Robert E. 1974. *Affective-Humanistic Education: Goals, Programs, and Learning Activities.* Belmont, CA: Fearon.

Van Til, William, Gordon Vars, & John Lounsbury. 1967. *The Modern Junior High School,* 2nd ed. Indianapolis, IN: Bobbs-Merrill.

Vitz, Paul. 1986. *Censorship: Evidence of Bias in Our Children's Textbooks.* Ann Arbor, MI: Servant Publications.

Walberg, Herbert J., & James W. Keefe (eds.). 1986. *Rethinking Reform: The Principal's Dilemma.* Reston, VA: National Association for Secondary School Principals.

Wallace v. Jaffree. 1985. 472 U.S. 38.

Waskin, Yvonne, & Louise Parrish. 1967. *Teacher-Pupil Planning for Better Classroom Learning.* New York: Pitman.

West Virginia State Board of Education v. Barnette. 1943. 319 U.S. 624.

Weinstein, Gerald, & Mario D. Fantini. 1970. *Toward Humanistic Education: A Curriculum of Affect.* New York, Washington, and London: Praeger.

Whitehead, John W., & John Conlan. 1978. Establishment of the Religion of Secular Humanism. *Texas Tech Law Review* 10, pp. 1–62.

Wight, Albert R. 1971. *Affective Goals in Education.* Salt Lake City, UT: Interstate Educational Resource Center.

Wight, Albert R. 1972. *Toward a Definition of Affect.* Salt Lake City, UT: Interstate Educational Resource Center.

Willower, Donald J., Terry L. Eidell, & Wayne K. Hoy. 1967. *The School and Pupil Control Ideology.* The Pennsylvania State University Studies. University Park: The Pennsylvania State University.

Wise, Arthur E., & Michael E. Manley-Casimir. 1971. Law, Freedom, Equality—and Schooling. In Vernon E. Haubrich (ed.), *Freedom, Bureaucracy, and Schooling* (pp. 46–73). Washington, DC: Association for Supervision and Curriculum Development.

Wood, George H. 1984. Schooling in a Democracy: Transformation or Reproduction. *Educational Theory* 34, pp. 219–39.

Wynne, Edward A. 1980. *Looking at Schools: Good, Bad and Indifferent.* Lexington, MA: Lexington.

Wynne, Edward A. 1985/1986. The Great Tradition in Education: Transmitting Moral Values. *Educational Leadership* 43, pp. 4–10.

Wynne, Edward A. 1988. Balancing Character Development and Academics in the Elementary School. *Phi Delta Kappan* 69, pp. 424–26.

Yulish, Stephen. 1980. *The Search for a Civic Religion: A History of the Character Education Movement in America, 1890–1935.* Washington, DC: University Press of America.

Zinn, Howard. 1980. *A People's History of the United States.* New York: Harper & Row.

Index

About the Author

JAMES A. BEANE, Ed.D. is on the faculty of the School of Education at the National College of Education. Previously, he was Professor of Education in the Department of Administration, Supervision, and Curriculum at St. Bonaventure University. Jim Beane has also been a teacher and a project director in regional education planning centers in New York State. He is co-author of *Self-Concept, Self-Esteem, and the Curriculum* (1986), *Curriculum Planning and Development* (1986), and *When the Kids Come First: Enhancing Self-Esteem* (1987). He has also published numerous papers in professional journals, consulted in many school districts, and served as a visiting professor at several universities. His major scholarly interests are the effects of schooling on the personal and social development of young people and the restructuring of curriculum organization.